Revealing Snapshots
PEOPLE AND EVENTS THAT SHAPED CHRISTIANITY

Revealing Snapshots
PEOPLE AND EVENTS THAT SHAPED CHRISTIANITY

Ralph E. MacKenzie

CLAIREMONT BOOKWORKS
San Diego, California

Copyright © 2014 by Ralph E. MacKenzie.

All rights reserved. No part of this publication may be reproduced, distributed or transmitted in any form or by any means, including photocopying, recording, or other electronic or mechanical methods, without the prior written permission of the publisher, except in the case of brief quotations embodied in critical reviews and certain other noncommercial uses permitted by copyright law. For permission requests, write to the publisher, addressed "Attention: Permissions Coordinator," at the address below.

CLAIREMONT BOOKWORKS
P.O. Box 179191
San Diego, CA 92177
www.clairemontbookworks.com

Unless otherwise indicated, Scriptures taken from the HOLY BIBLE, NEW INTERNATIONAL VERSION. Copyright © 1973, 1978, 1984 International Bible Society. Used by permission of Zondervan Bible Publishers.

Book Layout ©2013 BookDesignTemplates.com

Ordering Information:
Quantity sales. Special discounts are available on quantity purchases by corporations, associations, and others. For details, contact the "Special Sales Department" at the address above.

Revealing Snapshots / Ralph E. MacKenzie—1st Edition
Printed in the United States of America

20 19 18 17 16 15 14   1 2 3 4 5 6

ISBN 978-0-9912265-1-1

This book is dedicated to three people who have had a profound influence on my Christian life. The first two, Don and Sue Moore, were used by the Holy Spirit to bring me to Christ. I saw in them how they not only "talked the talk," but also "walked the walk."

The third person is Norm Geisler. He has been a teacher and a mentor, in addition to a faithful friend, for over sixty years. Norm has stood by me in difficult times as well as good. We co-authored together "Roman Catholics and Evangelicals: Agreements and Differences," published by Baker Books in 1995. It continues to serve as a well-balanced volume and enjoys broad acceptance even to this very day.

REVEAL

v. From the Latin (revēlāre) meaning to unveil; in other words, to make known that which was previously unknown.

SNAPSHOT

n. A brief appraisal, summary, or profile.

REVEALING SNAPSHOTS

n. Short vignettes that provide insight into the way in which people and events helped shape Christianity.

Contents

PART ONE: Apostolic to Post-Nicene 1

Apostolic Christianity 1

    THE ASCENSION OF JESUS (Acts 1:6-12) 2

    EARLY CHURCH/PENTECOST (Acts 2 and 4) 2

    GAMALIEL (Acts 5:34-40) 3

    STEPHEN (Acts 6-7) 4

    SIMON THE SORCERER (Acts 8) 5

    PHILIP AND THE ETHIOPIAN EUNUCH (Acts 8:26-40) 6

    SAUL'S CONVERSION (Acts 9:1-31) 7

    CORNELIUS AND PETER (Acts 10) 8

    THE COUNCIL AT JERUSALEM (Acts 15:1-21) 10

    THE COUNCIL TO GENTILE BELIEVERS (Acts 15:22-29) 11

    PAUL CIRCUMCISES TIMOTHY (Acts 16:1-3) 11

    THE MACEDONIAN CALL (Acts 16:6-10) 12

    THE CONVERSION OF LYDIA (Acts 16:13-15) 13

    THE DEMON-POSSESSED GIRL (Acts 16:16-21) 14

    PAUL AND SILAS IN THE PHILIPPIAN JAIL (Acts 16:19-34) 14

    PAUL AND SILAS LEAVE PHILIPPI (Acts 16:35-40) 16

    AT BEREA (Acts 17:10-15) 16

    AT ATHENS (Acts 17:16-21) 17

    PAUL BEFORE THE AREOPAGUS (Acts 17:22-34) 18

PAUL IN CORINTH (Acts 18:1-28) 19
PRISCILLA AND AQUILA (Acts 18:18-28) 21
APOLLOS AT EPHESUS AND CORINTH (Acts 18:24-28) 21
TWELVE MEN WITHOUT THE SPIRIT (Acts 19:1-7) 22
THE SEVEN SONS OF SCEVA (Acts 19:13-22) 23
PAUL'S FAREWELL TO THE EPHESIANS (Acts 20:17-38) 24
PAUL'S ARRIVAL IN JERUSALEM (Acts 21:17-26) 25
PAUL'S TRIAL BEFORE FELIX (Acts 24:1-27) 26
THE TRIAL BEFORE FESTUS (Acts 25:1-12) 27
FESTUS CONSULTS WITH KING AGRIPPA (Acts 25:13-22) 28
PAUL BEFORE AGRIPPA (Acts 25:23-27; 26:1-32) 29
THE JOURNEY TO ROME (Acts 27:1-44; 28:1-31) 30
LUKE—THE AUTHOR OF ACTS 32
JOHN—THE LAST APOSTLE 32
NERO 34
THE DESTRUCTION OF JERUSALEM 35

Ante-Nicene Christianity 35
THE DIDACHE 36
PERSECUTION IN THE SECOND CENTURY 36
POLYCARP 37
PERSECUTION IN THE THIRD CENTURY 38
THE MARTYRDOM OF PERPETUA AND FELICITAS 38
TERTULLIAN 39

Nicene Christianity 40
PERSECUTION IN THE FOURTH CENTURY 41

    NICHOLAS, BISHOP OF MYRA, LYCIA 41

    GREGORY THE ILLUMINATOR 42

    CONSTANTINE 43

    THE VINCENTIAN CANON 44

Creedal Christianity 45

    THE APOSTLES' CREED 45

    THE NICENE CREED 46

    THE ATHANASIAN CREED 46

    ATHANASIUS, BISHOP OF ALEXANDRIA 47

Conciliar Christianity 48

    COUNCIL OF NICEA 48

    COUNCIL OF CONSTANTINOPLE 49

    COUNCIL OF EPHESUS 50

    COUNCIL OF CHALCEDON 51

Post-Nicene Christianity 51

    MACRINA THE YOUNGER 52

    SIMEON STYLITES THE ELDER 52

    JEROME 54

    AUGUSTINE OF HIPPO 55

PART TWO: Middle Ages 57

    Early Middle Ages Christianity 57

        LEO THE GREAT 57

        BENEDICT OF NURSIA 58

        GREGORY THE GREAT 59

        CHRISTIANITY COMES TO THE BRITISH ISLES 61

COLUMBA	61
BONIFACE	62
THE RISE OF ISLAM	63
CYRIL AND METHODIUS	65
POPE SYLVESTER II	66
VLADIMIR OF RUSSIA	67
High Middle Ages Christianity	**68**
EASTERN VS. WESTERN CHRISTIANITY	68
THE EAST/WEST SCHISM	70
ANSELM OF CANTERBURY	71
THE CRUSADES	73
BERNARD OF CLAIRVAUX	74
BERNARD OF CLUNY	75
HILDEGARD OF BINGEN	76
FRANCIS OF ASSISI	77
DOMINIC	79
THOMAS AQUINAS	80
Late Middle Ages Christianity	**82**
THE RENAISSANCE	82
CATHERINE OF SIENA	84
THE BRETHREN OF THE COMMON LIFE	85
THE PRE-REFORMATION PERIOD	87
JOHN WYCLIFFE	88
JOHN HUSS	89
THOMAS A KEMPIS	90

    GIROLAMO SAVONAROLA 91

    DESIDERIUS ERASMUS 91

PART THREE: Early Modern to Early America 93

    Early Modern Christianity 93

        IGNATIUS OF LOYOLA 93

        WILLIAM TYNDALE 95

        FRANCISCO DE VITORIA 96

        TERESA OF AVILA 97

        LANCELOT ANDREWES 98

        THE INQUISITION 99

    Reformation Christianity 100

        MARTIN LUTHER 101

        PHILIPP MELANCHTHON 103

        JOHN CALVIN 104

        ULRICH ZWINGLI 106

        HEINRICH JOHANN BULLINGER 107

        ANABAPTISTS 108

        JOHN KNOX 109

        LADY JANE GREY 110

        ENGLISH REFORMATION 111

    Counter-Reformation Christianity 113

        PRE-TRENT CONFERENCES 114

        THE CONFERENCE OF HAGENAU 114

        DISPUTATION OF WORMS 115

        THE CONFERENCE OF RATISBON/REGENSBURG 115

    THE COUNCIL OF TRENT 116

    ISSUES ADDRESSED AT TRENT 116

    RENE DESCARTES 117

    PETER CLAVER 118

    BROTHER LAWRENCE 119

    BLAISE PASCAL 121

    JOHN BUNYAN 122

    JOHN LOCKE 123

    SIR ISAAC NEWTON 124

Enlightenment & Skeptics of Christianity 125

    THE ENLIGHTENMENT 126

    VOLTAIRE 126

    DAVID HUME 127

    JEAN-JACQUES ROUSSEAU 128

    IMMANUEL KANT 128

    FRIEDRICH SCHLEIERMACHER 129

Early American Christianity 129

    THE GREAT AWAKENING 130

    ISAAC WATTS 130

    DAVID BRAINERD 131

    JONATHAN EDWARDS 132

    GEORGE WHITEFIELD 132

    SAMUEL DAVIS 133

    COUNT VON LUDWIG ZINZENDORF 134

    JOHN WESLEY 134

  CHARLES WESLEY 135

  ISAAC BACKUS 136

  FRANCIS ASBURY 137

  ARCHIBALD ALEXANDER 137

  THE CLAPHAM COMMUNITY 138

  WILLIAM CAREY 139

  WILLIAM ELLERY CHANNING 140

  WILLIAM WILBERFORCE 141

PART FOUR: Modern to Postmodern 143

 19th Century Modern Christianity 143

  THE RESTORATION MOVEMENT 143

  ADONIRAM JUDSON 145

  JOHN NELSON DARBY 146

  THE OXFORD MOVEMENT 147

  ORESTES BROWNSON 148

  JAMES GIBBONS 149

  FREE METHODIST CHURCH 150

  FRANCIS THOMPSON 151

  LORD ACTON 152

  GEORGE MATHESON 153

  ALEXANDER MACLAREN 154

  EDWARD M. BOUNDS 155

  DAVID LIVINGSTONE 155

  SEVENTH-DAY ADVENTIST CHURCH 157

  SOREN KIERKEGAARD 158

JOHN HENRY NEWMAN 160
KARL MARX 161
FR. ALEXANDER MEN 162
ALEKSANDR SOLZHENITSYN 163
CHARLES HADDON SPURGEON 165
DWIGHT LYMAN MOODY 166
CHARLES DARWIN 168
JAMES HUDSON TAYLOR 169
THE FIRST VATICAN COUNCIL 170
ABRAHAM KUYPER 171
JULIUS WELLHAUSEN 172

20th Century Modern Christianity 173

THE CRISTERO WAR 173
WILLIAM (BILLY) SUNDAY 175
YOUNG MEN'S CHRISTIAN ASSOCIATION (YMCA) 176
THE SALVATION ARMY 176
SIGMUND FREUD 177
PAUL C. VITZ 179
ALBERT SCHWEITZER 181
THE FUNDAMENTALS 182
KARL BARTH 183
CHARLES HODGE 184
BENJAMIN BRECKINRIDGE WARFIELD 185
THERESE OF LISIEUX 186
GILBERT KEITH CHESTERTON 188

    WALTER ARTHUR MAIER 189

    PAUL SCHNEIDER 190

    FR. MAXIMILIAN KOLBE 191

    DONALD GREY BARNHOUSE 193

    DIETRICH BONHOEFFER 194

Postmodern Christianity 196

    DEAD SEA SCROLLS 196

    ECUMENISM 197

    SECULAR VS. SECULARISM 198

PART FIVE: The Church in Transition 201

Catholic Christianity 201

    VATICAN II 201

    THEOLOGICAL POSITIONS AT VATICAN II 203

    CATHOLICS AND EVANGELICALS 204

    LEON JOSEPH CARDINAL SUENENS 205

    MOTHER TERESA 206

    LIGHT AND LIFE MOVEMENT 208

    JOHN COURTNEY MURRAY 210

Evangelical Christianity 211

    HENRIETTA MEARS 211

    A. W. TOZER 213

    C. S. LEWIS 214

    T. S. ELIOT 216

    R. G. LeTOURNEAU 217

    RUDOLPH BULTMANN 219

ETA LINNEMANN 220

Ecumenical Christianity **222**

J. EDWIN ORR 222

THE ACTON INSTITUTE 224

MORTIMER ADLER 225

THE TAIZE COMMUNITY 227

AVERY CARDINAL DULLES 229

RICHARD JOHN NEUHAUS 231

VERNON C. GROUNDS 232

CHARLES W. COLSON 233

THOMAS C. ODEN 235

EVANGELICALS AND EASTERN ORTHODOXY 237

EVANGELICALS AND CATHOLICS TOGETHER 238

PART SIX: The New Millennium **241**

Contemporary Christianity **241**

WILLIAM C. CREASY 241

JOHN H. ARMSTRONG 242

DAVID E. BJORK 244

THE ALPHA COURSE 245

THE ALLIES FOR FAITH AND RENEWAL 247

HOMOSEXUALITY AND CHRISTIANITY 248

EMMAUS MINISTRIES 249

THE SAN DIEGO CHRISTIAN FORUM 250

CHRIS CASTALDO 252

ISLAM IN THE TWENTY-FIRST CENTURY 253

  THE AMERICAN ISLAMIC FORUM FOR DEMOCRACY 255

  CARLI JELENSZKY 256

  RANIERO CANTALAMESSA 259

Conclusion 261

  THE NEXT CHRISTENDOM 261

  MISSIONARIES TO THE UNITED STATES 262

  CATHOLICS AND EVANGELICALS IN DIALOGUE 263

  A PERSONAL STORY 264

Bibliography 267

Foreword

If church history has always bored you, then you have never read this book! The panorama of snapshots that pass along the horizon in this book will keep you glued to your armchair for hours. Drawing from decades as an author and teacher, Professor MacKenzie parades across the stage of church history some of the most fascinating—and sometimes unexpected—figures in the history of Christianity. These are people and events that helped shape Christianity. Some of them were under-reported or skipped over completely, women as well as men.

You will meet the rabbi who taught Paul when he was Saul the Pharisee. You will discover the person who turned the hinge of history and moved Christianity to the Western world. You will learn everything from the origin of Santa Clause to the Ethiopian eunuch who took Christianity to the African continent. Furthermore, you will come to know the bishop whose enemies called him "the black dwarf," but who saved Christianity from becoming the biggest cult in the Western world.

Do you know the bishop who preached against slavery in the eleventh century or the forerunner of the parachurch movement? Are you aware of the leader that gave rise to the Renaissance Movement? Well, if you read this book, you will be informed about these and many more.

Have you ever heard of Brother Lawrence, Count von Ludwig Zinzendorf, Leo the Great, or Teresa of Avila? Do you know the Christian lady who was queen of England for only nine days? Have you met the man who almost singlehandedly stopped the slave trade in England?

Do you know about the Conference of Ratisbon/Regensburg that could have saved one of the great splits in the Christian world? Do you know who Lord Acton was, Francis Thomson, Abraham Kuyper or Paul Vitz? Well, let me assure you that Professor MacKenzie's lucid and fascinating style will draw you into the circle of saints, great and small, which will leave you thirsting for more.

In addition to noted literary giants like G.K. Chesterton, Dietrich Bonheoffer and T.S. Eliot, there are many snapshots of lesser known but influential Christians from Leon Joseph Cardinal Suenens and Eta Linnemann to R.G. LeTourneau.

I can guarantee you a memorable reading experience whether it be about Mortimer Adler, Avery Cardinal Dulles, SJ, or Vernon C. Grounds. The snapshots of Thomas C. Oden, William C. Creasy, and David Bjork will bring life to your view of contemporary Christianity.

If I had come upon fascinating, exciting, and energizing portraits of Christianity like these earlier in my career, perhaps I might have learned to love to read more than Augustine, Anselm, and Aquinas. I highly recommend this book! To borrow a phrase from the author, it is a veritable cornucopia of literary and theological delight.

Norman L. Geisler, PhD
Professor of Apologetics
www.VeritasSeminary.com

Acknowledgments

This book has truly been a labor of love from conception to completion. Both friends and colleagues repeatedly encouraged and challenged me while producing this work. Words cannot express or acknowledge the contribution that my brother in Christ, David Costantino, has bestowed upon this project over the course of the past year. Both his time and various talents played an essential role in preparing the manuscript and guiding it along its journey to publication.

Furthermore, several others offered vital assistance along the way as well. For example, Jake Schell served as my developmental editor, restructuring the document in numerous places until we got it right. Then, Carissa Johnson, while completing her senior year at Liberty University and taking a full load, took this project on as an internship and served as my copyeditor and proofreader, which became for me a very humbling experience.

Later, Deb Eaton offered me a dozen different cover designs, until we finally settled on this stunningly beautiful cover. She is a truly gifted artist. Next to last, I would like to acknowledge three exceptional readers: Dr. Cliff Anderson, Dr. Barry McCarthy, and Mrs. Rachel Costantino. Each plowed through the final draft in a matter of days and offered up numerous ideas that improved the final copy. Lastly, were it not for the typing effort by my grandson Ben Trent and the countless hours my devoted wife, Donna MacKenzie, spent administrating the project and transforming my difficult handwriting into electronic copy, this manuscript would not have seen the light of day. To all, I am most grateful!

Introduction

Over the past two millennia since the time of Christ, people and events have served to either instigate departure from or return to biblical Christianity. This book introduces the reader to those people and events in a unique way. It uses short vignettes called snapshots to reveal insights into the way in which each person or event herein served or militated against Christian unity and orthodoxy.

Throughout this work, the reader will encounter many surprising characters. Here we briefly introduce you to three of them. The first is Athanasius who lived during the fourth century. Most likely educated in his native city, he received a classical education and was ordained a deacon in 319. He became the bishop's secretary and accompanied him to the famous Council of Nicea in 325. When Bishop Alexander died, Athanasius succeeded him as Bishop of Alexandria.

He was both black and short of stature, which caused his numerous theological detractors to refer to him as "the Black Dwarf." Today his admirers salute him for his dispute with Arianism, the heresy that denied the Trinity. This dispute led to his installation and overthrow as Bishop—five times. The final victory over Arianism occurred at the Council of Constantinople in 381. Though Athanasius didn't live to see the final victory, nevertheless, the "Black Dwarf" stands vindicated.

Next, please meet Hildegard of Bingen who lived eight hundred years later during the twelfth century. Born in Beckelheim, Germany, little is known about her youth, except for her sickliness as a child. At eight years old, a recluse named Blessed Jutta received her into her community directed by the Benedictines.

When Hildegard turned fifteen, she became a nun and in 1136 succeeded Jutta as Prioress. During her lifetime she experienced visions and wrote about them. Upon careful examination, Bernard of Clairvaux proclaimed the writings to be legitimate.

Hildegard went on to write hymns, music, and she traveled throughout Germany, speaking to large groups of clergy, several popes, and even Frederick I (Barbarossa), the Holy Roman Emperor. Not shy, she swiftly chastised any who did not meet her standards in holiness and personal behavior.

As a nun, she "broke the mold" so to speak. In 1979, at the eight-hundredth anniversary of her passing, she was canonized by Pope John Paul II. Then in 2012, Pope Benedict XVI declared Hildegard of Bingen, a Doctor of the Universal Church. She became the 34th Doctor and only the fourth female to receive this honor.

Lastly, moving ahead four hundred years, meet Martin Luther. Many consider him one of those people who divided the Church when he nailed his *Ninety-Five Theses* to the Wittenberg door in 1517, thus providing the catalyst for the Protestant Reformation, which is clearly an historical dividing point.

However, upon further investigation, it appears that Luther never intended to create a wedge that would subsequently divide the Church. Rather, he sought to restore—a Church divided by the sale of indulgences—to the Biblically sound Christian teaching of salvation by grace through faith in the work of Christ alone.

In other words, the sale of indulgences to obtain salvation represented the departure; the *Ninety-Five Theses* represented Luther's attempt to restore orthodoxy. These are just a few of the many surprises in store for the reader. Therefore, read on for more exciting eye-openers!

PART ONE

Apostolic to Post-Nicene

Apostolic Christianity

Had you been present at the Ascension, you would have observed a group of people numbering over one hundred—mostly Judeans, but also some visitors. There was a smaller group who seemed to be followers of the man who was addressing the crowd.

It was a clear day and after answering a few questions, the man began to rise in the air. He was immediately covered by a cloud that hid him from their sight. While the crowd was intently looking into the sky, two men dressed in white clothing admonished them, saying that the man would return to earth in the same way that he departed. The events that had just occurred caused some degree of anxiety and the crowd tried to learn what had just transpired. Perhaps you had ingested too much of the fruit of the grape the night before.

THE ASCENSION OF JESUS (Acts 1:6-12)

The Ascension of Jesus into heaven happened on the Mount of Olives between Jerusalem and Bethany. It is covered in Luke 24:50-53 and Acts 1:6-12, and the disciples who were present at the Ascension are listed in Acts 1:13. Jesus instructed them to return to Jerusalem. Peter states in Acts 2:33 that Jesus had been "Exalted to the right hand of God" and the Holy Spirit had been sent to indwell the believers. The cloud that hid Jesus from his observers was probably the Shekinah glory—the visible manifestation of the Divine. The "two men dressed in white" is a common description of angels.

A number of theological implications result from the Ascension of Christ. The first three Gospels mention Transfiguration, the Ascension, and the Parousia, which is a Greek word referring to the second coming of Christ; these three events present Christ's divine glory to humanity. The cloud that hid Jesus from his observers was present at the aforementioned events.

Another blessing made possible by the Ascension is the arrival of the Holy Spirit to carry on Christ's ministry here on earth. In heaven, the exalted Lord functions as our Advocate in the presence of His Father.

Finally, the Ascension made possible that our human nature, which the eternal Son of God adapted for Himself, was now present at the right hand of God.

This presence was made possible by the Incarnation and has significance for us concerning our salvation, both now and in the future kingdom.

EARLY CHURCH/PENTECOST (Acts 2 and 4)

Prior to his Ascension, Jesus promised to send a Comforter and the Comforter was the Holy Spirit. However, one might erroneously conclude that the Holy Spirit was here for the first time. Of course, that would be wrong as the Holy Spirit took part in the creation of the universe and played a role in the advancing of salvation history leading up to Pentecost.

Acts 2 details the coming of the Holy Spirit on Pentecost, including the filling of the Spirit, the manifestation of the gift of tongues, and Peter addressing the crowd which had gathered. Then we read about Peter's instructions to the believers about the formation of the church, following the apostles' teaching, fellowship, breaking of bread, and prayer.

In Acts 4, Peter and John addressed the Sanhedrin, the supreme and highest court of law at Jerusalem in New Testament times. The elders and teachers of the law were disturbed at the preaching of Peter and John and "... commanded them not to speak or teach at all in the name of Jesus." Peter and the other apostles answered, "We must obey God rather than men." When the Jewish leaders heard this, they wanted to execute them. Now we encounter the first "snapshot" of this work, Gamaliel.

GAMALIEL (Acts 5:34-40)

"But a Pharisee named Gamaliel, a teacher of the law, who was honored by all the people, stood up in the Sanhedrin and ordered that the men be put outside for a little while. Then he addressed them: 'Men of Israel, consider carefully what you intend to do to these men.' ... Gamaliel counseled: "Therefore, in the present case I advise you: Leave these men alone! Let them go! For if their purpose or activity is of human origin, it will fail. But if it is from God, you will not be able to stop these men; you only find yourselves fighting against God. His speech persuaded them."

Gamaliel taught Paul in his pre-Christian days. Gamaliel was a grandson of the liberal Hillel. He was held in such high esteem that he was designated "Rabban," or our teacher, a higher title than

"Rabbi," or my teacher. One wonders if this view of Gamaliel, so contrary to that of the majority of the Sanhedrin members, might indicate a special working of the Holy Spirit through General Revelation.

STEPHEN (Acts 6-7)

Stephen, who was "a man full of God's grace and power, did great wonders and miraculous signs among the people." Stephen had been one of seven men chosen from the Grecian Jews ordained by the apostles to minister to the widows who were being overlooked. Of the seven, Stephen seems to be considered the leader, and he was chosen to speak to the Sanhedrin. He was seized by members of the Synagogue of the Freedmen, who were people from different Hellenistic areas that had been freed from slavery.

Starting with Abraham, Stephen gave a detailed historical presentation of the events that ended with the people of Israel in Egypt. Then, Moses and Aaron were brought into the account; when suddenly Stephen's speech shifted from historical to censure. He declares, "You stiff-necked people ... You are just like your fathers. You always resist the Holy Spirit! Was there ever a prophet your fathers did not persecute? They even killed those who predicted the coming of the Righteous One. And now you have betrayed and murdered him."

Stephen's introduction of Jesus and his crucifixion by these Jewish leaders was the last straw; they turned into a murderous mob and began stoning him. "But Stephen, full of the Holy Spirit, looked up to heaven and saw the glory of God, and Jesus standing at the right hand of God. 'Look,' he said, 'I see heaven open and the Son of Man standing at the right hand of God.'" Why was Jesus "standing" rather than remaining seated? F. F. Bruce, in his book, *The Book of Acts: The New International Commentary,* offers this explanation: "It may be, however, that a standing posture is mentioned here because the Son of Man at God's right hand is not only viewed as King and priest, but also—and this is most relevant to Stephen's special situation—as a witness. Stephen has been confessing Christ before men, and now he sees Christ confessing His servant before God. The proper posture for a witness is the standing posture. Stephen, condemned by an earthly court, appeals for vindication to a heavenly court, and his vindicator in that Supreme Court is Jesus, who stands at God's right hand as Stephen's advocate, his 'paraclete.'" It should be understood that the above quote by F. F. Bruce is his interpretation and not accepted by all authorities.

"While they were stoning him, Stephen prayed, 'Lord Jesus, receive my spirit.' Then he fell on his knees and cried out 'Lord, do not hold this sin against them.' When he had said this he fell asleep. And Saul was there, giving approval to his death." The church had received its first martyr. This event was witnessed by a Jewish Pharisee named Saul. We will meet him in due course, bearing a different name. Stephen is honored in the Canon of the Roman Mass; while in the Eastern Church, his feast is held on December 27. Blessed are those who die in the Lord. The Church has honored the faithful Christians who followed Jesus in death by assigning them a feast day on the church calendar.

SIMON THE SORCERER (Acts 8)

The Old Testament makes it clear that sorcery, also called magic, was strictly forbidden in Israel. Some of the offences covered under this category may be found in II Chronicles 33:6, including human sacrifice, sorcery, divination and witchcraft, and the consultation with mediums and spiritists.

Simon the Sorcerer, called Simon Magus, plays an important role in early Christian history. He is often accused of being the father of Gnostic heresies. He was a Jewish sorcerer and a false prophet. "Now for some time a man named Simon had practiced sorcery in the city and amazed all the people in Samaria." He boasted that he was a great man.

Simon heard Phillip preaching in the name of Jesus, saw many people getting baptized, and joined them. He was also impressed with the signs and miracles he witnessed. Then Peter and John placed their hands on those converted and they received the Holy Spirit. When Simon saw this, he offered the apostles money and said, "Give me also this ability so that everyone on whom I lay my hands may receive the Holy Spirit."

But Peter said to Simon, "May your money perish with you, because you thought you could buy the gift of God with money! You have no part or share in this ministry, because your heart is not right before God." Simon seemed to admit his sinfulness and asked for prayer that God might forgive him. Some have advanced the question: Was Simon truly converted?

When the Gospel is presented, the message is gladly received. But sadly on some occasions, the response is a counterfeit one. There is no further mention of Simon after this event. The state of his soul must be left in God's hands.

The Simon of this account is occasionally confused with another sorcerer and false prophet named Bar-Jesus who Paul and Barnabas encountered when they visited Cypress. That event can be found in Acts 13.

PHILIP AND THE ETHIOPIAN EUNUCH (Acts 8:26-40)

Next we look at Philip, who labored closely with Stephen, and his encounter with the Ethiopian eunuch. An angel of the Lord instructed Philip to travel south on the road that goes from Jerusalem to Gaza. He soon met an Ethiopian eunuch, an officer in charge of the treasury of Candace, queen of the Ethiopians. When Philip approached the chariot, he heard the man reading Isaiah the prophet. Philip asked if he knew what he was reading and when he replied that he did not, he invited Philip to join him in his chariot. The eunuch, a Gentile who was a Jewish proselyte, had been to Jerusalem to worship and was returning home. Luke viewed him within a Jewish context.

It is uncertain how Jews would have viewed a eunuch worshiping at Jerusalem given that Deuteronomy 23:1 states that no emasculated male could be a part of the Jewish community. However, Isaiah 56:3-5 speaks of eunuchs being received by the God of loving kindness. The official was reading Isaiah 53, a well-known Messianic prophecy. "The eunuch asked Philip, 'Tell me, please, who is the prophet talking about, himself or someone else?' Then Philip began with that very passage of Scripture and told him the good news about Jesus." The Ethiopian spotted some water by the road and asked Philip to baptize him. After they came out of the water, the Spirit took Philip away and the eunuch saw him no more, and he went on his way rejoicing. Christianity was introduced to Ethiopia in the fourth century, and it would be interesting to know if this incident was used in that missionary effort.

SAUL'S CONVERSION (Acts 9:1-31)

In keeping with the custom, "Saul" was given his Hebrew, Jewish name. Later "Saul" was changed to "Paul" because of his Roman, Hellenistic background. The name change may have occurred because Paul was now entering the Gentile phase of his ministry. It has been suggested that if Paul had not become a Christian, his talents coming forth from his intellectual gifts would have led him to be recognized in world history. Paul would become second only to Jesus the Savior Himself as the major influence for the spread of Christianity worldwide.

Saul's conversion is well known, we remember him from the stoning of Stephen. After he hears and receives Jesus, Saul—now

Paul—remains with the disciples in Damascus. Paul wastes little time before he begins what he will become famous for. "At once he began to preach in the synagogues that Jesus is the Son of God." His message had difficulty receiving a hearing. "All those who heard him were astonished and asked, 'Isn't he the man who raised havoc in Jerusalem among those who call on his name? And hasn't he come here to take them as prisoners to the chief priests?'" But the tide had turned in favor of Paul and his message became more powerful. He debated the Jews living in Damascus proving that Jesus was the Christ.

"When he came to Jerusalem he tried to join the disciples, but they were all afraid of him, not believing that he really was a disciple." Barnabas brought him to the apostles and confirmed Paul's powerful conversion. This former pharisaical Jew from Tarsus would go on to pen thirteen out of the twenty-seven books that comprise the New Testament. Saul's conversion is so important in church history that it is the only event recorded three times in the Book of Acts.

CORNELIUS AND PETER (Acts 10)

"At Caesarea there was a man named Cornelius, a centurion in what was known as the Italian Regiment." Centurions were officers in the Roman army. Two are mentioned by name in the New Testament: Cornelius and Julius—who escorted Paul and other prisoners to Rome and treated Paul kindly; and two others unnamed—one at Capernaum and the other at the cross.

Cornelius is described by Luke as devout and God-fearing, and as a non-Jew who believed in the monotheism of the Jews, read the Scriptures, and practiced some of the Jewish rites. He was respected by the Jews, because he prayed and gave alms to the people of Israel.

One day in the afternoon, Cornelius had a vision in which he saw an angel who called him by name. Cornelius was afraid and asked, "What is it, Lord?" The angel replied, "Your prayers and gifts to the poor have come up as a memorial offering before God." He was instructed to send men to Joppa and bring back a man named Simon Peter, who stayed at Simon the tanner's house by the sea. Cornelius sent some men to Joppa, to find Peter and begin the return to Caesarea.

During the journey, Peter went up on the roof of a house to pray. There, he fell into a trance and saw something come down from heaven like a large sheet. "It contained all kinds of four-footed animals, as well as reptiles of the earth and birds of the air. Then a voice told him, 'Get up Peter. Kill and eat.'" He was puzzled and replied that he had never eaten anything impure or unclean. The voice spoke to him a second time. "Do not call anything impure that God has made clean."

Initially, he found this very difficult to understand and obey. Peter was soon to learn that the vision's message was broader as to what he could eat, but impacted Jewish and Gentile relationships as he had known them.

When the party arrived in Caesarea and met Cornelius, he fell at Peter's feet in reverence. Peter told Cornelius to stand up—that he was a man not worthy of worship. They went inside and met a large group of people. Peter addressed them: "You are well aware that it is against our law for a Jew to associate with a Gentile or visit him. But God has shown me that I should not call any man impure or unclean." Then Peter asked Cornelius why he was sent for. Cornelius told of the vision he received from God and that the gathering was ready to hear from Peter.

Peter stated that God accepts men from every nation who honor him and do what is right, mentioning the good news of peace, that Jesus Christ is Lord of all. Even though the Jews killed Jesus by hanging him on a tree, God raised him from the dead.

During this message, the Holy Spirit descended on the group. The Jewish believers were astonished that the gift of the Holy Spirit had been bestowed on the Gentiles who were present. Since the Spirit had anointed them, Peter ordered that they be baptized in the name of Jesus. We next see the apostles and Christian leaders at the Jerusalem Council will declare that Gentiles were to share in the promises to Israel; the Council was to be of greatest importance to the developing Church.

THE COUNCIL AT JERUSALEM (Acts 15:1-21)

This gathering at Jerusalem in AD 50 had a great impact on the early Church. We learn that the Gentiles were to be blessed by the promises to Israel. This was a recurring message in the Old Testament. For example, Genesis 18:18 tells that the Messiah is to be a descendent of Abraham and "all nations on earth will be blessed through him." The Christian movement had always understood a connection to the religion of Israel. We have already seen that connection at work in the episode between Cornelius and Peter.

Paul, Barnabas and other believers were sent from Antioch to Jerusalem to meet with the apostles and elders to deal with the issue of whether a Gentile must submit to the Jewish circumcision. When Paul and Barnabas arrived in Jerusalem, they told the leaders there what God had accomplished through their efforts during their missionary journey through Iconium, Lystra and Derbe. "The whole assembly became silent as they listened to Barnabas and Paul telling about the miraculous signs and wonders God had done among the Gentiles through them."

James related that Peter had spoken about how God had shown his plan to establish from the Gentiles a people for himself. James, the Lord's brother, presided at the Council. He was known as "James the Just" for his piety and scrupulousness in keeping the law. Associates also used the term "Old Camel's Knees" because of his constant praying. Luke's mention of the silence that fell over the assembly after Barnabas and Paul spoke indicates that a turning point had arrived. However, Galatians 2:11-21 reveals that Peter would eventually give in to Jews, of the "stricter sort," on this issue. James' main input to the decision of the council was to indicate that Gentiles did not have to become Jews in order to be converted to faith in Christ.

THE COUNCIL TO GENTILE BELIEVERS (Acts 15:22-29)

The leaders at the Council decided to send their decision to Antioch, accompanied by Paul, Barnabas, Silas, and Barsabbas. The letter stated that the Judaizers went beyond their authority by insisting that Gentile believers must be circumcised and adapt to a Jewish lifestyle.

The council members went on to say that it seemed good to the Holy Spirit and to them not to burden the Gentile believers with anything beyond the following requirements: "You are to abstain from food sacrificed to idols, from blood, from the meat of strangled animals and from sexual immorality. You will do well to avoid these things." The Holy Spirit guided the early Church in dealing with the vexing problems concerning ethical and moral restrictions between Jewish and Gentile believers.

PAUL CIRCUMCISES TIMOTHY (Acts 16:1-3)

Paul faced the circumcision issue when he wanted to add Timothy to his team. Timothy's mother was Jewish and a believer; however, Timothy's father was Greek. Since Timothy's father was Greek, should Paul perform the circumcision rite on Timothy in spite of his belief that circumcision was not necessary for Gentile converts? However, Timothy, because of his Jewish mother, was a Jew in the eyes of the Jewish community; a child's religion is identified with his mother's lineage. Consequently, Paul circumcised him. For Paul, being a good Christian did not mean being a bad Jew.

Later, a different situation arose. Paul received a revelation from God that instructed him to preach the Gospel among the Gentiles. He assembled a team to assist him. The group included Barnabas, a Levite from Cyprus, and Titus, who was a Gentile. However, some Jewish Christians in Jerusalem insisted that Titus be circumcised.

Paul denied their demands because he felt that Titus would have the opposite problem that Timothy had, since he would be working with non-Jews. The success of spreading the biblical message was more important than these cultural issues that had been dealt with at the Jerusalem Council.

THE MACEDONIAN CALL (Acts 16:6-10)

The Macedonian call, also referred to as the Macedonian vision, ranks high in historical turning points. Because of Paul's obedience, the Christian message went westward and, consequently, Europe and the Western world were evangelized. Paul was prevented by the Holy Spirit from further preaching in the province of Asia.

Paul, accompanied by Timothy and Silas, traveled throughout the region of Phrygia and Galatia. They went down to Troas and during the night Paul had a vision of a Macedonian asking for help. He took this as a call from God to evangelize Macedonia. Macedonia was a region in southeastern Europe and became a Roman province in 148 BC. Many commentators suggest that Paul met Luke at Troas, perhaps for medical advice. Luke may have pointed out that Macedonia was in need of hearing the Gospel. The party now moved to Philippi. At this point, Luke shows unobtrusively that he has now joined the missionary party as a fourth member. The "we" passages in Acts make this clear.

Just imagine how world history could have developed differently; thank you, Paul.

THE CONVERSION OF LYDIA (Acts 16:13-15)

In Judaism, a congregation was made up of ten men; thus, Philippi was without a synagogue. Therefore, on the Sabbath, Paul and his companions traveled outside the city, searching for a Jewish place of prayer. About a mile and a half west of the city, they found a group of women gathered to read from the Law and the Prophets, to comment on their readings, and if possible, to hear an exposition and receive a blessing. Paul and his friends sat down with these women and began a conversation.

One of the women was from Thyatira, a city in western Asia Minor. Thyatira was once a part of the ancient Kingdom of Lydia, and was still considered to be Lydia. Hence, the woman was called Lydia. Thyatira was known for making purple dyes and for dyeing clothes—activities that were carried on by women at home. Lydia was an artisan in purple dyes and had come to Philippi to ply her trade.

She was referred to as a "God-fearer," having probably received instruction at a synagogue in her native Thyatira. Lydia was probably either a widow or never married, and some of her women friends may have been relatives and servants living in her home. She immediately received the Gospel message and was baptized along with members of her household. Then she invited the missionary party to stay at her home and they did.

From such a small incident, the church at Philippi began. We gather from his letter to the Philippians that it was one of Paul's most-loved congregations. Soon her home became the center of Christian outreach and worship in Philippi. Although the culture that the church inherited from Judaism was clearly patriarchal concerning the station and status of women, the church learned by the example of the Savior the truth of Galatians 3:28: "There is neither Jew nor Greek, slave nor free, male nor female for you are all one in Christ Jesus."

THE DEMON-POSSESSED GIRL (Acts 16:16-21)

Here we meet two of the converts mentioned by Luke among Paul's converts at Philippi. They were different in culture, station, and mental and physical condition in life, which indicated the power of Jesus' name to bring salvation in diverse situations.

The first was Lydia, the independent business woman of sterling character and God-fearing mind. The second was a person very different; an unfortunate demon-possessed slave girl who was exploited by her owners for material gain. Luke described her as a person inspired by Apollo, the god especially noted for the giving of oracles and worshipped at the shrine of Delphi in central Greece.

She followed the missionaries through the streets of Philippi, proclaiming that they were servants of the Most High God, bringing the way of salvation. The missionaries found her "unsolicited testimonials" to be counter-productive to their mission. Paul finally exorcised the demon that possessed her, commanding, in the name of Jesus, that he depart from her, which immediately happened.

"When the owners of the slave girl realized that their hope of making money was gone, they seized Paul and Silas and dragged them into the marketplace to face the authorities." What Paul did for the slave girl was not appreciated by her owners; in removing the demon, he had eliminated their income.

PAUL AND SILAS IN THE PHILIPPIAN JAIL (Acts 16:19-34)

There was a great amount of anti-Semitism among the people—"these men are Jews ... advocating customs unlawful for us Romans to accept and practice ..." which caused bigotry to flare up and complicate resolution of the issue. The crowd was incited to anti-Semitic violence by the slave girl's owners and the people turned on Paul and Silas. However, Rome did not share this local anti-Semitism.

The authorities stripped and severely flogged the two missionaries as disturbers of peace and had them jailed and put in stocks. Paul and Silas, being Roman citizens, should not have been subjected to such violent treatment. Later, when writing to the Corinthian church, Paul looked back on this episode as one of the afflictions he suffered as a servant of Christ. For the sake of the gospel, Paul had been in prison more frequently, been flogged more severely, and with Silas had been exposed to death again and again.

Instead of bemoaning their situation, "about midnight Paul and Silas were praying and singing hymns to God, and the other prisoners were listening to them." Then an earthquake shook the prison, doors opened, and chains fell off all the prisoners. The jailer awakened, saw the doors open, and assumed the worst—a guard who allowed his prisoners to escape was liable to the same sentence as the prisoners would have received.

The jailer, assuming all the prisoners had escaped, drew his sword to kill himself. But Paul, saw him in the doorway, and shouted from within the prison, "Don't harm yourself! We are all here!" Paul, Silas and the other prisoners had stayed in their cells. The praying and singing, the earthquake, the opening of the doors, and the loosing of the chains had the effect of vindicating God's servants. Paul and Silas were preparing for the jailer's conversion.

The jailer rushed in and fell trembling before Paul and Silas. He cried out, "What must I do to be saved?" Paul and Silas presented to the Philippian jailer the same Gospel that had been proclaimed since Pentecost, "Believe in the Lord Jesus and you will be saved."

Because this was all new to the jailer, Paul and Silas explained to him and his family "the Word of the Lord." The jailer and his family, to judge by their actions, believed in Christ and received the Holy Spirit. The jailer washed the wounds of Paul and Silas, and he and his family were baptized. Then he took the missionaries into his home and fed them. The family was filled with joy because they had come to believe in God. This was Luke's third example of the power of Christ at Philippi. And Paul and Silas no doubt felt the rods and stocks well worth experiencing, given the joy that was brought into the jailer's home.

PAUL AND SILAS LEAVE PHILIPPI (Acts 16:35-40)

By the next day, excitement had abated, and the officials decided that the two vagabond Jews had been taught a lesson and could be released. But when the jailer reported the message that they are free to leave, Paul contended that an act of injustice had been committed against the political rights of Roman citizens. Thus, those who were the cause of the injustice should be the ones to make it right.

Paul's message was conveyed to the officials, and they were dismayed to learn that these two Jews were Roman citizens. They feared that the possibility of a complaint reaching Rome would leave them in an awkward position. They went to the jail and requested Paul and Silas to leave Philippi. Paul's insistence on an official apology may have served as a protection to the members of the church that had been planted during his stay there.

AT BEREA (Acts 17:10-15)

When the missionary group went to Thessalonica, they sought out the local synagogue, hoping to find Jews and perhaps "God-fearing" Gentiles as well. Paul reasoned with them from the Scriptures that Christ had to be crucified and rise from the dead. The result was that some Jews were persuaded, but the majority of those responding were "God-fearing" Gentiles.

As in other areas where Paul and Silas had ministered, the Jews who resisted the Gospel were incensed at the Gentiles' response to Paul's preaching and stirred up a riot. The situation became intense and the brothers sent Paul and Silas to Berea, which is modern Veria. Berea was a city of southwestern Macedonia in the district of Emathia.

On arriving at Berea, Paul and his companions went to the synagogue to proclaim the Gospel as was their custom. Unlike the reception they received in Thessalonica, "Now the Bereans were of more noble character than the Thessalonians, for they received the message with great eagerness and examined the Scriptures every day to see if what Paul said was true."

The result was that many believed, including some prominent Greek women and many Greek men—not just converts from among Gentile "God-fearers" but converts who were pagan Gentiles. Luke gave the Jews undying fame by characterizing them as being "more noble" than the Thessalonian Jews because they tested the truth of Paul's message by Scripture instead of judging it by existing political and cultural standards.

AT ATHENS (Acts 17:16-21)

Paul waited for Silas and Timothy to join him before beginning his mission in Athens. But the overt idolatry he saw around him led him to present the claims of Christ to the Jews and "God-fearing" Gentiles on the Sabbath and those who would listen in the marketplace on weekdays.

Athens had lost the political influence she had held in days past, but she still continued to represent the highest level of culture reached in classical antiquity; the sculpture, literature, and oratory of Athens had reached its pinnacle in the fourth and fifth centuries BC. In philosophy, she held the leading place, being the native city of Socrates and Plato, as well as the adopted home of Aristotle, Epicurus, and Zeno. Paul, a Hellenistic Jew, was well aware of Greek philosophy and very adept at using it to present the case for Christianity, which he would display in due course. Indeed, God chose well in identifying Paul to be the person to present the Gospel to the Gentiles.

In the marketplace, "a group of Epicurean and Stoic philosophers began to dispute with him. Some of then asked, 'What is this babbler trying to say?' Others remarked, 'He seems to be advocating foreign gods.' They said this because Paul was preaching the good news about Jesus and the resurrection." The Greek philosophers then took Paul to the Areopagus, Mars Hill.

PAUL BEFORE THE AREOPAGUS (Acts 17:22-34)

The Areopagus, the Council of Ares—Latin equivalent of "Mars Hill"—was northwest of the Acropolis. The Greek philosophers explained Paul's message to the authorities so that he might either receive the freedom of the city to preach or be censored and silenced.

Paul began his presentation by observing that the citizens of Athens were very religious. "For as I walked around ... I even found an altar with this inscription: TO AN UNKNOWN GOD. Now what you worship as something unknown I am going to proclaim to you."

Luke tells us that Paul addressed the nature of God and man's responsibility to him. God does not live in temples "made by hands" and is not dependent upon anything he has created. Further: "From one man he made every nation of men, that they should inhabit the whole earth; and he determined the times set for them and the exact places where they should live." Paul did not refer to Jewish history or quote Scripture for he realized that it would have no impact on those who were unfamiliar with this material.

Instead, he used what Christian apologists have used for time immemorial—General Revelation. God speaks to us in two ways; through Scripture, known as "Special Revelation," and "General Revelation" by using physical and human nature and historical events. In the Old Testament, the psalmist says, "The heavens proclaim his righteousness, and all the peoples see his glory." In the New Testament, Paul told the Romans that God shows his invisible attributes through physical creation and human nature.

So, Paul quoted from his hearers' own poets: "For in him we live and move and have our being," from the Cretan poet Epimenides in his *Cretica, c. 600 BC*, "We are his offspring," from the Cilician poet Aratus in his *Phenomena*. Paul was arguing that the poets, who the listeners recognized as authorities, legitimatized his message. He ended his presentation saying, "For he has set a day when he will judge the world with justice by the man he has appointed. He has given proof of this to all men by raising him from the dead."

While the resurrection of Jesus had a confirming effect on the early Christians, the majority of this audience rejected Paul's presentation. Some said, "We will hear you again." The response by the Greek philosophers was not overwhelming. Currently, there are some interpreters who think the apostle used a flawed apologetical approach to win converts. They forget Luke's final comment: "A few men became followers of Paul and believed. Among them was Dionysius, a member of the Areopagus, also a woman named Damaris, and a number of others."

PAUL IN CORINTH (Acts 18:1-28)

Paul went to Corinth in AD 51. Because of its geographic location,

Corinth was a prosperous city in the eighth century BC. When Paul arrived, the city's population was over two hundred thousand, made up of local Greeks, freed men from Italy, Roman military veterans, businessmen, Orientals from the Levant, and a large number of Jews. Corinth was the center of worship for the goddess Aphrodite, whose temple included a thousand sacred prostitutes available to service the population. To "Corinthianize" meant to be sexually immoral, a title which still applied in Paul's time.

Jewish law declared that theological students must learn a trade. Paul was a tentmaker and leather worker. Hence, in Corinth, he came in contact with a Jewish Christian couple, Aquila and Priscilla, who also plied in that trade and in whose shop Paul worked. The couple had been forced to leave Rome because of the Edict of Claudius, who was emperor in AD 49–50. They were probably converted at Rome. Paul calls Priscilla and Aquila his fellow workers in Christ Jesus.

Then Silas and Timothy joined Paul in Corinth and brought him the good news that the church at Thessalonica was in good shape. They also brought money as a gift from the congregation at Philippi. The ministry at Corinth consisted of Paul's proclamation in the synagogue—which was rejected by the majority of Jews—then a direct outreach to Gentiles followed. One of the first to accept Paul's message at Corinth was Crispus, the leader of the synagogue, whose whole family "believed in the Lord." He was not the first believer, but was one of the most prominent, and his conversion led to other conversions. He was one of the few who Paul personally baptized.

The work of evangelism at Corinth was promising. "One night the Lord spoke to Paul in a vision: 'Do not be afraid ... do not be silent. For I am with you ... because I have many people in this city.' So Paul stayed for a year and a half, teaching them the word of God."

PRISCILLA AND AQUILA (Acts 18:18-28)

In the spring of AD 52, Paul departed Corinth for Jerusalem and then to Syrian Antioch. He was accompanied by Priscilla and Aquila. The order of the names that Luke uses here may reflect the preeminent position that Priscilla had attained in the ministry or her higher social position.

Before leaving Corinth for Jerusalem, Paul had his hair cut off because of a vow he had made. During his time at Corinth when the ministry was not doing well, he had taken a Nazarite vow as he asked God for special assistance with his ministry. The church in Corinth improved, and Paul wanted to fulfill his vow by giving his hair as a burnt offering in the temple. This could only be fulfilled after a thirty-day period of purification in the Holy City. For more information concerning these vows, see Numbers 6:1-21.

Some have called this a "Nazarite-like" vow, because they feel uneasy that Paul at any time in his Christian ministry should take a Jewish vow; however, he considered himself a Jewish Christian. But at the conclusion of three missionary journeys to the Gentile world, Paul could still state that he was "a Pharisee, the son of a Pharisee." Pharisees were always a minority group; under Herod, they numbered something over 6,000. They were the most rigorous, some would say a fundamentalist sect, in Judaism.

In addition to his Pharisaical training, Paul was a Hellenistic Jew, schooled in Greek culture and philosophy and a committed Christian believer. He knew the difference between Jewish positions that undermined the Gospel and those which were merely cultural constructs.

APOLLOS AT EPHESUS AND CORINTH (Acts 18:24-28)

Luke tells about Apollos, another disciple from church history. Between Paul's time at Ephesus and his return to the city on his third missionary journey, Apollos came to Ephesus in the summer of AD 54. He was a learned man with a thorough knowledge of the Scriptures. "He had been instructed in the way of the Lord, and he spoke with great favor and taught about Jesus accurately, though he knew only the baptism of John."

When Priscilla and Aquila heard Apollos preach in the synagogue, they realized that he had some deficiencies in his knowledge of the Christian message. They then invited him to come to their home and "explained to him the way of God more adequately."

Apollos' understanding of the new faith seems to have come through the disciples of John the Baptist—"he knew only the baptism of John." With further instruction from Priscilla and Aquila, Apollos accepted all God had done in the crucifixion and resurrection of Jesus and in the coming of the Holy Spirit at Pentecost. There is no indication that Apollos was baptized at this time. Perhaps his earlier baptism of repentance by John was viewed as Christian because it points Apollos to Jesus. Furthermore, 1 Corinthians reveals the respect that Apollos received among the Christians and that he was well regarded also by Paul.

The Christians of Ephesus encouraged him and sent a letter of commendation, probably penned by Priscilla and Aquila, to the believers at Corinth. There he debated with the Jews and shared from the Old Testament that Jesus was the Messiah.

TWELVE MEN WITHOUT THE SPIRIT (Acts 19:1-7)

"While Apollos was at Corinth, Paul took the road through the interior and arrived at Ephesus." Ephesus was on the western coast of Asia Minor, between the Koressos Mountains and the Aegean Sea. It was settled in the eleventh or twelfth century BC by Athenians as an opening to the resources of the Asian steppes.

When arriving in Ephesus, Paul encountered some disciples

and asked, "Did you receive the Holy Spirit when you believed?" Now, where or when true believers are found, including in the Old Testament where salvation history began, the Holy Spirit has been active among people. However, Paul is inquiring about whether or not they had experienced the "special" activity by the Holy Spirit that was first present at Pentecost. This activity included signs and wonders, the speaking in unknown tongues and the laying on of hands by the apostles, which God used to illustrate this new spiritual phenomenon.

This spiritual occurrence was critical to the development of the early Church, and whenever the Person and activity of the Holy Spirit has been ignored or undervalued, the Church has suffered. It should be noted that Jesus did not begin His ministry until He received the anointing of the Holy Spirit; He also acted only in the Spirit's power and not in His own.

When Paul asked these men the question, they answered that they were not aware of the presence of the Holy Spirit. Paul investigates further, "Then what baptism did you receive?" "John's baptism," they replied. Then Paul explained that John's baptism was a baptism of repentance, which pointed to the one coming after him, Jesus. "On hearing this, they were baptized into the name of the Lord Jesus. When Paul placed his hands on them, the Holy Spirit came on them, and they spoke in tongues and prophesied."

THE SEVEN SONS OF SCEVA (Acts 19:13-22)

Incantations and the use of magical names were used to exorcise evil spirits in the ancient world, and they seemed to be present at Ephesus. For example, "Some Jews who went around driving out evil spirits tried to invoke the name of the Lord Jesus over those who were demon-possessed. They would say, 'In the name of Jesus, whom Paul preaches, I command you to come out.'"

"Seven sons of Sceva, a Jewish chief priest, were doing this.

One day, the evil spirit answered them, 'Jesus I know, and I know about Paul, but who are you?'" Then the demon-possessed man overpowered the seven brothers and beat them severely, and they ran out of the house naked and bleeding. Even demons know when to take advantage of an apt situation.

News of this event was widespread throughout Ephesus. All who heard were overcome with reverential fear and learned not to misuse the name of Jesus or treat it casually. On a positive note, many believers renounced their secret acts of magic, and some magicians were converted. Luke finds parallels between Peter's ministry and Paul's. Both heal lame men and have successful encounters with sorcerers. Little wonder that so many Orthodox and Roman Catholic churches have the names of St. Peter and St. Paul in their titles.

PAUL'S FAREWELL TO THE EPHESIANS (Acts 20:17-38)

It is impossible to imagine how Paul could have included anything more in this final address to the Ephesian elders. Nothing is left out. He touched on his service at the church and mentioned his sorrow at times over the rejection by his own people, the Jews. Regardless of the difficulty of the issue involved, he addressed it publicly and in their houses. He declared that both Jews and Greeks must turn to God, in repentance, and have faith in Jesus Christ. And, led by the Holy Spirit, he went to Jerusalem, with no knowledge of what the future will bring.

Paul relates that wherever he had ministered, the Holy Spirit had warned him that imprisonments and difficulties would impact his life. "However, I consider my life worth nothing to me, if only I may finish the race and complete the task the Lord Jesus has given me—the task of testifying to the gospel of God's grace." Has any Christian ever stated the task that we are commissioned to address any more clearly or succinctly than this?

Sadly, none of the Ephesian Christians would ever see Paul again. He reiterated that he had been faithful in the proclamation of the Gospel and counseled them to do likewise. Then a warning, "I know that after I leave, savage wolves will come in among you and will not spare the flock. Even from your own number, men will arise and distort the truth in order to draw away disciples after them." Paul told them to keep their guard up.

Now Paul committed them to God and told them that they should help the weak by quoting the words of Jesus: "It is more blessed to give than to receive." This is a rare instance of a comment by Jesus not found in the canonical Gospels. "When he had said this, he knelt down with all of them and prayed. They all wept as they embraced him and kissed him. What grieved them most was his statement that they would never see his face again. Then they accompanied him to the ship."

PAUL'S ARRIVAL IN JERUSALEM (Acts 21:17-26)

When Paul and his companions reached Jerusalem, they were warmly received by the believers there. The following day, the group visited James, with all the elders present. Paul greeted them and gave a report on the success of their mission to the Gentiles.

The reaction to the report was positive; however, there was some disturbing news. In spite of the thousands of Jews who were converted, they had received some false information. "They have been informed that you [Paul] teach all the Jews who live among the Gentiles to turn away from Moses, telling them not to circumcise their children or live according to our customs. What shall we do? They will certainly hear that you have come." Those who make this claim are Jews who are ignorant of the conclusions reached at the Jerusalem Council.

James and the elders apparently regarded these rumors as false and offered a solution to the problem. If Paul were to be seen taking part in one of the Jewish customs that he was reported to have discounted, it would have been thought that he remained an observant Jew. Four men in their mist had contracted some ceremonial defilement and were to undergo a purification rite in the temple, a temporary Nazarite vow. Paul was advised to join with them in this rite and the Jerusalem believers would see that he conformed to the ancestral customs.

James and the elders assured him that they had no wish to nullify the pronouncements of the Jerusalem council and impose unnecessary legal requirements on Gentile converts. Paul agreed and the next day accompanied the four Nazarites into the temple.

PAUL'S TRIAL BEFORE FELIX (Acts 24:1-27)

Paul arrived in Jerusalem, was arrested, spoke to the crowd there and addressed the Sanhedrin. Then, the Jews conspired to kill Paul, without success. He was transported, under arrest; to Caesarea where he stood trial before Felix.

Felix was a freed man of the emperor Claudius, who was appointed procurator of Judea in AD 52. Two characteristics will stand out in the following narrative: the governor had disregard for justice and was consumed with avarice.

Ananias, the high priest, had come to Caesarea with some elders and a lawyer named Tertullus, who presented the charges against Paul before the governor. Tertullus proceeded to tell Felix how privileged the citizenry of Caesarea were for having Felix as governor and Paul "to be a trouble maker, stirring up riots among the Jews all over the world. He is a ringleader of the Nazarene sect and even tried to desecrate the temple; so we seized him."

Paul replied by saying that he was glad to make his defense before Felix. "My accusers did not find me arguing with anyone at the temple, or stirring up a crowd in the synagogues or anywhere else in the city." However, Paul admitted that he worshipped the

God of Israel, as a follower of the Way, which his accusers called a "sect."

Then Paul gave a brief history of his activities after he came to Jerusalem, bringing gifts for the poor and presenting offerings. He cannot understand what all of the fuss is about "unless it was this one thing I shouted as I stood in their presence: 'It is concerning the resurrection of the dead that I am on trial before you today.'"

Felix seemed to grasp the implication of the charges that were being leveled at Paul. After all, he had been in Palestine for ten years, which was enough time for him to understand that the issues involved were completely religious in nature, even though offered in the guise of political sedition. Nonetheless, Felix put his decision on hold until the commander Lysias came down to Caesarea. As a Roman citizen, Paul was given a measure of freedom and allowed visits from friends to care for his needs. "When two years had passed, Felix was succeeded by Porcius Festus, but because Felix wanted to grant a favor to the Jews, he left Paul in prison."

THE TRIAL BEFORE FESTUS (Acts 25:1-12)

Porcius Festus succeeded Felix in AD 59, and for the Jewish population of Palestine, he was a welcome replacement. Three days after arriving in the province, Festus traveled up from Caesarea to Jerusalem, where he met with the chief priests and Jewish leaders. They suggested, as a favor to them, that he have Paul brought to Jerusalem for trial. Luke tells us that they were planning an ambush to kill him on the way. Unwittingly, Festus upset their plans: "Festus answered, 'Paul is being held at Caesarea and I myself am going there soon. Let some of your leaders come with me and press charges against the man there, if he has done anything wrong.'"

When Festus arrived in Caesarea, he convened court and had

Paul appear before him. After the Jews who came down from Jerusalem made their rather weak presentation, Paul spoke in his own defense: "I have done nothing wrong against the law of the Jews or against the temple or against Caesar." Paul states that he has spoken neither against Jewish or Roman law.

To do the Jews a favor, Festus asked Paul if he was willing to return to Jerusalem and stand trial before him there. Paul recognized that if he returned to Jerusalem, he would be under the jurisdiction of the Sanhedrin. Paul replied, "I am now standing before Caesar's court, where I ought to be tried...I appeal to Caesar!" "After consulting with the legal experts who made up his advisory council, Festus replied, 'You have appealed to Caesar, to Caesar you will go!'" The law in this period protected Roman citizens who invoked the right of "appeal to the emperor" from coercion by provincial officials. By the beginning of the second century AD, citizens were automatically remanded to Rome by provincial governors to be examined for a variety of offenses.

FESTUS CONSULTS WITH KING AGRIPPA (Acts 25:13-22)

"A few days later, King Agrippa and Bernice arrived at Caesarea to pay their respects to Festus." Marcus Julius Agrippa II was the son of Agrippa I and the great-grandson of Herod the Great. He was raised in Rome at the court of Claudius and like his father, he was a favorite of the emperor.

At his father's death in AD 44, he was only seventeen years old—too young to rule over his father's domains. Agrippa was put in charge of several minor kingdoms until AD 53, when Claudius gave him the tetrarchy of Philip and Varus. As ruler of the adjoining kingdom to the north, Herod Agrippa II came with his sister Bernice to visit Festus, the new governor of Judea.

Festus discussed Paul's conflict with the Jewish leaders and questioned why they had asked for Paul's death. He confessed that he was unable to understand the ramifications of these issues, which seemed to him to be not real offenses punishable under Roman law but theological differences of a Jewish intramural nature. This information stirred Agrippa's interest. "Then Agrippa said to Festus, 'I would like to hear this man myself.' He replied, 'Tomorrow you will hear him.'"

PAUL BEFORE AGRIPPA (Acts 25:23-27; 26:1-32)

The next day Agrippa and his sister entered the audience room, joined by the high ranking officers and the leading men of the city. Then, at the command of Festus, Paul was brought in. For Luke, this defense was the most important of Paul's five defenses. All the attention centers on Paul himself and the Gospel, not on the charges brought forth by the Jews.

Paul now addressed King Agrippa and spoke in more detail on the points that he had made before in his four defenses. He spoke about his life pre-conversion and his position as a Pharisee: "I too was convinced that I ought to do all that was possible to oppose the name of Jesus of Nazareth. And that is just what I did in Jerusalem. On the authority of the chief priests I put many of the saints in prison and when they were put to death, I cast my vote against them."

Then Paul told of his conversion experience when he heard a voice from heaven saying in Aramaic, "'Saul, Saul, why do you persecute me? It is hard for you to kick against the goads.' Then I asked, 'Who are you, Lord?' 'I am Jesus, whom you are persecuting,' the Lord replied." Speaking directly to King Agrippa, Paul said that he was obedient to the voice from heaven. He preached first in Damascus, then in Jerusalem and in all Judea, and also to Gentiles. "That is why the Jews seized me in the temple courts and tried to kill me." Festus had had enough. "At this point Festus interrupted Paul's defense. 'You are out of your mind, Paul!' he shouted. 'Your great learning is driving you insane.'"

Then Paul addressed the king: "King Agrippa, do you believe the prophets? 'I know you do!' Then Agrippa said to Paul, 'Do you think that in such a short time you can persuade me to be a Christian?'" Paul then prayed to God that all present who had heard his testimony would be saved. Then they all arose and left the room.

Discussion of what they had heard convinced them that Paul was not doing anything that deserved death or punishment. "Agrippa said to Festus, 'This man could have been set free, if he had not appealed to Caesar.'"

THE JOURNEY TO ROME (Acts 27:1-44; 28:1-31)

Luke's account of Paul's voyage to Rome stands as one of the most exacting pieces of descriptive writing in the whole Bible. Luke's use of the term "we" implies that it is an eyewitness account. "When it was decided that we would sail for Italy, Paul and some other prisoners were handed over to a centurion named Julius, who belonged to the imperial Regiment." Luke had a high regard for this centurion. "The next day we landed at Sidon; and Julius, in kindness to Paul, allowed him to go to his friends so they might provide for his needs."

Traveling from Palestine to Crete, a wind of hurricane force swept from the island. "Paul spoke to the sailors: 'Last night an angel of the God whose I am and whom I serve stood beside me and said, 'Do not be afraid Paul. You must stand trial before Caesar; and God has graciously given you the lives of all who sail with you.'"

At dawn, the Romans saw a bay with a sandy beach and decided to run the ship aground. Then it was every man for himself. Roman military law said that the guard who let his prisoner escape would suffer the same penalty the escaped prisoner would have suffered. Then the soldiers decided to kill the prisoners, lest they escape while getting to land, but the centurion Julius proved his determination to protect Paul and prevented this. God in his providence brought them all safely to shore. Many, like Luke, undoubtedly saw the relationship between the promise and their safety and praised the God Paul served.

"Once on shore, we found out that the island was called Malta." While ashore, Paul healed many people through prayer and the laying on of hands. From what Luke relates, it seems Paul looked on his time in Malta as a high point in his ministry.

After three months, Julius arranged for another ship to take his group of prisoners into Italy. "When we got to Rome, Paul was allowed to live by himself, with a soldier to guard him." With this verse, the last "we" section closes. Luke must have remained with Paul through most if not all of his detention at Rome, being visited from time to time by such friends as Epaphras, John Mark, Demas, and Jesus, who was surnamed Justus.

"Three days later he called together the leaders of the Jews. When they had assembled, Paul said to them: 'My brothers, although I have done nothing against our people or against the customs of our ancestors, I was arrested in Jerusalem and handed over to the Romans. They examined me and wanted to release me, because I was not guilty of any crime deserving death. But when the Jews objected, I was compelled to appeal to Caesar—not that I had any charge to bring against my own people.'"

A second meeting called the leaders to Paul's quarters. Luke tells us that it lasted "from morning till evening." Paul insisted that because of Israel's attitude, the message of "God's salvation" had been sent directly to the Gentiles where it would find a positive response.

Luke closes the Book of Acts thusly: "For two whole years Paul stayed there in his own rented house and welcomed all who came to see him. Boldly and without hindrance he preached the Kingdom of God and taught about the Lord Jesus Christ."

LUKE—THE AUTHOR OF ACTS

Luke authored both the third Gospel and the Acts of the Apostles. We learn about life during this period, when Paul and Luke journeyed together, by reading the "we" sections in the Book of Acts (16:10-17; 20:5-21; 27:1-28).

According to Colossians 4:14, Luke was a physician. Professional physicians used their skills in Bible times. However, their work was largely considered to be magical. Circumcision is the only type of surgery mentioned in the Bible.

Most sources say that Luke was a Gentile, an inference drawn from his use of the Greek language. These sources also indicate that he was from Antioch, and if correct, he was possibly one of the first members of the Christian community in that city.

The literary style of Luke's Gospel and Acts indicates that their author was a well-educated person with considerable gifts of expression. Luke's gifts as a historian have been recognized by many scholars who have viewed his work against its classical background and concluded that he ranked among the best of the historians of his day.

According to a tradition found in Anti-Marcionite sources, Luke was unmarried. He composed his Gospel in Greece and died at the age of eighty-four. Luke is both the Patron of doctors and artists. In the middle ages, a picture of the Blessed Virgin Mary found in Rome was ascribed to him.

Luke was a beloved friend and companion of Paul in the journeys related by him in the Book of Acts. Hence, he deserves special mention.

JOHN—THE LAST APOSTLE

Possibly the best known and the most revered verse in the Bible is:

"For God so loved the world that he gave his one and only Son, that whoever believes in him shall not perish but have eternal life." This was written by John, the last living apostle. He was a son of Zebedee and brother of that James who suffered martyrdom under Herod Agrippa I. His mother seems to have been Salome, who may have been a sister of the Virgin Mary. If this was the case, then John was a cousin of Jesus and they knew each other from childhood. John's father Zebedee was a fisherman on the Sea of Galilee, and John, along with his brother James, aided their father in his occupation. The Apostle John was a disciple of John the Baptist and, like Jesus, was also related to him. John returned to his fishing business and worked with his brother and sometimes with Peter. Because of the testimony of John the Baptist and being led by the Holy Spirit, he became a disciple of Jesus and traveled with Him to Galilee.

The first mention of John found in the New Testament is Matthew 4:21. Jesus called him and his brother James to follow him, and later they were appointed apostles. Jesus named the two Boanerges, or "sons of thunder," because of their vehement temper. But the natural defects of their character were overcome by the work of the Holy Spirit and John became a man "whom Jesus loved." He was one of the three apostles whom Jesus chose to be with him at the Transfiguration, at the agony in the Garden, and at the Last Supper, and he sat next to Jesus at the table.

On the cross, Jesus commended his mother Mary to John's care. Five books of the New Testament are ascribed to John—the fourth Gospel, three Epistles, and Revelation, which he probably wrote in AD 95 on the island of Patmos, where he was exiled for preaching the word of God and the ministry of Jesus.

In the book of Revelation, Jesus tells John, "Write, therefore, what you have seen, what is new and what will take place later." The Lord tells John to write a description of the spiritual condition that existed in the seven churches—Ephesus, Smyrna, Pergamum, Thyatira, Sardis, Philadelphia, and Laodicea.

John was released from Patmos after the death of Domitian and returned to Ephesus, where he entertained Polycarp, Papias, and Ignatius as his pupils. While in Ephesus, the seven churches probably enjoyed John's care and Jesus' admonishments about their spiritual condition, or lack thereof. Polycarp's disciple Ignatius tells us that John continued to live in Ephesus until his death during the reign of Trajan. John was likely the only apostle who died a natural death; all the other apostles were martyred.

NERO

Nero's father was Domitius Ahenobarbus, "brazen beard," who was from an illustrious family but had a vicious life. Nero's mother Agrippina was a sister of the emperor Caligula; and through her mother she was the great-granddaughter of the emperor Augustus, which gave her son a strong claim to the throne.

Nero was proclaimed emperor of Rome in AD 54; but his atrocities and poor governance finally destroyed the credit of his house. He finally ended his reign by committing suicide in the face of the revolts of AD 68. Although Nero is not named in the New Testament, he must have been the Caesar to whom Paul appealed. Nero probably heard Paul's case in person, for he was interested in provincial cases. Some have held that Paul was probably martyred, along with Peter, near Rome in the last year of Nero's reign and death in AD 68.

In AD 64, much of the city of Rome was destroyed by fire. To divert the suspicion that Nero had started it for his own entertainment, he accused the Christians of being to blame for the fire. Nero conducted mass arrests and among other atrocities, he burnt his victims alive in public.

THE DESTRUCTION OF JERUSALEM

The leadership of the Jerusalem church was in the hands of James, the brother of the Lord. A devout, law-abiding Jew, he was honored by his followers, but in AD 62, he was murdered at the direction of the Jewish leaders. His death left the Jerusalem church without a leader. At the same time, tensions between the Jews and the Romans increased. Finally, the Jews revolted in AD 66, refusing to perform the daily sacrifice for the emperor. The tragic, intense war that followed cost more casualties than any previous conflict.

In the midst of all the carnage, the leadership of the Jewish people moved from the politicians into the hands of religious leaders. History has shown that occasionally when politicians give way to theologians, trouble is on the horizon.

When the Roman general Vespasian, who later became emperor, was frustrated over a lack of success and left; he put his son Titus in charge of the army. He brought in catapults, siege towers, and battering rams to the walls, which led to hunger and pestilence to rage throughout the city. A soldier threw a torch against the tapestries that Herod had hung along the temple walls, and the fire burned uncontrolled throughout the city. Thousands and thousands of Jews committed suicide. The end was near; the destruction of the Temple in AD 70 and the national entity of the Jewish people occurred to a great degree because of the civil war that occurred among the Jews themselves. In some cases, "creed" determines "deed."

Ante-Nicene Christianity

With the passing of the last apostle, John, we now exit the apostolic era and enter a period of church history known as the Ante-Nicene era. We begin with the *Didache*.

THE DIDACHE

A widely circulated second century Christian document, the *Didache* is mentioned in a collection of literature known as the *Apostolic Fathers*. It shares space with such works as the Epistles of Clement, Barnabas, Martyrdom of Polycarp, and the Shepherd of Hermas. The longer title, "The Teaching of the Lord, through the Twelve Apostles, to the Gentiles," reveals its purpose, which is to teach Christian truth. New Testament books cited in the *Didache* include: Romans, 1 Corinthians, 1 Thessalonians, and the Book of Revelation.

The *Didache* contains two sections, the "way of life" and the "way of death." The former instructs baptismal candidates as to how they should conduct themselves as Christians. The community baptized in the name of the "Father and of the Son and of the Holy Spirit," and give instructions regarding fasting and prayer. The "way of life" describes Jesus as "the holy vine of David thy child." Lastly, it discusses the Eucharist, also known as Holy Communion or the Lord's Supper.

The second section called the "way of death," describes events surrounding the Christian's departure from this life. Some authorities believe that the *Didache* served the same purpose for the early Christian community as did the Apostles Creed. Precise dating of the *Didache* remains a mystery.

PERSECUTION IN THE SECOND CENTURY

Claudius Nero became emperor in AD 53 and was the first ruler to persecute Jews and Christians, because he felt they were a threat to his rule. Titus Flavius Domitian became emperor in AD 81 and at the end of his reign he continued the persecution.

In the beginning of the second century, Justin Martyr, arguably the finest Christian scholar of the time, refused to swear allegiance to the emperor. He was scourged and beheaded under Marcus Aurelius, who became emperor in AD 161 and ruled until his death in AD 180. He was succeeded by Commodus. During his reign, the number of martyrs was relatively low. Severus became emperor in AD 193. While Christians lived in peace in the beginning, eventually he too began to persecute the church.

We have deliberately refrained from describing the tortures used by those who persecuted Jews and Christians for their refusal to denounce their faith. Suffice to say that man's cruelty toward each other knows no bounds. What's more distressing is to know that this behavior has not been completely absent later on between Christian groups.

POLYCARP

Polycarp is one of the leading Christian figures in Roman Asia in the middle of the second century. He was a determined defender of orthodoxy, addressing such heretics as the Marcionites, who rejected the validity of the Old Testament witness for Christians, and the Valentinians, the Gnostics who believed that devotees gained a special kind of spiritual enlightenment that was not available to the uninitiated.

Polycarp had been a disciple of the apostle John and thus was an important link to the early Church. He was well known as a leader among the Christians and was arrested and told to reject his faith in Christ or be burned at the stake. In a new translation of *Eusebius: The Church History* by Paul L. Maier, Eusebius describes Polycarp's decision. "But the governor pressed him, 'Take the oath and I will set you free. Curse Christ!' But Polycarp replied, 'For eighty-six years I have been his servant, and he has never done me wrong. How can I blaspheme my King who saved me?'" With this statement, Polycarp sealed his fate; he joined the expanding list of Christian martyrs who gave their lives for Jesus.

PERSECUTION IN THE THIRD CENTURY

Although Christianity was still considered a threat to the Roman government, the violent persecutions lessened in intensity. The church experienced growth in the later second century. The third century saw persecution intensify and become more severe. Christian leaders were being put to death, and some decided to leave the area.

Also, early in the third century, Emperor Septimius Severus started the civil wars that weakened the empire. He wanted all of his subjects under the worship of "the Unconquered Sun." All gods were accepted, as long as the "Sun" reigned over all.

This is syncretism, the attempt to combine different doctrines and systems, resulting in the formation of a new religion that bears little resemblance to the original elements. This practice was not acceptable to Jews and Christians. Consequently, Septimius Serverus decided to ban both Jewish and Christian religions and outlawed them on penalty of death. Today, people experience syncretism as the Gospel is lost and Christianity conforms to what is popular in the culture.

THE MARTYRDOM OF PERPETUA AND FELICITAS

The term "martyr" came to be used in particular for those who lost their lives because they were Christians. In the persecution of Christians, during the second and third centuries, there were many martyrs.

Perpetua was a well-to-do Christian woman who had an infant child. Little is known about her conversion to Christ and how she lived her Christian life. She lived with her husband, son, and slave in Carthage, today known as Tunis in North Africa. This area was an important Christian community, and her story was well known among them.

Some accounts say Felicitas was Perpetua's slave and was in her eighth month of pregnancy when she was arrested. Roman law held that it was illegal to execute a woman with child. She was distressed since she was also a believer and wished to accompany Perpetua in martyrdom. God heard her prayer and she delivered the child prematurely. Christian friends took the children.

When Emperor Septimius Severus decided to abolish Christianity, he began his campaign in North Africa. Five new Christians were singled out for arrest, one of whom was Perpetua. When her father learned of this, he came at once to visit her in prison.

He was a pagan and saw a way for Perpetua to be freed. He implored her to denounce Christianity. She refused his plea. Her father visited her several more times pleading more passionately for her to denounce Christ, but to no avail. The five new Christians, including Perpetua and Felicitas, were subjected to terrible torture by wild animals and finally put to death by the sword.

The event so affected Augustine of Hippo that he preached four sermons on the details of the ordeal. We can be confident that Stephen and many subsequent Christian martyrs experienced the "Beatific Vision," also known as the presence of God.

TERTULLIAN

Brought up in Carthage as a pagan, Quintus Septimius Tertullian received a good education in literature and rhetoric; he may have practiced as a lawyer. He was the author of a number of works dealing with apologetics and theology in Latin, as well as a few writings in Greek. Tertullian also addressed heresies including Gnosticism, which came into the church in the second century. Its errors are clearly referenced in the New Testament. False teachers denied that Christ had "come in the flesh."

On one occasion, Tertullian wrote a letter to his wife, who was also a Christian. The letter finishes with a lovely picture of Christian marriage. The following has been excerpted from the letter by Tertullian entitled "To My Wife," found in the Cluny Collection.

"How shall we ever be able adequately to describe the happiness of that marriage which the Church arranges, the Sacrifice strengthens, upon which the blessing sets a seal, at which angels are present as witnesses, and to which the Father gives His consent? For not even on earth do children marry properly and legally without their fathers' permission.

"How beautiful, then, the marriage of two Christians, two who are one in hope, one in desire, one in the way of life they follow, one in the religion they practice. They are as brother and sister, both servants of the same Master. Nothing divides them, either in flesh or in spirit. They are, in very truth, two in one flesh; and where there is but one flesh there is also but one spirit. They pray together, they worship together, they fast together; instructing one another, encouraging one another; strengthening one another." This is a beautiful example of spousal love in the early Church.

He also was interested in the central position that martyrdom had in the development of Christianity. Tertullian was aware of Stephen, the Church's first martyr; and more recent to his time, Christians such as Polycarp, Justin Martyr, and Ignatius of Antioch. Tertullian was well known for his statement: "The blood of the martyrs is the seed of the church." His style was brilliant, masterful, and difficult. He resides among the most famous of the African Church Fathers.

Nicene Christianity

The Nicene era includes the period immediately leading up to, including, and immediately following the Council of Nicea in AD 325.

PERSECUTION IN THE FOURTH CENTURY

Valerius Diocletianus Diocletian was a Roman Emperor from AD 284–305. A person endowed with energy, organizational skills, and a logical mind, his goal was to stabilize the Empire and return it to its past glory.

At first the Christians enjoyed peace which had not existed for them in Rome for some time. Diocletian spread the ruling power among himself and three junior emperors, which worked well as long as he represented ultimate authority. Given the egocentricity of his junior partners, this was not to last.

Persecution against the Church soon broke out, the first problems occurred in the army. Most of the church leaders at the time held that Christians should not be soldiers; however, there were many believers in the legions. In spite of the fact that both his wife and daughter were believers, the emperor decided to ignore the church leaders on this issue.

The worst persecution since Nero and Severus ensued. An edict issued at Nicomedia enjoined the destruction of churches and the burning of Christian books. The persecution resulted in a large number of martyrs. In AD 305, Diocletian, formally abdicated, lived his last years tending his garden at his palace at Spalato. A positive change was coming that would impact the lives of average Christians of the time and the direction of western civilization as well.

NICHOLAS, BISHOP OF MYRA, LYCIA

Though one of the most popular saints—in both Greek and Latin Churches—information on Nicholas remains sketchy. Born of wealthy parents in Parata in Asia Minor, he grew up an orphan. Later, he gave away his possessions to the poor and sick, made a pilgrimage to Jerusalem, and upon return, was elected bishop of

Myra. Nicholas devoted himself to the conversion of sinners and the care of orphans, making numerous gifts to the latter. Stories depict him arranging dowries for poor servant girls, tossing bags of money into homes which faced starvation, and coming to the aid of lost sailors and prisoners.

He is regarded as the patron saint of sailors, and churches were built so that they could be seen as landmarks from the sea. Bishop Nicholas was imprisoned during the Diocletian persecution and upon release, he attended the Council of Nicaea and served his diocese for several decades afterward. He died in Myra. He is patron saint of Russia and of Greece. Nicholas is also the patron saint of children, bringing them gifts on the sixth of December, which leads to "Santa Claus," an American corruption of Saint Nicholas.

After dealing with the material addressing the cruel and shocking behavior of emperors and personages such as Caligula, Nero, Domitian, and Septimius Severus, it is comforting to read about St. Nicholas. Parents should tell their children at Christmas about him; he might not have worn a red suit and white beard and flown in a sleigh pulled by reindeer, but "Saint Nicholas" was indeed a "saint."

GREGORY THE ILLUMINATOR

Armenia was a state between Persia and the Roman Empire. Christianity was founded there by Gregory "the Illuminator," also called the Apostle of Armenia. Gregory had been converted while in exile in the Roman Empire. Upon his return to Armenia, he was successful in bringing King Tiridates III to Christ and baptizing him in AD 303.

Thus the rulers of Armenia had become Christians before Constantine in Rome. Soon, the majority of the population followed their king and converted to Christianity, and the Bible was translated into Armenian.

In AD 450, the Persians invaded Armenia and attempted to install their pagan religion in the country. This happened before the Council of Chalcedon, and the Armenians hoped that the Roman Empire would aid them as fellow believers; it was not to be.

In the eleventh century, the Turks took the country and their harshness led many Armenians to immigrate to Asia Minor. The Turks followed them and ruled with an iron fist. In the early twentieth century, hostility still continued between the two groups. Gregory "the Illuminator" had the right spiritual goal, but history has not been kind to the Armenians.

CONSTANTINE

Constantine was born in Naissus, a military post near the Danube. His father Constantius was an officer in the army. He rose in rank and political stature, and in AD 293, Emperor Maximian made Constantius his Caesar. Constantius learned that one of his concubines was a Christian named Helena. Before he abandoned her, she had a son—Constantine. In doing so, Helena changed the course of history, helped her son move the Roman Empire to end the persecution of Christians, and introduced the "Dawn of Christendom."

Helena took many trips to Palestine to locate a number of sites mentioned in the New Testament concerning the last days of Jesus' life and crucifixion. She and her son built a number of churches on sites that they determined to be the actual locations of the events recorded in the New Testament. Christians, Jews, and others travelling these days in Israel owe a large debt of gratitude to Constantine and his mother Helena for establishing the locations which drew tourists from all over the world to the Holy Land.

In AD 313, Emperor Constantine the Great ended Rome's persecution of Christians and led the way to Christianity becoming the state religion of the Roman Empire. The capital of the empire moved from Rome to Byzantium and changed the name to Constantinople, which now is known as Istanbul. The new church had many names: the Byzantine Church, the Eastern Church, the Orthodox Church. The centers of the Eastern Church are Constantinople, Jerusalem, Antioch, and Alexandria, which developed autonomously.

Also, early in AD 313, Constantine and Licinius—who earlier had been rivals to the Emperor—issued a proclamation entitled the Edict of Milan. This document recognized the legality of the Christian churches and tolerated all religions equally. Later in his reign, Constantine would go further and establish Christianity as the favored religion of the Roman Empire. He and his mother, Helena, impacted the world for a thousand years.

THE VINCENTIAN CANON

Vincent was possibly a soldier during a time of barbarian invasions. He became a monk at the Abbey of Lerins, off the coast of France. He wrote soon after the Council of Ephesus on subjects including faith, divine authority, and the work of the Councils.

Augustine wrote extensively on soteriological subjects, among which was the doctrine concerning the nature of sin. In his words, before the Fall, man was free both to sin and to not sin. But after the Fall, the only option left to man was the freedom to sin.

This didn't sit well with Pelagianism, which taught that humans enter this world with complete freedom to sin or not to sin. It rejects the doctrine of original sin, in which children have no sin until they decide to sin on their own. Clearly, Augustine and Pelagius did not often dine together. Vincent was a semi-Pelagian and opposed Augustinianism. Despite his stress on tradition, he maintained that the ground of Christian truth was Holy Scripture and the role of the Church was to guarantee its right interpretation.

Vincent penned the "Vincentian Canon," which has been frequently used as a reliable guide for Christian orthodoxy: "what has been believed everywhere, always, and by all." There is general agreement by Eastern Orthodoxy, Roman Catholicism, and orthodox Protestantism that this refers to the doctrines that were formulated by the Creeds and Councils that emerged by the fifth century.

Creedal Christianity

The early Church was not a collection of different theological positions. All the evidence suggests that it was a cohesive community that held a comprehensive set of beliefs, even if these were not always in writing. For the average believer, who may well have been illiterate, it was necessary to come up with a statement of essential Christian doctrines. It was because of this pastoral need that the creeds emerged.

THE APOSTLES' CREED

The Apostles' Creed is an early summary of Christian beliefs. It is repeated every Sunday in many churches. It was not written by the apostles—in spite of its title—but was used as a baptismal confession in second century Rome.

"I believe in God, the Father Almighty, the Maker of heaven and earth, and in Jesus Christ, His only Son, our Lord. Who was conceived by the Holy Ghost …" The above contradicts Marcionism, which was an early heresy that distinguished between the Creator in the Old Testament and the Redeemer God in the New Testament.

"He [Jesus] descended into hell …" This is not in the early creed. "Hell" is a mistranslation of "Hades," the Greek word for the Hebrew "Sheol," the abode of both the righteous and the unrighteous who await their fate.

"The third day he arose again from the dead …" This statement counters Gnosticism—a movement in the early Church that taught that matter was evil and that denied the humanity of Jesus. It also appears currently in the New Age Movement.

THE NICENE CREED

The Nicene Creed was drawn up at the Council of Nicaea in AD 325 to defend the orthodox faith against Arianism, which was anti-Trinitarian. The Nicene Creed stated that Christ is of the same substance as the Father, not a similar substance. Arianism taught that the Son of God was not eternal but created by the Father from nothing, and that therefore, He was not God by nature.

Arianism, though condemned by Arius' bishop Alexander at a synod at Alexandria, spread and continued to excite the masses. Emperor Constantine, who at first supported the Nicene faith, soon wavered, because of the influence of his sister Constantia, who favored Arianism. Constantine's positive governance did not extend to his theology; he was overruled at Nicea and Arianism was condemned.

The theological debate went back and forth until Arianism held the upper hand and threatened to win out over Orthodoxy. We will learn more of the conflict when we cover the place that Athanasius had in the controversy. He succeeded Alexander as bishop of Alexandria, and Athanasius' name is firmly embedded in the dispute.

THE ATHANASIAN CREED

The Athanasian Creed first made its appearance in Gaul, South France, in about the fifth century. It was said to be the work of Athanasius because it reflects the arguments he employed against the heresies that he faced during his lifetime, including Arianism and disputes over the divine and human natures of Christ.

This creed was written in Latin and was unknown in the Greek

East until the twelfth century. It then spread rapidly and for many Christians, Eastern and Western, it became the touchstone of Christian orthodoxy.

However, in the eighteenth century, it was attacked as unchristian by liberals influenced by Deism and the Enlightenment, movements that had infiltrated the Church at this time. The Creed opens with the statement that if one does not hold to the faith believed in the early Church, "one without doubt shall perish everlastingly." Progressive members in the Church of England found this statement to be offensive to their delicate theological sensibilities and attempted to have the Athanasian Creed removed from the service of their church; fortunately, they were unsuccessful.

There is a balance in the Creed between the Church and the believer within it. It touches every theological issue that was debated during the first five centuries. It is the most accurate collection of classical orthodoxy one can find.

ATHANASIUS, BISHOP OF ALEXANDRIA

Probably educated in his native city, Athanasius became deacon and secretary to Alexander, bishop of Alexandria. He attended him at the Council of Nicaea and succeeded Alexander as bishop in AD 328. He refused to compromise with Arianism and incurred the enmity of the heresy during the reigns of Constantius and Constantine.

Athanasius was black and short of stature, which caused his theological opponents to dub him the "black dwarf." The dispute with Arianism led him to be installed and deposed five times as Bishop of Alexandria. He was untiring in his opposition to anti-Trinitarianism.

Athanasius didn't restrict his efforts to addressing issues surrounding the Trinity. Before AD 318, while still in his twenties, he wrote a treatise on the Incarnation that addressed some of the most difficult aspects of this doctrine. Athanasius also developed an interest in the primitive monkish communities in the desert and was acquainted with Anthony of Egypt. They collaborated in supporting the Nicene party in the Arian controversy, and Athanasius wrote a biography of the monk, *Life of Anthony*.

Also at this time, a controversy developed over which books should be included in the New Testament canon. The book most at risk was Hebrews, which most of the early fathers knew was not written by Paul. The most influential theologian present, Augustine, was sure that Paul was not the author. Although the authorship of Hebrews remained obscure, Hebrews touches on a number of doctrines: the person of Christ, His real humanity, sinlessness, His heavenly priesthood, and His sacrifice at the Cross of Calvary. In addition, its literary composition and expository power is unsurpassed in the New Testament.

In his thesis, *The Easter Letter*, Athanasius closes the argument and defines the New Testament canon, which became the principal teaching instrument of the Church. Athanasius' resolute character as well as his theological acumen contributed much to the Church in the fourth century.

Conciliar Christianity

We now turn to the four major councils in the fifth century. Of course some issues are covered both in the creeds and councils.

COUNCIL OF NICEA

In AD 325, bishops came together in Nicea, a city in Asia Minor, close to Constantinople. This council would come to be known as the First Ecumenical Council. Three hundred bishops attended, mostly from the East, but also many from the West. The council discussed procedures for election and ordination of elders and bishops, and also the order of procedures in various ecclesiastical settings. The crucial issue that faced the bishops was the Arian controversy. Several groups involved that didn't agree, including strict Arians and a small group of bishops who were opposed to Arianism and worried that the movement would strike at the heart of the Christian faith. The leader of this group was Bishop Alexander of Alexandria and a young man who at the time was only a deacon. That man was Athanasius, who would become famous as the champion of Nicene orthodoxy. The council concluded that the Son of God is of one substance with the Father, which was denied by Arius.

COUNCIL OF CONSTANTINOPLE

Emperor Theodosius I held a council to heal the split in the Eastern Church over the long controversy concerning Arianism. Attendance was small, including 150 orthodox and 36 heretical bishops. The result would be the reiteration of the condemnation of the Arian heresy reached at Nicea. Arianism was the view that because God is one, Jesus could not have been truly God.

Athanasius did not live to see the final victory of the cause that consumed him most of his life. However, the "black dwarf" was finally vindicated. Unfortunately, Arianism is currently active in the form of the Jehovah's Witnesses and the Unitarian, Universalist denominations.

This council dealt with another heresy. Apollinarius, Bishop of Laodicea, taught that in the Incarnation, the divine logos replaced the human psyche, so that Jesus' humanity was restricted to his human body. Thus, Apollinarianism was condemned as well. Also, Sabellianism was present at First Constantinople and also condemned.

Sabellius, an early third century theologian, taught that there was only one divine Person, not three as in Christian Trinitarianism. It was denounced as well. If Christians were more familiar with the theological controversies dealt with in the early centuries, they would avoid many doctrinal difficulties.

COUNCIL OF EPHESUS

The Council of Ephesus considered the issue of Nestorianism, which divides the Person of Christ into two persons, divine and human. Emperor Theodosius II was uncertain in ecclesiastical affairs. In AD 428, he appointed the Antiochene professor of theology, Nestorius, Patriarch of Constantinople. Nestorius was deposed three years later at the Council of Ephesus.

Nestorianism was, in effect, the belief that although Jesus Christ was one person—God and man united—his two natures, one human and one divine, existed side by side and hence were separable. This heresy so stressed the separation of the two natures of Christ that it was almost as if he were two people. One result of this view was that Jesus' suffering for mankind was seen as an act of Jesus in His humanity but not in His deity. This did not sit well with the attending bishops at the council and they rejected it.

The second topic to be addressed involved the nature and status of the most Blessed Virgin Mary. It was at this council that the cult or cultus of the Blessed Virgin Mary received official sanction. It should be noted for Protestants who are leery to what they perceive as too much attention toward the mother of Jesus that the Roman Catholic word "cult" here is not used in a pejorative way, but in the classic sense of a religious system or community. The term *Theotokos* was to protect the divinity of the fruit of the Virgin's womb. Unfortunately, things escalated and, for a variety of reasons, some cultural and some theological, the Virgin Mary began to attract more attention. This issue has not gone away and Part Five will address the modern views.

COUNCIL OF CHALCEDON

The Council of Chalcedon, the Fourth Ecumenical Council, was held in the city of Chalcedon in Asia Minor, opposite Byzantium. An Ecumenical Council means one which is binding on all Christians. It was ordered by Emperor Marcian to deal with the Eutychian heresy.

Chalcedon affirmed the statements of Nicaea and Constantinople, holding them to be a sufficient statement of the orthodox faith concerning the Person of Christ. However, it took exception with the new error of Eutyches, who held that Jesus had only one nature.

Eutyches had been an Archimandrite Abbot of a large monastery at Constantinople. He lacked theological subtlety and held that, while Jesus was "of one substance with the Father," he was not "of one substance with us." This was in opposition to the teaching of Tertullian, who centuries earlier taught that in Christ there are "two natures in one Person." In rejecting this heresy, Chalcedon reaffirmed the decisions of the three great councils: Nicea, Constantinople, and Ephesus.

The East accepts First Nicea, First Constantinople, Ephesus, and Chalcedon; Eastern Orthodoxy adds the following additional councils: II Constantinople, III Constantinople, and II Nicea; hence the title: "The Church of The Seven Councils."

During this period, the Church was concerned with the Person of Christ: "Who He was." Later, culminating with the Reformation, it would address the subject of "What He did." All cults and heresies depart theologically from the doctrines that developed from this time frame.

Post-Nicene Christianity

This period covers the aftermath of the Council of Nicea in AD

325. Several key figures stand out on the historical stage, beginning with Macrina the Younger, Simeon Stylites the Elder, Jerome, and finally Augustine of Hippo.

MACRINA THE YOUNGER

Macrina was born in Caesarea, Cappadocia, the eldest of their ten children of Basil the Elder and Emmelia. Her paternal grandmother was Macrina the Elder. She was the sister of the Cappadocian Fathers, Basil, and Gregory of Nyssa.

Macrina received excellent training, based more on the study of the Bible than on secular literature; she also helped educate her younger brothers and sisters. When she was twelve years old, her father arranged a marriage for her with a young man from a good family. However, the husband-to-be died before the marriage could be consummated, Macrina decided to become a perpetual virgin and pursue Christian perfection.

By her strength of will, she had a deep influence on her brother Basil, persuading him to forgo a promising secular career for the Christian priesthood. Upon the death of her father, Macrina and her mother developed a convent on the family estate in Pontus. Here, they and their servants and other companions practiced asceticism and studied Holy Scripture.

When her mother died, Macrina disposed of her wealth to live a life of complete poverty and prayer. She accomplished much by her pious efforts, which was very rare among women of this era.

SIMEON STYLITES THE ELDER

Before the life of Simeon Stylites is examined, some background is helpful. Although monastics existed throughout the Roman Empire, the Egyptian desert provided the most fertile site for its growth. An important goal for early monks was solitude.

According to Justo L. Gonazlez in *The Story of Christianity*, we learn of the desert monks and nuns: "It is impossible to tell who was the first monk—or nun—of the desert." Two will be mentioned here. The first is Paul of Thebes (died about AD 340), who fled to the desert to escape persecution, where he lived for one hundred years in solitude and prayer. The other is Anthony of Egypt (died AD 356), who gave away his possessions in AD 269 and in AD 285 retired to life in the desert. They were well known by Jerome and Athanasius.

Now meet Simeon Stylites, who most certainly wasn't the founder of the Monastic movement, but was clearly one of the most unusual and eccentric practitioners of that lifestyle. Monks living in communities were called cenobites; Anchorites/Solitaries were monks who lived alone or in solitude—a hermit or a recluse. In *A History of Christianity,* Paul Johnson states, "Thus we can say with reasonable certitude that Simeon Stylites was an illiterate, born on the Syrian border (c. 389). He was dismissed from a monastery for excessive asceticism and went to live in a cistern, where he had himself walled up with no food during Lent." Concluding that he deserved more severe surroundings, Simeon moved near Antioch, where he lived on a column. At first, the column was nine feet high, but it was eventually replaced by others—the final pillar being over fifty feet from the ground.

One might think that this situation would mean that Simeon would not be able to communicate with other people. However, visitors were able to ascend the column for prayer and advice by using a ladder. Simeon Stylites died in AD 459, after spending 37 years on his column, from which he preached often and administered cures. Leaders including the Emperor Theodosius II and his wife Eudocia had great respect for Simeon and listened to his counsel. He wrote a letter to Emperor Leo in favor of the Council of Chalcedon, which was well received.

J. D. Douglas, Walter A. Elwell and Peter Toon in *The Concise*

Dictionary of the Christian Tradition offer the following comments concerning Simeon Stylites: "His unusual lifestyle attracted thousands of spectators; led to the conversion of unbelievers; and, because of the respect he gained, added an influential voice in support of orthodoxy." A twenty-first century Christian might take exception to Simeon's proclivities, but he was certainly true to the Gospel.

JEROME

Jerome was born at Strido, near Aquileia, on the Adriatic coast. He studied in Rome, was baptized, and then travelled to Gaul. Returning to Aquileia, he and some friends led an austere life. He then settled as a hermit in the Syrian Desert for five years. On returning to Antioch, he was ordained priest. He was in Rome from AD 382 –385, where he served as secretary to Pope Damasus. The following year, Jerome settled at Bethlehem and devoted the remainder of his life to study.

He was one of the more fascinating characters of the fourth century. His holiness was not humble but proud and haughty, and he did not accept criticism well from others. Those who experienced his scorn were not only heretics but also John Chrysostom, Ambrose of Milan, Basil of Caesarea, and Augustine of Hippo. Those who crossed him he called "two-legged asses."

Jerome was also obsessed with sex. He hoped to overcome this burden but was tormented by sexually explicit dreams. Meanwhile, he found help with a group of wealthy, devout women who lived nearby. It was with that group that he felt free to discuss scholarly questions—especially concerning the Bible. Whether this new relationship addressed his problems with his former dreams is not known.

Jerome's writings were unsurpassed in the early Church. His greatest accomplishment was his translation of most of the Bible into Latin from the original tongues. This work, the Vulgate, would remain the best translation of the Bible for many years. Jerome also wrote a number of commentaries in which he brought his many interpretive skills to bear.

He also inadvertently agreed with the Reformers by advocating the acceptance by the Church of the Hebrew Canon of Scripture, thus excluding those books that came to be called the Apocrypha—or for Roman Catholic readers, the deuterocanonical books or "second canon."

While commenting on the dispute between Augustine and Jerome, Geisler and MacKenzie in *Roman Catholics and Evangelicals: Agreements and Differences* offer the following information: "Although the Roman Catholic canon has eleven more books than the Protestant Bible, only seven extra books appear in the table of contents of Roman Catholic Bibles. This makes the total forty-six—the thirty-nine in the Protestant and Jewish Old Testament, plus seven more complete books. There are, however, four more books or pieces of literature that are added to other books that do not appear in the table of contents. So with seven complete books and four other pieces of literature found in Daniel and Esther, the Roman Catholic canon has eleven more books than does the Jewish Bible and Protestant Old Testament." When Augustine learned of Jerome's decision to exclude the Apocrypha from the canon, he was greatly displeased. He felt strongly that it should be included.

AUGUSTINE OF HIPPO

Augustine of Hippo was born at Tagaste, North Africa in AD 354. His father was a pagan and his mother was a devoted Christian. Augustine went to school at Madaura and then at Carthage in AD 370. At the University of Carthage, he studied rhetoric.

There he fell into a lifestyle of licentious living and took a mistress, whom he lived with for fifteen years. She bore him a son,

Adeodatus. At this time, Augustine became a disciple of Manichaeism; a major heresy in the ancient world that placed an emphasis on asceticism as a way of salvation.

In AD 383, he went to Rome and opened a school there. Upset by the riotous living of his students, he accepted a position as the chair of rhetoric at Milan. Meanwhile, his mother Monica, disturbed by his lifestyle and earnestly praying for his conversion, followed her son to Milan. They came under the influence of Bishop Ambrose, who was famous for his oratorical skills and outstanding as a supporter of orthodoxy. Shortly after, Augustine was converted in AD 386.

Augustine returned to Tagaste, where he founded a monastery and led a life of prayer and meditation. In AD 391, Augustine was ordained a bishop at Hippo. His public disputes with Manichaeans, Donatists, and later with Pelagianism would occupy him for the rest of his life. Two of Augustine's writings stand out namely, his *Confessions* and *City of God*. *Confessions* is a spiritual autobiography where he spares no detail of how God led him to faith in Christ.

Then, when Rome was plundered by the Goths in AD 410 and the Christian world despaired of the result this would have on their faith, Augustine penned the thesis which addressed this incident: *The City of God*. It makes the case for the real existence of two cities, each built on love: the city of God is built on the love of God and the earthly one is built on love of self. In Matthew 16:18, Jesus makes it clear which city will endure.

Some would argue that Augustine was the finest theologian Christianity has ever produced—apologies to committed Thomists. Still, he certainly shaped the theological framework of both Reformed and Roman Catholic systems.

PART TWO

Middle Ages

Early Middle Ages Christianity

Centered primarily in Europe, the Early Middle Ages spanned the period of time from the fifth to the tenth centuries. It began roughly with the decline of the Roman Empire. For example, this era witnessed the sack of Rome in AD 410 by Alaric, King of the Visigoths. Then, in AD 455, Rome was sacked again by Genseric, King of the Vandals. Finally, the last Roman Emperor, Romulus Augustulus, fell in AD 476. Thus began the Middle Ages. We begin Part Two with Leo the Great.

LEO THE GREAT

Two popes stand out in the fifth and sixth centuries. We will treat Leo the Great first. Leo was born in Tuscany, Italy. He was a deacon under Celestine I and arch-deacon under Sixtus III. In AD 440, he was sent to Gaul on an assignment and subsequently recalled and made pope.

Pope Leo was a competent preacher; ninety-six sermons and letters survive. He addressed heretics, including Manichaeans, Nestorians, and Pelagians, and put in place requirements for and the responsibilities of priests and bishops. In AD 452, Italy was invaded by Attila the Hun, who ransacked the city of Aquileia.

From there they advanced to Rome. It was then that Leo left Rome and traveled to meet "the Scourge of God." What transpired in that encounter is not known, but Attila decided not to attack Rome and turned northward, where he died shortly thereafter. Leo was still pope in AD 455 when another horde, the vandals, devastated the city. But the pope led negotiations with the Vandal leader Genserie and avoided the burning of the city, though he took many captives. Leo sent missioners to aid and redeem as many of the captives as possible.

Needless to say, these events and others like them gave Leo great authority in the city. Leo was convinced that Jesus had made Peter the rock of the church, and as his successor, it was his duty to lead the flock when trouble surfaced. Leo the Great died in AD 461 and was declared a Doctor of the Church in 1754. He is honored by Roman Catholics and other Christians as well.

BENEDICT OF NURSIA

Benedict was born around AD 480 of wealthy parents and studied at Rome. The riotous lifestyle there led him to withdraw from the world and live in a cave at Subiaco. Here he lived as a hermit for some time. A community grew up around him and he formed twelve monasteries comprised of twelve monks each and abbots provided by himself. Local jealousy developed toward Benedict and when an attempt to poison him failed, he left Subiaco and moved with a band of monks to Monte Cassino. Here he began to devise a system of regulations to govern monks to live together according to biblical standards.

These regulations would become known as Benedict's Rule. Most importantly, the regulations became the gold standard for monastic life. "Listen!" Benedict directed in his prologue, to the voice of God for direction on where one is to serve in prayer, faith, and good works. Monastic rules were blueprints for an ordered and celibate lifestyle that had been growing in the Christian Church for two hundred years. In about fifty pages, Benedict wrote Rules noteworthy for its biblical directives, spiritual insights, and practical wisdom.

Benedict died in AD 550. About thirty years after his death, some of Monte Cassino's monks traveled to Rome and gave Pope Gregory a copy of Benedict's Rules. The pope was very impressed. Not only did Pope Gregory write Benedict's biography, which has become famous, he also did much to push Benedict's Rules as a model for monasticism in the West. Gregory's endorsement of the rule did much to give direction for future monastic orders and provided guidance for Christianizing the societies of Europe and evangelizing pagans for Christ.

It is no accident that when Joseph Cardinal Ratzinger was elected to be the Bishop of Rome, he chose as his papal name, Benedict. A more fitting example of godliness, dignity, and wisdom could scarcely be found in church history.

GREGORY THE GREAT

Gregory was born in Rome around AD 540 to a well-situated family at the time Justinian reigned in Constantinople. The Rome that Gregory knew was very different from the ancient glory of the Empire. After years of repeated sieges, the city was in an advanced state of neglect and mismanagement. Many of her monuments and buildings had been torn down to repair her walls.

Scant is known of Gregory's early years in this devastated city. We know that after his ordination, Gregory was made a papal deacon to Pope Pelagius II and served the pope *as nuncio*, the title of the pope's representative, at Constantinople. Pelagius died in AD 590 of the plague and for six months, no pope ruled in St Peter's Basilica. When church leaders tried to elect Gregory pope, he refused the office and fled the city. He was found and dragged back to Rome. After notifying Constantinople, officials consecrated him St. Peter's successor in AD 590.

Gregory the Great was pope until AD 604. He was the fourth and last of the traditional Latin Doctors of the Church and the father of the medieval Papacy. In the late medieval era, the outstanding scholastic teachers were given the title, "Doctor."

Gregory's early letters indicate his unhappiness over having been forced to take on the responsibilities of the papacy. These tasks were heavier than normal because of the breakdown of civil order at the time. He found himself drawn into temporal and political affairs as well as spiritual and ecclesiastic concerns; he also organized the distribution of food to the starving. Gregory stated that he was not dispensing his own property but that which belonged to the poor, given originally by St. Peter, to care for his flock. Given his own monastic background, Gregory was a promoter of monasticism and liturgy. His name was so closely identified with plain song, the official music used in the liturgy of the Roman rite, that it came to be known as "Gregorian Chant."

However, it is not only for these reasons that Gregory is called "the Great." He did not neglect doctrine and theological formulations. Augustine of Hippo had suggested the possibility of a place of purification for those who died in sin; Gregory affirmed its existence. Hence, the doctrine of purgatory became "De fide," must be believed, for Roman Catholics.

The doctrine of penance, where the sins of the repentant sinner are forgiven, was stressed. Gregory believed that in the Mass, Christ was sacrificed anew—although an "un-bloody" sacrifice. Because of all these achievements and pronouncements, Gregory has been called by some the first "pope" in the modern sense. He was so racked by pain from gout that by the time of his death, he could no longer walk. Gregory was buried in Saint Peter's with the epitaph, "council of God."

CHRISTIANITY COMES TO THE BRITISH ISLES

Many evangelicals believe missionary activities started later in church history; not so. The apostles and disciples spread throughout the then unknown world telling the Good News about Jesus and announcing the Gospel. Except for the apostle John, who died a natural death on the Isle of Patmos, all of the apostles suffered martyrdom for their efforts.

Gregory the Great had a passion for missions. One of his greatest contributions to Christianity was his zeal for converting pagans to the Gospel of Jesus Christ. Perhaps the best known missionary sent out by Gregory was Augustine of Canterbury—not to be confused with Augustine, the famous bishop from Hippo.

Augustine of Canterbury traveled to Kent, England in AD 597 and was successful in converting King Ethelbert to Christianity. The king's wife was already a believer. The Christian example provided by the king and queen brought many of their subjects to embrace Christianity.

COLUMBA

One of the greatest of the Middle Age missionaries, Columba, who was born in Ireland, became a missionary to Scotland. He arrived on the island of Iona in AD 563 and established a monastery there that served as his headquarters. The monks he sent out played a crucial role in the evangelization of both Scotland and England.

Columba went forth for missionary labors among the Picts in the northern two-thirds of Scotland. He succeeded in converting King Brude of the Picts. Then in AD 574, the new king of the Scots of Dal Riada came to Iona to receive his conformation at Columba's hands.

Interestingly, he was a biblically-based conservationist, a forerunner to the modern environmentalists. He believed that Christ had redeemed all of creation and argued that to reject the beauty of the earth was to reject the kingship of Jesus Christ, the Lord of all life.

It should be said that Britain was evangelized twice—first by Christians in the Roman Legions during the first three centuries. Secondly, by Celtic monasticism that kept the faith alive in the north and was assisted by Columba and his successors along with the Roman Christians who accompanied Augustine of Canterbury to the south.

BONIFACE

The apostle of Germany, known as Winfred, was born in Devonshire, England in AD 680. He studied at a monastery near Exeter. At fourteen, Winfred entered the Benedictine monastery of Notshalling. Later, as the director of the school, he wrote the first Latin grammar for English students. Winfred was ordained at thirty and began preaching. He was well trained in Scripture and educated in grammar, rhetoric, and poetry.

In AD 716, Winfred went to Germany, but the political situation caused him to return to England. While away, his abbot—a superior of a monastery—had died and Winfred was chosen to replace him. It would have been an honor, but he wanted to be a missionary. Two years later, he traveled to Rome to meet the pope and asked to be made a missionary.

Pope Gregory II saw gifts in Winfred that would qualify him to be a missionary, so he changed his name to Boniface after a Roman Christian martyred in the Arian controversy. Boniface means "good works." The pope sent Boniface back to Germany, where he began evangelizing and suppressing heresy. As to his deportment and methodology, some historians claim that he was short tempered with pagans, heretics, and even fellow orthodox Christians. This behavior hampered his evangelistic efforts. Boniface became archbishop of Mainz, but in spite of some success in establishing churches, he ran afoul of a group of pagans and suffered martyrdom. This was a tragic end for one who was gifted, but had mixed results as a missionary, because of his assertive personality.

THE RISE OF ISLAM

Islam arose from the teaching of Muhammad. The name Islam means "submission to the will of Allah." One finds Islamic terms spelled differently in English: Mohammed vs. Muhammad and Moslem vs. Muslim; the latter spellings are currently preferred. Timothy George in *Is the Father of Jesus the God of Muhammad?* offers: "Muslims are sometimes called Muhammadans, after the prophet Muhammad … But Muslims themselves take the word *Muhammadan* as an insult. For all their devotion to Muhammad, they regard him neither as divine nor as the founder of their religion. Muhammad did not claim to be sinless or perfect, and unlike Jesus, he did not receive worship from other human beings." The collection of revelations supposedly given by Allah to Muhammad is known as the Qur'an. The word Qur'an is Arabic for "the recitation."

The founder of Islam, Muhammad, was born in Mecca, Arabia. He worked in his youth as a camel driver, and later, he became a successful merchant. Fifteen years following his marriage, he became concerned with the superstition of the Arabs and spent much time in meditation. At age forty, Muhammad felt himself to be elected by Allah to preach the true religion. He exhorted the people of Mecca to abandon their polytheistic customs and believe in Allah, the true God. This preaching endangered Muhammad's income and he fled Mecca.

He arrived in Medina, where he was enthusiastically received, and established a theocratic state there. Muhammad subjugated the city of Medina and ultimately brought all of Arabia under his control. He became judge, lawgiver, and social arbiter of his followers, establishing principles incorporated later in the Qur'an.

The creed of the new religion is expressed in the formula: "There is no god but Allah, and Muhammad is His messenger." There are five religious pillars of Islam: (1) the Confession of Faith (*Shahada*) requires every Muslim to verbally confess, "There is no god but Allah and Muhammad is His prophet;" (2) Prayer (*Salat*) requires reciting the creed and worshipping five times a day in the direction of Mecca; (3) Fasting (*Sawm*) is required during the month of *Ramadan*; (4) Pilgrimage (*Hajj*) at least once during a lifetime to Mecca, if one is physically and economically able; and (5) Almsgiving (*Zakat*) purifies ones heart from selfishness and greed.

The major beliefs in Islam are: Allah is one and the Trinity is blasphemy. Jesus Christ is one of the many prophets of Allah; however, Muhammad is the last prophet and supersedes Jesus. Jesus was sinless, but he did not atone for anyone's sins and did not die on the cross. Some say that Judas was substituted for Christ on the cross.

It isn't necessary to distinguish between the names "God" and "Allah"—both have the same referent. Some Arab Christians use the term "Allah" for God. Muslims are the most rigid monotheists in the world. They accept the Old Testament and the Christian Gospels but believe they have been corrupted; the Qur'an corrects these mistakes.

Norman Geisler and Abdul Saleeb, in their book *Answering Islam: The Crescent in the Light of the Cross,* offer the following information about the core of this religion. "The strength of Islam is neither in its rituals nor in its ethics, but in its grasp of one great idea: monotheism. Among the religions of the world there is not one that has a shorter creed than Islam and not one whose creed is so well known and so often repeated." Islam clearly emphasizes the rituals and ethics of their religion.

CYRIL AND METHODIUS

Often called "the Apostles of the Slavs," Cyril was born in AD 826, and Methodius AD 815. Both men were born in Thessalonica, today modern Salonika. In the ninth century, this city was an important center of commercial and political life within the Byzantine Empire. In addition, the city occupied a notable position in the intellectual and social life in that part of the Balkans.

Methodius was the older brother and his baptismal name was probably Michael. His younger brother Constantine was known by his religious name, Cyril. Methodius entered a monastery at the foot of Mt. Olympus in Bithynia, known as the Holy Mountain. His brother Cyril studied in Byzantium, where he received Holy Orders. While still a young man, Cyril became Librarian of the Archive attached to the great Church of the Holy Wisdom in Constantinople and held the position of secretary to the patriarch of that city. Cyril soon wished to be relieved of these posts and ultimately accepted a position teaching philosophy in the school of higher learning in Constantinople. He gained the epithet of The Philosopher, by which he is still known.

He ultimately joined his elder brother Methodius. While in the Crimea, the brothers identified what they believed to be the church where the remains of Saint Clement, Pope of Rome, were buried. They collected his relics and brought them to Rome to present them to Pope Hadrian II. Then the event which was to determine the of their lives occurred.

Prince Rostislav of Greater Moravia made a request to Emperor Michael III, to send to his people "a Bishop and teacher ... able to explain to them the true Christian faith in their own language."

Those chosen were Cyril and Methodius, who set out and probably reached Greater Moravia by the year AD 863, at the crossroads of East and West. They undertook a mission among the Slavic people to which both of them devoted the rest of their lives.

They had taken with them the texts of the *Sacred Liturgy*, which they had prepared and translated into the old Slavonic language. Cyril invented an alphabet called Cyrillic and thus became the founder of Slavonic literature. The missionary activity of the two brothers was accompanied by notable success. About three years later, they traveled to Rome, and Pope Hadrian II approved the Slavonic liturgical books. Methodius had to carry out the next stages by himself as his younger brother, became gravely ill and died shortly afterwards in Rome. On June 2, 1985, Pope John Paul II honored the evangelizing work of Saints Cyril and Methodius in his Fourth Encyclical Letter.

POPE SYLVESTER II

Gerbert of Aurillac was born about AD 940 in Auvergne, France of humble parents. He began his service to the Church and studied first at the monastery of his hometown.

Gerbert then traveled to Spain, where he studied at Barcelona and also at Cordova and Seville, under the direction of Arabian instructors. There, he concentrated on mathematics and the natural sciences, showing advanced progress. From Spain, Gerbert proceeded to Rome with his theological teacher, Bishop Hatto of Vich. John XIII recommended him to Emperor Otto I, who sent him to Reims, where Archbishop Adalbero appointed Gerbert a teacher at the cathedral school.

Beginning in AD 983 and over next twelve years, Gerbert was appointed to a number of ecclesiastical positions with mixed results. During that period, his career in the Church changed for the better, and he was sent to the court of the youthful Emperor Otto

III, where Gerbert became the Emperor's teacher. In AD 998, Gregory V made him Archbishop of Ravenna.

Gregory V died a year later and Gerbert was elected his successor, influenced by the emperor. He took as his papal name, Sylvester II, and became the first French pope. Sylvester took his new position as the head of the Church seriously. As pope, he was concerned about abuses by the clergy, including simony—the sale of ecclesiastical pardons, and concubinage—co-habitation of unmarried people. Most importantly, the clergy should be men with spotless lives.

During his reign, he was held in high esteem for his learning; however, some common people thought of him as in league with the devil, and legends surrounded his name.

There is abroad these days the notion among secularists that Christianity was the enemy of modern science. This view is challenged by a volume written by James Hannam, *The Genesis of Science: How the Christian Middle Ages Launched the Scientific Revolution*. He is a graduate of Oxford and Cambridge, where he earned two PhD degrees in physics and the history of science.

His book mentions, among the historical and scientific accomplishments of Pope Sylvester, the introduction of the use of Arabic figures into Western Europe and the invention of the pendulum clock. Prior to becoming pope, Gerbert used a musical instrument called a monochord to teach harmonics. He also was extremely knowledgeable concerning astronomy; he built models of the universe. These are but a sample of Sylvester's accomplishments. Hannam calls Sylvester II "the mathematical pope."

VLADIMIR OF RUSSIA

Vladimir, called "the Apostle of the Russians and Ruthenians," was grandson of Olga and illegitimate son of Sviastoslav, grand duke of Kiev. He was given Novgorod to rule by his father. A number of civil skirmishes broke out and when order was restored, Vladimir was sole ruler of Russia, well known for his barbarism and immorality.

He became aware of the spread of Christianity and legend has it that in the late tenth century, Prince Vladimir, who had been raised a pagan, desired to adopt a religion in order to stabilize his kingdom. To this end, he sent out envoys to examine the major religions—Eastern Orthodoxy, Roman Catholicism, and Islam—and advise him as to which would be best suited for his domain. When the emissaries returned to Kiev, they recommended the faith of the Greeks, for they reported that when they attended the Divine Liturgy in the cathedral of Hagia Sophia in Constantinople, "We did not know if we were in heaven or on earth." Vladimir had found his religion.

Vladimir was converted, reformed his life, and married Anne, daughter of Eastern Emperor Basil II. On his return to Kiev, he invited Greek missionaries to Russia, led his people to Christianity, borrowed canonical features from the West, and built schools and churches. Vladimir and Anne became fitting Christian role models for their people. He is patron of Russian Catholics.

High Middle Ages Christianity

Sandwiched between the Early Middle Ages and the Late Middle Ages, the High Middle Ages spanned from the eleventh to the thirteenth centuries. The beginning of this period was highlighted by a major split in Christianity, namely East versus West, which we will cover next.

EASTERN VS. WESTERN CHRISTIANITY

To understand the controversies which plagued Eastern and Western Christianity, we must go back to the early church. That Christianity was Eastern before it was Western is shown by the fact that it was an Eastern Christian—Ananias from Damascus, Syria—who baptized Paul in Acts 9:19.

The Roman Empire legalized Christianity in AD 311. Emperor Justinian established five patriarchates to govern the rapidly growing ranks of believers: Jerusalem, Alexandria, Antioch, Rome, and Constantinople—four of these are in the East. The Eastern branch of Christianity, which had produced champions of the faith such as Athanasius, Tertullian, Cyprian, John Chrysostom known as "the Golden Mouthed," and Augustine, became more and more estranged from the Western Church, which swore fidelity to the Bishop of Rome.

A number of disputes over political, cultural, and theological issues finally led in 1054 to the rupture between the East and West—the Great Schism. Following the Great Schism, the Fourth Crusade—which had been commissioned to free the Holy Land from Muslim control—ravaged the city of Constantinople. This three-day pillage in 1204 finalized the division between East and West. A great number of Orthodox believers were slaughtered by Catholic soldiers and this tragedy has not been forgotten.

While there are disagreements, both groups agree that tradition—along with Scripture—provides spiritual guidance and theological formation for the church. In addition to the first four ecumenical councils, which Eastern Orthodoxy, Roman Catholics, and Protestants accept as authoritative, the East adds II Constantinople, III Constantinople, and II Nicea; hence, the title, "the church of the Seven Councils." Roman Catholicism, on the other hand, was "open ended," and accepted a larger number of councils as authoritative—the latest being the Vatican II Council in 1962-65.

However, Orthodoxy does not deny to the Holy and Apostolic See of Rome a "primacy of honour"—"a pride of place" or "first among equals"—and under certain conditions, the right to hear appeals from all parts of Christendom. Note that the word "supremacy" is not used. For Orthodoxy, all bishops are equal regardless of their ecclesiastic jurisdiction. Fr. Alexander F.C. Webster, Eastern Orthodox Chaplain at the University of Pennsylvania, puts it thusly, "... the shoes of the fisherman fit more than one pair of apostolic feet."

"What must I do to be saved?" This question posed by the Philippian jailor to Paul and Silas in Acts 16 deals with the most important doctrines in Christian theology. For Eastern Orthodoxy, soteriology (salvation) finds its source in the theological method developed in the Nicene Creed and enumerated by Athanasius. While Roman Catholicism and Reformed Protestantism use justification as the first doctrine in salvation, Orthodoxy prefers the term *theosis*, which means "divinization " or "deification." The Orthodox appeal to Scriptures such as 2 Peter 1:4, where the apostle speaks of "participating in the divine nature," and Colossians 2:10, where Paul says we have been given "fullness in Christ."

Eastern Orthodox bishop Timothy Ware, in his volume *The Orthodox Church*, addresses these doctrines. "The Orthodox idea of deification must always be between God's essence and His energies. Union with God means union with the divine energies, not the divine essence, the Orthodox Church, while speaking of deification and union, rejects all forms of pantheism." On the doctrines concerning salvation, the Orthodox are orthodox.

THE EAST/WEST SCHISM

The veneration of icons was a subject of great discussion in the Eastern Church from AD 725–842. Icons are flat paintings, wrought in ivory and other materials, representing the Lord, the Blessed Virgin Mary, and other saints that are honored in the Greek Church.

Influences against the veneration of icons were present in the

Eastern Empire, at the end of the seventh century. The Monophysite heresy, which minimized the humanity of Christ, and the Paulician sect did not help the iconoclastic cause. Evangelistic efforts among the Jews and Muslims were said to be difficult due to the presences of icons in the East.

The battle between the "iconoclastics"—image breakers—and the "iconodules"—worshipers of images—was intense. The controversy raged for years, but the West refused to accept the imperial edicts. When the Seventh Ecumenical Council gathered at Nicea, it distinguished between *latria,* which is due only to God, and a lesser veneration, *dulia,* which is to be given to images. Timothy Ware comments on the place of icons in his jurisdictions. "Because icons are only symbols, Orthodox do not worship them, but reverence or venerate them. John of Damascus carefully distinguished between the relative honour of veneration shown to material symbols, and the worship due to God alone." The honor of images won over the destroyers of icons in the East.

The final rupture between East and West occurred in the eleventh century. The Bulgarian archbishop, Leo accused the West of error because it made clerical celibacy a universal rule and celebrated communion with unleavened bread. Reconciliation was not forthcoming. On June 16, 1054, when the patriarch was about to celebrate communion, Cardinal Humbert, on behalf of the pope, appeared at the great Church of the Holy Wisdom, also known as the Cathedral of Saint Sophia. Humbert placed on the high altar a sentence of excommunication from the Roman Catholic Church.

ANSELM OF CANTERBURY

Anselm was the most penetrating Christian thinker between Augustine and Thomas Aquinas. Anselm entered a monastic school in Normandy. He took monastic vows, and in 1063 became Prior of the school. His strong Christian witness and intellectual prowess led to him becoming a teacher and spiritual director.

He answered an invitation to come to England and there won the respect of King William I and many of the barons. The archbishopric was vacant, and the King was persuaded to appoint an archbishop. He chose Anselm, who reluctantly agreed and was consecrated in 1093. Like Thomas Aquinas, Anselm owed much to Augustine, whose guiding principle, "faith seeking understanding," he adopted for his own.

Among other writings, Anselm wrote *cure Deus Homo*—"why God became man." In this famous work, he redirects thinking on the nature and purpose of the atonement that had been in place since the Apostolic Era. The view held at the time was the "ransom theory." This position stated that the atonement was an antidote over the forces of sin and evil, a deliverance of humanity from the clutches of Satan. Augustine held this view.

Anselm's contribution is called the "Satisfaction Theory." It understands the atonement as compensation to the Father; sin is conceived as the robbing of God of the honor which is due to Him. Our case seems hopeless; hence, the God Man. The Reformers would form their view of salvation based on Anselm's model.

Anselm was not only a deep thinker, but he was interested in Christian social work as well. In 1102 in his capacity as archbishop, he delivered one of the first and strongest attacks on the slave trade in England. Slavery would not be ended for more than seven hundred years.

Anselm's practical and devotional writings abound with passages of sincere evangelical warmth. Following is an example that Anselm constructed as a homily to be delivered by clerics for those who were in extremis. "Dost thou believe that thou canst not be saved but by the death of Christ? The sick man answereth, Yes. Then let it be said to him: Go to, then and whilst thy soul abideth in thee, put all thy confidence in this death alone,...cast thyself wholly on this death, wrap thyself wholly in this death ... Lord, I place the death of our Lord Jesus Christ between me and thy judgment; and with thee. And if he shall say unto thee, that thou art a sinner, say, I place the death of our Lord Jesus Christ between me and my sins ... If he shall say that he is angry with thee, say, Lord, I place the death of our Lord Jesus Christ between me and thou anger." One could use these words when comforting a person approaching death.

In 1720, Clement XI declared Anselm a "Doctor of the Church." I believe that he qualifies as one of the outstanding portraits in this volume.

THE CRUSADES

For centuries, Christians had looked on the Holy Land as the area where their faith began. However, the presence of Islam there made religious pilgrimages often hazardous. The use of the term crusades refers to the number of campaigns which originated from Western Europe to the Eastern Mediterranean. They had for their goal the recovery of the Holy Land from Islam and its retention in Christian hands. This would require the Ottoman Empire's expanding power to be curtailed.

The First Crusade in 1095 was instituted by Urban II at the Council of Clermont. Soon a rather unorganized mob set out for Jerusalem under the leadership of Peter the Hermit. During the journey, they lived off the land and had to fight other Christians who defended their crops and possessions. This rabble army practiced their war against the infidel by killing thousands of Jews. They laid siege to Antioch, and during the battle a large number of combatants on both sides were massacred. The Crusades finally caught sight of Jerusalem on June 7, 1099. A fierce battle occurred and a horrible bloodbath ensued. All defenders were killed, women were raped, and infants thrown against walls. Secular historians have distorted these events; although it must be said, this was not our finest hour.

There were seven more crusades, including one that included Richard the Lionhearted of England and Phillip II Augustus of France. Also, several "children's crusades" resulted in masses of children and adolescents marching eastward, only to die or be enslaved by those whose territories they crossed.

BERNARD OF CLAIRVAUX

Bernard was born in 1090 of noble parents in Fontaines, France. He showed an early interest in the monastic orders and entered the monastery at Citeaux with thirty other young men. Three years later, he was asked by his abbot to select a place for a new monastery. Bernard established a house at Clairvaux that, under his leadership, became one of the centers for the Cistercian Order. The Order soon became one of the most influential religious forces in Europe. Bernard's power increased when one of his former students, a Cistercian monk, was elected as Pope Eugenius III in 1145.

Bernard was also involved in the Second Crusade. His preaching was very different from some of the early preachers who counseled bringing down fire and brimstone on the crusader's foes. His passion was the study of the Scriptures and devotion centered on the humanity of Jesus. Indeed, it was his saintliness rather than the force of his intellect which made him well known in Europe and was the cause of the rapid growth of the Cistercian Order in the twelfth century. He insisted that God should be loved simply and purely because He is God. Bernard was canonized in 1174, and was created a "Doctor of the Church" in 1830.

Incidentally, contemporary with Bernard was a friend of his named Malachy, a bishop from Ireland. Malachy has become posthumously famous for his papal prophecies. In *Lignum Vitae*, published in 1595, a papal list, attributed to Malachy, allegedly predicted the last 112 popes with surprising accuracy. This recently became important, because Pope Benedict, the 111th pope, suddenly, and without warning, abdicated his papacy, making room for the 112th pope. Could he possibly be the last pope?

In the second quatrain of his hymn to honor Malachy, Bernard revealed that the name Malachy means angel. Thus, the question arises, since angel means messenger, is it possible that Malachy's purpose, among other things, was that of an eschatological Papal messenger? Whatever the case may be, Bernard was given the high honor of ushering this saint into the awaiting arms of the "angels who took him," as described in *The Life and Death of Saint Malachy the Irishman*. Finally, as legend has it, intriguingly they were so close that both Bernard and Malachy were buried in the same grave.

BERNARD OF CLUNY

Bernard was a poet; he was a Benedictine monk at Cluny during the time of Peter the Venerable in the twelfth century. He composed sermons and a dialogue on the Trinity, and was the possible author of a collection of monastic regulations.

The following quote is found in John Delaney and James Tobin's book, *Dictionary of Catholic Biography*. "His most famous work is *De contemptu mundi*, a poem of some 3,000 lines, written about 1140. It is a brilliant and virile satire against contemporary immorality, the simony of bishops, insolence and incompetence of papal legates, weaknesses of the popes themselves, and monastic leanings toward luxury. Matching his angry lashing of the enormity of sin is the flowing lyricism of his praise of meditation, virtuous living, and the grandeur of union with God in heaven. The poem apparently was known to Dante, it had great effect and was widely quoted by apologists of both sides during the Reformation." This is a caustic observation on the Church of the twelfth century.

The September 29, 2012 devotional in *Closer Walk* shares the following hymn by Bernard of Cluny that describes the Christian's final home in heaven:

"They stand, those halls of Zion, all jubilant with song,
And bright with many an angel, and the martyr throng.
The Prince is ever in them, the daylight is serene;
The pastures of the blessed and decked in glorious sheen.
O sweet and blessed country, the home of God's elect!
O sweet and blessed country that eager hearts expect!
Jesus, in mercy bring us to that dear land of rest;
Who art, with God the Father and Spirit, ever blest."

HILDEGARD OF BINGEN

Hildegard was born in Bockelheim, Germany in 1098. The early biographers give little information about Hildegard's early family life, but indicate that she was a weak and sickly child. Her parents were religious and promised the child to the service of God. At eight years of age, Hildegard was given to Blessed Jutta, a recluse who lived in a cell near Diessenburg, in a community that had developed under Benedictine direction. When Hildegard was 15 years old, she became a nun, and in 1136, she succeeded Jutta as Prioress. As a child, she had experienced visions which continued in her new position. She spoke of them to her confessor, who directed Hildegard to put them in writing, and they became her principal work, *Scivias*.

Pope Eugenius III, after examining the writings, discussed them with St. Bernard of Clairvaux, who pronounced them valid and authorized their publication. At that time she moved her community to Rupertsberg, near Bingen, and built a convent there.

Hildegard wrote hymns and music for her nuns and corresponded with a large number of people including popes, kings, clerics, and the laity. She rebuked and warned all without regard to their position. She traveled throughout Germany, speaking to clergy and writing poetry and scientific studies on the human body and natural history. Hildegard broke the mold for what has been understood as the average mystic who was a nun in the twelfth century. Mysticism is a religious practice that looks for a direct knowledge of God—as opposed to an intellectual knowledge of Him.

During her lifetime, Hildegard of Bingen was honored as a saint and also declared a sorceress by some. In her day, she bore the title, "Sibyl of the Rhine." In 1979, the 800th anniversary of her death, Pope John Paul II referred to her as "an outstanding saint."

Then on October 7, 2012, Pope Benedict XVI declared Hildegard of Bingen a Doctor of the Universal Church. She becomes the 34th Doctor and the fourth female to receive the title.

FRANCIS OF ASSISI

Francis was born in 1181 in Assisi, Umbria, Italy, into a well-to-do family. He led a pleasure-seeking life as a youth. During a border dispute between Perugia and Assisi, he was taken prisoner and was incarcerated for several months.

Upon release, Francis returned home and became disillusioned with his worldly lifestyle. During an illness, he decided to change and began to devote himself to prayer and working with the poor. While on a pilgrimage in Rome, Francis interacted with beggars around St. Peter's Church and, exchanging his clothes with one, he spent the rest of the day begging. This experience set the tone for the rest of his life.

On returning to Assisi, he devoted himself to serving lepers and repairing a nearby ruined church. One morning, while worshipping in the church in Portiuncula, he heard the words of the Lord read from Matthew 10, telling his disciples to leave all. Francis took this reading as a personal call, discarded his staff and shoes, and determined to set out to save souls.

He attracted a number of like-minded followers and composed a simple role of life for himself and his associates, based on material from the Gospels. On a visit to Rome in 1209, Francis obtained approval to establish this new community from Pope Innocent III. Thus the order that bears his name was born: "The Franciscan Order."

The new order attracted many disciples, and Francis continued to preach, served the poor, and traveled twice to Syria to evangelize among the Muslims. Francis experienced shipwreck, as did Paul the Apostle before him, while on one of his missionary journeys. Some sources state that Francis received the "stigmata," which refers to the wounds and scars corresponding to those suffered by Christ during the crucifixion. A number of stigmata incidents have been reported to have occurred on persons of exceptional holiness. He died in Assisi, and was canonized in 1228. Clearly, Francis' passion for service remains a model for Christians today.

Cardinal Jorge Mario Bergoglio, born in 1936 in Buenos Aires, Argentina, was elected the 266th pope of the Roman Catholic Church on March 13, 2013. The first Latin American pope, trained in the Jesuit order, surprised the Church when he chose as his papal name Francis. While doctrinally orthodox like Francis of Assisi, the pope also resembles him as humble, unassuming, and holding concern for the poor and the downtrodden.

Another modern Catholic scholar who happens to be the preacher to the Papal Household, Fr. Raniero Cantalamessa, has written extensively on Francis of Assisi. See in particular: Raniero Cantalamessa, *Come, Creator Spirit: Meditations on the Veni Creator.*

DOMINIC

Dominic was born in 1170 in Caleruega, Old Castile, Spain. He studied at the University of Palencia and was ordained before he finished. Dominic and Bishop Diego were sent to Italy on a mission that proved unsuccessful. Following this, the two went to Rome to ask permission to found a new order that would address the heresy of the Albigensians. The request was denied.

Dominic and Diego were instead sent to Languedoc to instruct the Cistercians to adopt a more austere lifestyle. Their preaching attracted many converts as their university training enabled them to best their opponents. In 1208, Dominic traveled with the army that was involved with a crusade against the Albigensians.

Dominic attended the Ecumenical Council at Rome in 1215, where his request to establish an order of preachers was again denied. Dominic was fervent in preaching against what the Church viewed as heresy. He finally was successful a year later, when he received papal approval to establish the Order of Preachers, the Dominicans. The new order experienced great growth and in Lombardy, 100,000 persons were converted. He went on to form an order for the laity known as Militia of Christ.

Two Councils convened at Bologna, which resulted in Dominicans traveling to Hungary, Greece, and England, with a center being established at Oxford. Its purpose was to attempt a balance between the intellectual life, popular needs, and spiritual concerns.

The Dominicans soon rivaled the Franciscans in size and success, while both adapted the role of mendicancy—the use of begging to sustain the ministry. The Dominicans stressed poverty as a means of refuting heresy, while the Franciscans valued study, academics, and preaching as more effective in addressing theological error. Though the somber Spaniard Dominic was not as well-known as his contemporary Francis of Assisi, he was a humble man, always ready to preach the Gospel and win people to Christ. Dominic was a capable leader and organizer. Tradition has it that he instituted the devotion of the Rosary, but this is disputed by some historians.

The list of church leaders and theologians who were Dominicans is impressive: Thomas Aquinas, his mentor, Albert the Great, and Catherine of Siena, who as a young girl, joined the "Sisters of the Penance of St. Dominic." On the other hand, some Dominicans were considered to be problematic. Meister Eckhart, who was a German mystic, was accused of heresy in 1326 but died during the proceedings. Also, Girolamo Savonarola was hanged as a schismatic and heretic in Florence. Dominic died in Bologna in 1221 and was canonized in 1234. Dominic was a man who held to authentic Christian doctrine, but was characterized by some as "austere."

THOMAS AQUINAS

Also called "Doctor Angelicus," the Doctor of the Angels was born in 1225 at Roccasecca, the youngest son of Count Landulf of Aquino, who was related to the Emperor and King of France. At the age of five, Thomas was sent to a Benedictine school at Monte Cassino. In 1240, while at school in Naples, he was attracted to philosophy and decided to join the recently founded Dominican Order.

Thomas went to Paris in 1245, where he came under the direction of Albertus Magnus-Albert the Great; indeed a fortunate coupling for the Church. Albertus introduced Thomas to Aristotelian philosophy. Thomas accompanied his mentor to Cologne, was ordained in 1250, returned to Paris, and became a master of theology.

Thomas received his doctorate, aided Albert in establishing the system of studies adopted by the Dominicans, and lectured in cities throughout Italy. Pope Gregory X sent him to the Council of Lyons in 1274, but he died on the way. One of the reasons that the council was convoked was to heal the rupture caused by the East/West Schism; it is interesting to speculate what impact Thomas would have brought to the council if he had arrived.

Aquinas has enriched the Church with his contributions in philosophy and theology. John J. Delaney states in *Dictionary of Catholic Bibliography*: "[e]xcept for the limitations of thirteenth century science, what St. Thomas had to say about God and man, creation and purpose, mind and matter, will, the soul, knowledge, human conduct, motives, habits, acts, grace, and faith remains fundamental in Catholic thinking and has been papally approved as such." Delaney makes the point that Thomas' theological statements have stood the test of time.

Also, Thomas made a distinction between reason and faith. F. L. Cross comments on this distinction in *The Oxford Dictionary of the Christian Church*. "If in a large area reason is paramount, many of the fundamental Christian verities (the Trinity, the Incarnation, the creation of the world in time, original sin, purgatory, the resurrection of the body etc.) lie wholly beyond its province. But while such doctrines cannot be established by reason they must not be considered contrary to reason." This distinction is rejected by Evangelicals who are fideists—those who reject the use of reason in discussing doctrine.

For a treatment of Thomistic positions on ethics see: Norman L Geisler and Ralph E. Mackenzie, *Roman Catholics and Evangelicals: Agreements and Differences* and Norman L. Geisler, *Thomas Aquinas: An Evangelical Appraisal*. Both volumes address areas of doctrinal differences between evangelical Protestants and Roman Catholics.

Late Middle Ages Christianity

The Late Middle Ages spanned from the fourteenth to the sixteenth centuries. It was during the early part of this period that Europe suffered the most deadly disease outbreak in its history. The Black Death became the legendary pandemic known as bubonic plague. It began in 1347 and killed a third of the human population. With that in view, we begin the last segment of the Middle Ages with a more inspiring event called the Renaissance, to which we now turn our attention.

THE RENAISSANCE

Before the Renaissance, the moral climate around Rome was less than stellar; practices such as simony—the purchase or sale of ecclesiastical pardons, and nepotism—favoritism shown by persons in high office to relatives—were rampant. Clerics paraded their mistresses and children with impunity. Also, priests and other clerics were poorly educated and did a negligible job of teaching their parishioners.

The Renaissance is defined as "rebirth" or "revival." This period involved a renewal of art, literature, and learning in Europe in the fourteenth through sixteenth centuries. It began in Italy and spread throughout Europe and other countries, which marked the transition from the medieval to the modern world. The Renaissance would lead to an improvement in the area of moral and ethical standards.

The Renaissance implies a negative judgment on the preceding age. This movement is generally understood as developing between the fourteenth and sixteenth centuries. It was also the period of rediscovery of the literature of classical antiquity. The awakening of interest in classical learning coincided with the invention of the printing press, which discovery would facilitate the

Reformation. Books now were more accessible and scholars were able to compare different editions of Cicero, Jerome, and the New Testament.

The term "humanism" developed at this time. While some humanists were not orthodox, many humanists were sincere Christians who believed in sin and the limits of human achievement. The Renaissance saw a revival of interest not only in the classical literature, but also the early church Fathers, the biblical texts, and the heritage of Judaism.

The theology of the Middle Ages was called "scholasticism." This was an impressive synthesis of human learning and the revelation of Scripture, the finest expression of which was the work of Thomas Aquinas. Preceding the Renaissance, the realism of Thomas had given way to "Nominalism," which withdrew the data of faith from the realm of reason and paved the way for the disintegration of scholasticism. This was called the *Via Moderna* against the method of Augustine and Aquinas.

All of these factors paved the way for the Reformation. Luther was educated in Nominalism, while Calvin was trained in humanism, as was Melanchthon. Unfortunately, the Renaissance provided the tools with which the thinkers of the Enlightenment would attempt to use to dismantle Christianity. One of the most important figures among the Christian humanists was Desiderius Erasmus, called the Prince of the Humanists, whom we will be addressing again in due course.

The Renaissance also impacted the whole area of culture: painting, sculpture, and architecture. Michelangelo painted the ceiling of the Sistine Chapel. He also was a superb architect who designed St. Peter's in Rome and was also famous for designing the uniforms worn by the Swiss guards at the Vatican. Leonardo da Vinci painted the Last Supper and the Mona Lisa and drew sketches of devices far ahead of their time. Painting in this time was devoted to accuracy in form and anatomy.

The popes who ruled between 1447–1521 were for the most part affected by the spirit of the Renaissance as well. Nicholas V was interested in rebuilding the great churches of Rome and formed the Vatican Library. Julius II worked toward the unification of the papal states of Italy and was the one who commissioned Michelangelo to decorate the Sistine Chapel. The Renaissance should never be confused with the "Enlightenment;" the former was for the most part positive, while the latter was not.

CATHERINE OF SIENA

Catherine was born in 1347 in Siena, central Italy, south of Florence, the youngest of twenty-five children. She became a Dominican tertiary at sixteen and began to work with lepers three years later. While still quite young, she received visions and had many difficulties at home.

Her deep spirituality attracted a large group of followers, including many of noble rank. Several of these disciples were Dominicans who were knowledgeable in theological issues and helped Catherine avoid the errors that consumed other mystics. While at Pisa during Lent in 1375, she received the Stigmata, which is the reproduction of the wounds of the Passion of Christ in the human body. The first saint known to have received the Stigmata is St. Francis of Assisi. The Stigmata can be "actual," bleeding wounds, or "invisible," there is no bleeding or tearing of the flesh only sensation of pain. Sources confirm that Catherine experienced the latter.

She spent her remaining years attempting to resolve the Great Schism, which lasted from 1378-1417. This Schism was over who should occupy the Papal Chair.

Catherine died in Rome and was canonized in 1461, and made the "patron of Italy" in 1939. In 1970, Paul VI gave her the title of

"Doctor of the Church." Teresa of Avila joined Catherine in receiving the honor at the same time. Therese of Lisieux joined them in 1997 when Pope John Paul II elevated her as the 33rd doctor and the third woman to be declared a "Doctor of the Church." Both Teresa and Therese will appear in this volume later.

THE BRETHREN OF THE COMMON LIFE

The decline of the Middle Ages began after the Fourth Lateran Council in 1215 and continued until the close of the fifteenth century. Most historians—Roman Catholic and Protestant alike—agree that the Church had become morally corrupt and in need of reform.

Two movements that addressed the need to reform the church were the "humanists," who were the products of the Renaissance, and a number of church schoolmen who have been characterized as "mystics." Representative of the former group was Desiderius Erasmus, who was called the "Prince of Humanists." The mystics were a varied group; some—such as Hugo of St. Victor, Bonaventura, and Thomas Aquinas—were orthodox in their theology. Others were less precise in their theological formulations. An example was the German Dominican Meister Eckhart, who was accused of pantheism.

Both humanistic and mystical influences can be seen in the development of the movement known as the "Brethren of the Common Life." This group grew out of the teaching and preaching of Geert de Groote. He was a brilliant scholar and was appointed professor of philosophy and theology at Cologne in 1366. Eight years later, Groote was converted to Christ and his lifestyle—which previously had been self-indulgent—became simple and devout. After three years spent in a monastery near Arnhem, he became a missionary preacher, although he was never ordained a priest.

After Groote's death, his disciple Florentius Radewyns founded the Brethren of the Common Life in 1379. Religious communities were established throughout the Netherlands. They adopted a simple lifestyle. The Brethren of Common Life was non-monastic in the matter of vows; disciples were left free, whether clerics or laymen, to continue their ordinary vocations. The movement spread to Germany and Switzerland and became noted for its stress on Bible reading, meditation, and pursuit of holiness. The personal spirituality, which the movement nurtured among laypeople, would prepare for the message of the Reformation soon to follow.

Among important leaders who were impacted by the Brethren of the Common Life were Hadrian VI, elected Pope in 1522; Gabriel Biel, scholastic philosopher and founder of the University of Tübingen; and Thomas á Kempis, author of *The Imitation of Christ* and a biography of Gerhard de Groote. Martin Luther, who would become a leader of the German Reformation, came under the influence of the movement. Heinrich Bullinger of Zürich, a colleague of John Calvin, had been impacted as a schoolboy by the piety of his teachers who were members of the Brethren group. The aforementioned Desiderius Erasmus also studied with the Brethren.

By the end of the Middle Ages, the spiritual health of the Church had been severely compromised. However, Jesus promised in Matthew 16:18 and elsewhere that the message of the Gospel would never be completely overcome. The presence of movements in history like the Brethren of the Common Life validates this promise. I have often felt that contemporary ministries like Campus Crusade for Christ, InterVarsity Christian Fellowship, and the Roman Catholic movement Opus Dei would feel at home with the "Brethren."

THE PRE-REFORMATION PERIOD

It is not common knowledge that, prior to the Reformation, men and movements sought to redirect the Roman Catholic Church. Indeed, virtually all historians—Roman Catholic and Protestant alike—agree that the Church had become morally corrupt and was in need of reform.

The close of the fifteenth century proved to be a turning point in Western history. The church as well as the general culture would be drastically changed. In the church, while clerical celibacy was to be enforced, many disregarded it, openly flaunting their illegitimate children.

While some reformers spoke out against the corruption, it existed throughout the clergy, both priests and bishops, as well as some popes. Among the most notorious offenders include Pope Sixtus IV, who was highly immoral and plotted to assassinate a ruling Florentine family that was killed at Mass by two priests. Pope Alexander VI became one of the most notorious of all the popes. He used his office to favor his children—eight in all; even marrying his daughter Lucrezia to important princes multiple times.

Doctrinal problems existed as well. Some Catholic observers thought that the teaching of the church had gone astray. Since the fall of Constantinople, scholars from the East with views that were different from those common in the West flooded Western Europe and Italy in particular. The manuscripts these scholars used alerted Western scholars to the many changes that had occurred in the copying of ancient texts; now the Greek text of the New Testament could be compared with the Latin Vulgate.

Catholic poet Sebastian Brant summed it up thusly, "St. Peter's bark is tempest-tossed, I fear the vessel may be lost." The situation looked dire; however, help was on the way.

JOHN WYCLIFFE

John Wycliffe was born in 1329 into a wealthy English family who owned property near Richmond in North York, England. He became Warden of Canterbury Hall in Oxford from 1365–1367.

Wycliffe attended Oxford University and had become master of Balliol College by 1360. He studied for his master's degree, which he received a year later. Upon ordination, he became rector of a church in Lincolnshire. Wycliffe became an absentee pastor, which was common in those days, to provide a means to finance his academic studies. He took exception to the skepticism that prevailed at Oxford and was present at academic institutions throughout Europe.

Wycliffe was a popular teacher, and his lectures were well attended. He chose Augustine as his main theological guide. Nominalism, the theory of knowledge that denies the objective reality of universal principles, was popular at the time, and like Augustine, Wycliffe was a realist and therefore stood against it.

By 1370, he had become Oxford's leading philosopher and theologian. Wycliffe developed political ideas that had radical social implications. Not only should unjust civil leaders be disenfranchised, but church leaders should be judged according to scriptural standards as well.

His ideas caused much controversy because in addition to his political positions, he addressed a number of doctrines that he disagreed with, which, of course, put him at cross-purposes with clerical authorities. Many of Wycliffe's theological adjustments would appear in the systems that would develop in the future Reformation.

During this time, the church was extremely wealthy, owning about one-third of all land in England, but claimed that it should be exempt from paying taxes. Wycliffe made it clear that these issues were a blot on the reputation of clergy who were claiming to reflect leadership over Christian churches.

These views, coupled with Wycliffe's disagreements with the church which would surface during the Reformation, caused him to lose support in Oxford; his Eucharistic position would be the last straw. It would be condemned by the University in 1381. After his death his remains were exhumed, burned and cast into the river Swift.

He has been called the "Morning Star of the Reformation." His greatest legacy to that movement was to stress the need for the Bible to be translated into the common language of the people. The Wycliffe Bible Translators Movement has carried on Wycliffe's goal in current times.

JOHN HUSS

John Huss was born in 1372 at Husinec, Bohemia, now Czechoslovakia, of poor parents. He entered Prague University, where he proceeded to earn his BA, MA and BD degrees. In 1401, he became the Dean of Philosophical Faculty at the school. Huss was ordained priest in 1400 and became a well-received preacher at the Bethlehem Chapel at Prague. Although he believed in the "real presence" in the Eucharist—"transubstantiation," Huss was an admirer of Wycliffe and stressed the authority of Scripture.

Because of the close links between England and Bohemia since the marriage between King Richard II and Anne of Bohemia, Wycliffe's radical doctrines found their way to Prague. His attack on transubstantiation was met with little favor. Wycliffe's opposition to clerical corruption and his appeal for a change from the hierarchical church to the invisible church of the elect fell on sympathetic ears.

Huss's preaching these novel doctrines led him to be excommunicated by the archbishop. Huss added to his difficulties by attacking the sale of indulgences. In 1414, he was promised safe conduct to a council meeting at Constance. He was captured, tried, and convicted of heresy. John Huss went bravely to a martyr's death a year later. We learn of the prayer that Huss offered as he was dying in Justo L. Gonzalez's book, *The Story of Christianity, Vol 1.* "Lord Jesus, it is for thee that I patiently endure this cruel death. I pray thee to have mercy on my enemies.' He was heard reciting the Psalms as he died." By the time of his death, Huss became a national hero. The University of Prague declared him a martyr.

THOMAS A KEMPIS

Thomas Hemerken was born in 1380 at Kempen, near Düsseldorf, Germany, and was the son of a blacksmith. He studied in Deventer under Florentius Radewyns and in 1399 joined the Augustinian "Brethren of the Common Life." He was ordained in 1413 and was made a sub-prior in the movement.

Thomas spent almost the rest of his life writing, preaching, and copying manuscripts and was widely consulted as a spiritual guide. Williston Walker in A *History of the Christian Church* examines one of Thomas' best known works saying, "[the] noblest product of this simple, mystical, churchly piety is the *Imitation of Christ*—a book the circulation of which has exceeded that of any other product of the Middle Ages." The purpose of this manual is to teach Christians how to develop spiritual maturity by following Christ as their model. The *Imitation* has become a favorite devotional text among Protestant evangelicals as well. Thomas a Kempis and his spiritual formation, learned with the Brethren of the Common Life, have enriched the Body of Christ far beyond their origin in the fifteenth century. For a beautifully illustrated volume, see William C. Creasy's translation from the Latin manuscript of *The Imitation of Christ*.

GIROLAMO SAVONAROLA

Savonarola was born in 1452 in Ferrara, Italy. He at first decided on a medical career, but he changed course and joined the Dominicans in Bologna in 1474. Several years later, he was sent as a missionary to northern Italy.

After struggling at first, Savonarola's preaching improved and he soon became noted around Italy for his fiery sermons. He began preaching in Florence and attacking corruption in the government and the Church. When the government leaders changed, Savonarola believed that God wanted to use him to address issues that the Church was facing. He prophesied on the development of the Church in apocalyptic terms, and in 1494 instituted a democratic form of government in Florence, which some would say resembled a theocracy—government by God.

However, his criticism included Pope Alexander VI and the papal court. Savonarola was excommunicated in 1497, and things went downhill from there. He continued to rail against Pope Alexander and finally he was arrested, tortured, hanged, and burnt at the stake in Florence. Whether Savonarola deserved his fate is disputed among some authorities who rather hold that he should be added to the list of saints.

DESIDERIUS ERASMUS

Erasmus was born in 1469 in Rotterdam, Holland, the illegitimate son of Gerard of Gouda. He became an orphan at age fourteen and was placed in a monastery against his wishes. The bishop of Cambria took Erasmus under his care, ordained him in 1492, made him his secretary, and encouraged him to pursue an academic career.

This is the second time we have encountered Erasmus; he was mentioned when we treated the "Brethren of the Common Life" at

Deventer in the fourteenth century, where Erasmus was involved in the movement. We will visit him again when he debates Martin Luther during the Reformation.

He completed his studies in Paris, tutored, and traveled to England in 1498, where he met Thomas More. More encouraged Erasmus to study Greek and direct his attention to scriptural commentary. Upon returning to the continent he published a number of works including the *Greek New Testament*. Also, Erasmus produced a number of works from the church Fathers, including Jerome, Hilary, John Chrysostom, and Augustine, to name a few.

A treatment of Erasmus, known as the "Prince of Humanists," is found in F. L. Cross' *The Oxford Dictionary of the Christian Church*. "The most renowned scholar of his age, Erasmus was a man of vast, if not always deep, erudition, of uncommon intellectual powers, but adverse to metaphysical speculation ..." Furthermore, in *Church History in Plain Language*, Bruce L. Shelley writes about Erasmus reflecting the image of a reformer. "Erasmus's followers thought they heard a true reformer in him. He laid the egg, they said, that Luther hatched." Shelley identifies the impact that Erasmus had on the Reformation.

Erasmus, while remaining a Roman Catholic, was dismayed by theologians whom he found to be hostile and dismissive of new ideas. He wrote about this condition in *The Praise of Folly*, where he suggested the early church and the Fathers be used for reform, not the latter scholars. For Erasmus, theology was to be a guideline to Christian living. For him "creed determines deed."

PART THREE

Early Modern to Early America

Early Modern Christianity

The Early Modern era roughly began with the invention of the printing press by Gutenberg in 1450, which brought us the first Bible using a printing press with movable type. The Bible was the Latin *Vulgate*. The *Vulgate* was the Bible used by Ignatius of Loyola, the founder of the Jesuits, to whom we will now turn our attention.

The Snapshots covered in this section are about persons who were and remained Roman Catholic, as well as those who were persuaded of the legitimacy of the Protestant movement. Among the latter group, William Tyndale paid for his decision by suffering martyrdom. The inquisition was the Catholic response to Protestantism.

IGNATIUS OF LOYOLA

Ignatius was born in 1491 at the family castle of Loyola in the Basque province of Guipuzcoa, Spain, not far south of the Pyrenees. He was the youngest of thirteen children born to a well-to-do family.

Ignatius joined the army and received a wound in his right leg at the siege of Pampeluna in 1521. During his recovery, he read *The Life of Christ* and the biographies of the Church Fathers, which led him to become a soldier of Christ. Upon recovery he embarked on a pilgrimage to Montserrat. There Ignatius developed the main points of what became his *Spiritual Exercises.* This work was published in Rome. Ignatius began his studies in 1524 and received his Master of Arts degree ten years later. From Montserrat he went to Manresa, where in retirement, he gave himself up to a life of prayer and extreme mortification.

Five years prior to the Council of Trent, an event transpired that would change the life of Ignatius and the course of church history. In September of 1540, he received approval from Pope Paul III to found a new order known as the Jesuits. James L. Garlow writes about this order in *How God Saved Civilization.* "The Jesuits would become one of the greatest reforming and missionary forces of the Catholic Church. On August 15, 1534, Ignatius and six of his friends gathered in Paris and vowed to live lives of poverty and chastity. By 1539, it was obvious that this was a permanent community, so they wanted the blessing of the pope, which they received in 1540." What is not well known is the Jesuits were heavily involved in missionary activity.

The Jesuits became a potent presence in the Counter Reformation, attempting to stem the tide of Catholics becoming Protestants. Also, soon after the order's formation, Loyola began to send Jesuits out to the mission fields, not only throughout Europe, but also worldwide. The Jesuits were committed to education and established universities wherever they went.

In the seventeenth century, the Jesuits encountered serious problems within the Roman Catholic Church. They became entwined in debate with the Dominicans over God's sovereignty and human responsibility. Also Jesuit missionaries came under attack on the question of accommodation in the Chinese Rites controversy. The controversy stemmed from the question, how much missionaries should adapt themselves to the culture of the people who they are attempting to reach. Protestant missionaries have grappled with this problem as well.

This led to the abolition of the order in 1773; however, it was reestablished in 1814. It is presently the largest religious order for men and has ministries worldwide. Ignatius of Loyola was canonized in 1622.

WILLIAM TYNDALE

William Tyndale, a native of Gloucestershire in West central England, was born in 1494. He studied at Magdalen Hall, Oxford, and later at Cambridge. He was scholarly, earning a BA and MA at Oxford, and was proficient in Greek, Hebrew, and Latin. Philosophically he was a descendant of Wycliffe, and was disturbed by ignorance among the clergy, both scholarly and biblical, and the lack of English translations of the Bible.

Tyndale wanted to translate the Bible into English, but was rebuffed by the bishop of London. He then went to Germany and settled at Hamburg, never to return home. When the Renaissance scholar Erasmus published a Greek edition of the New Testament, Tyndale discovered the truths of justification by faith and the priesthood of all believers. He had an unquenchable passion to make the Bible available to every Englishman.

Denied permission from ecclesiastical authorities in England, Tyndale distributed scripture in England from Europe, including sites in Hamburg, Worms, and Antwerp. In 1525, his New Testament found its way into England. Ecclesiastical authorities there, including King Henry VIII, were incensed with this unlicensed translation.

William Tyndale agreed with Luther on the authority of the Bible and on justification by faith. However, he accepted Zwingli's position on the Eucharistic sacrament. Perhaps at the suggestion of Henry VIII, he was imprisoned near Brussels. There, in 1536, Tyndale was strangled and burnt at the stake. In dying, Tyndale said, "Lord, open the King of England's eyes."

How successful were Tyndale's efforts? Coverdale's and Mathew's Bibles were edited and revised by Tyndale. The King James Version reflects eighty to ninety percent of Tyndale. Even more importantly, Tyndale's translation proved lasting as seventy-five percent has found its way into the Revised Standard Version. Tyndale does indeed deserve the title "The Father of the English Bible."

FRANCISCO DE VITORIA

Francisco de Vitoria was born in 1485 in Vittoria, Navarre, Spain. He entered the Dominican Order in 1502 and studied at the Convent of San Pablo in Paris, where he was ordained priest in 1509.

De Vittoria taught arts and philosophy at the Convent of St. James and became 'doctor theologiae.' F. L. Cross writes in the *Oxford Dictionary of the Christian Church* about this well-known Dominican. "A humanist as well as a philosopher and theologian, he developed a method which, without disregarding philosophical speculation, made the scriptures and the Fathers the foundation of theological teaching."

De Vittoria disliked the Spanish methods of colonization in America, and wrote what would be accepted as international law, some of which is accepted today. De Vittoria was perhaps the first just-war theorist in the Middle Ages. He was a committed Thomist and, basing his approach on Augustine of Hippo and Thomas Aquinas, he developed what would become the just war theory, holding that no war should be allowed which brought evil to Christendom or the world at large. Francisco deserves recognition for being a just war theorist in the Middle Ages. This position is held by many scholars today.

TERESA OF AVILA

Teresa of Avila was born in 1515 to an old Spanish family. She was schooled by Augustinian nuns and entered the Carmelite monastery of the Incarnation at Avila. Teresa became ill and she was forced to return to her family. Upon her recovery and against her father's wishes, Teresa decided to become a nun, joining the Carmelites at Avila in 1536.

She became ill again and did not recover for five years. Teresa began to experience visions and hear voices, fearing that they were from the devil. Her spiritual life took a positive turn when she experienced a vision of Christ.

Teresa started a convent at Medina del Campo, where she met a young monk who in due course would be known as John of the Cross. Justo L. Gonzalez, in *The Story of Christianity,* exposes Teresa's sense of humor. "She was joined in her efforts by St. John of the Cross, a man so short that, when she met him, St. Teresa is said to have quipped, 'Lord, I asked you for a monk, and you sent me half of one.'"

Teresa of Avila was a woman of resolute character and a competent organizer. Teresa left to John the task of starting a number of men's monasteries while she traveled throughout Spain, founding convents and preaching her reforms. Teresa was determined to address the laxity which was prevalent in the convents of her day. As a spiritual writer, her influence was widespread. Combining mystical experiences with her activity as a reformer and organizer, she showed that the two activities are not mutually exclusive. Teresa of Avila became the second woman to be honored with the title of "Doctor of the Church," joining Catherine of Siena.

LANCELOT ANDREWES

Lancelot Andrewes was born in 1555 at the parish of All Hallows, Barking, England. He was educated at Pembroke Hall, Cambridge, where he was elected Fellow in 1576 and four years later a catechist. In 1601, Andrewes became Dean of Westminster.

Andrewes preached often at the royal court. One of the translators of the King James Version of the Bible, Andrewes was very devout and spent a good part of the day in prayer. A person of great scholarship, he spoke fifteen languages. While he was Dean at Westminster Abbey, his preaching transformed the services. There was an aura of genuine godliness about him.

Bishop Andrewes objected to the individual interpretation of Scripture, holding that this should be done in the Church. He did, however, encourage his listeners to develop a personal relationship with Christ. He spoke often about the importance of the Holy Spirit and referred frequently to the early Church Fathers. However, Andrewes did not regard the Church Fathers as infallible.

James I was captivated by Andrewes' preaching. Roger Steer in his book, *Guarding the Holy Fire,* discusses Andrewes, a Bible translator and a preacher extraordinaire. "No one has spoken so well since the days of the apostles, said the King after one of his sermons. Another Andrewes sermon delighted the King so much that he slept with the text of it under his pillow." As with Andrewes, King James was also skilled in a number of languages and a devotee of the early Church Fathers.

Andrewes believed that the church should be guided by: "One Bible, two Testaments, three Creeds, four Councils, and five Centuries."

THE INQUISITION

The "Inquisition" means the clerical persecution of heresy by church courts. Bruce L. Shelley investigates the Inquisition and its notorious history in *Church History in Plain Language*. "The early form of the Inquisition appeared in 1184, when Pope Lucius III required bishops to 'inquire' into the beliefs of their subjects. In short, they held an 'inquiry' or inquest. Heresy or harboring a heretic brought immediate excommunication." The idea of the Inquisition is not found in Scripture.

Likewise, the term excommunication doesn't appear in the New Testament. However, the concept can be found in the Pauline corpus—I Corinthians 5:5 and II Corinthians 2:5-11. Paul renders a verdict that the man should be separated from the congregation for participating in activity not found even among pagans.

In the early church, heresy was punished by excommunication; however, the inquisition would not develop its dreaded stature until the sixteenth century. The early Church Fathers generally disapproved of the physical techniques used to determine heresy.

The Inquisition, properly termed, came into being when in 1232 the Emperor Frederick II of Palermo, Sicily, put in place an edict to the whole Empire that the heresy hunting would be the undertaking of state officials; Church and State would come together. The inquisitors were not drawn from the bishops, but mainly from the Dominicans and the Franciscans, the thinking being that their theological training would better equip them for their task.

The so-called Spanish Inquisition began at the end of the fifteenth century. It was primarily concerned with investigating baptized Jews thought to have returned to Jewish practices. Later Protestants were sought out as well.

Cruel means were used, which often led to death. However, Rodney Stark, Professor of Sociology at the University of Washington, has done extensive research in this area. He also investigated the Spanish Inquisition in his book, *For the Glory of God,* and is not hesitant to declare historians have vastly exaggerated the amount of violence it caused. "For example, aside from a few specialists, most historians still seem to assume that the Spanish Inquisition burned large numbers of heretics, witches, Marrano Jews and other deviants in public autos-da-fé, and that to have fallen into the hands of the inquisitors was an almost certain sentence of death. All false!" That is why I enjoy church history! It's not always the way it has been reported. In any event, after the Spanish Inquisition ended in 1808, it was restarted six years later, but finally suppressed in 1834. Thank God.

Reformation Christianity

Since the East/West Schism, the Protestant Reformation was the most significant event to impact Christendom. Louis W. Spitz, in *The Renaissance and Reformation Movements, Vol. 2,* discusses that one is hesitant to choose between the East/West Schism and the Protestant Reformation as to which was the more devastating to the Church. Indeed, "Europe entered the sixteenth century at least nominally unified by the Catholic Church; it emerged from the Reformation with a variety of evangelical communities and Protestant groups competing with the old church and with each other for the faith and devotion of men." The Schism split the East from the West; the Reformation fractured the Western Church.

As time has passed and feelings have cooled, church historians, both Roman Catholics as well as Protestants, are taking a fresh look at positions which held sway surrounding the Reformation. We will discuss some of these issues in due course.

A Catholic historian, Alan Schreck, takes a balanced approach to this event in the *Compact History of the Catholic Church*. "Most Catholics, though, including the popes, did not take the reform of their Church seriously until the Protestant reformers spoke out boldly and left the unity of the Catholic Church. One positive result of the Protestant Reformation is that it began a more diligent effort of reform and renewal within the Catholic Church." Since the Vatican II Council, there are a number of historians, Protestant as well as Catholic, who are reassessing the facts surrounding the Reformation.

It is beyond the scope of this introduction to present a comprehensive and detailed treatment of Church History; rather we are offering insights into people, events, and movements which have been under developed or unknown by the average Christian reader.

We began with a look at Martin Luther, who was arguably the "godfather" of the Reformation Movement.

MARTIN LUTHER

Martin Luther was born in 1483 and was the son of a miner at Mansfeld, in Saxony, Germany. He was educated at the Cathedral School at Magdeburg, at Eisenach and at Erfurt University. Luther's father had planned for his son to become a lawyer, but Martin disagreed. Luther entered the monastery of the Augustinian Hermits at Erfurt; his father was not pleased. He was ordained a priest in 1507 and was sent as a lecturer to the University of Wittenberg.

Luther was consumed with "scrupulosity," which occurs when a troubled conscience, prompted by imaginary reasons, causes one to dread sin where it does not exist, making majors out of minors. But help was on the way; Luther was blessed to have a caring leader and confessor in his monastery, Johannes von Staupitz.

Luther's confessor and mentor, knowing of his young charge's struggles, directed him to study Scripture. Luther received a Doctor of Theology and began teaching theology and biblical studies at Wittenberg in 1513.

It is not so well known that Staupitz did not follow his pupil into the Reformation. Authors John Delaney and James Tobin in their volume, *Dictionary of Catholic Biography*, deal with Martin Luther's leader and confessor, Johannes von Staupitz. "He was accused of Lutheran tendencies, resigned his vicar generalship, became a Benedictine in 1522, and was appointed abbot of St. Peter's, Salzburg, Austria." This last decision of Staupitz notwithstanding, he deserves a commendation for directing his prize pupil to accept Jesus' death on the cross as full payment for his sins.

Luther's "conversion" possibly came about when he began to prepare lectures on the Bible. When teaching from Paul's epistle to the Romans, he became aware of justification by faith alone. Luther shaped the Reformation with the posting of the Ninety-Five Theses in 1517. The declaration mainly addressed the issue of indulgences, but it certainly got the people's attention.

Erasmus, "The Prince of humanists," whom we met earlier when we covered "The Brethren of the Common Life," enters the fray. He differed with Luther over the issue of "free will," and it caused a rupture in their relationship.

Unfortunately, there is also a phase in Luther's life which is not becoming; it deals with his view of the Jewish people and the Gospel. At first the Jews welcomed the Reformation because it divided their enemies. However, when mass conversions on their part were not forthcoming, Luther turned on them in fury.

Martin Luther has inspired both admiration and hatred, depending on one's view of the necessity of the Reformation. Both Roman Catholic and Protestant scholars have reevaluated the event and have come to some interesting conclusions. We will return to Catholic and evangelical Protestant issues when we cover the modern era.

PHILIPP MELANCHTHON

Philipp Melanchthon was born in 1497 in Bretten, Germany. He studied at Heidelberg and Tübingen. While teaching at Tübingen, he was appointed to the newly founded chair of Greek in Luther's University of Wittenberg in 1518.

Two men could not have been less alike; Luther was a religious revolutionary, while Melanchthon was a quiet systematic theologian. Luther was suspicious of philosophy and Christian humanism. Melanchthon, on the other hand, enjoyed the support of the most prominent Christian humanist of the day, Desiderius Erasmus.

Melanchthon became well-known at Wittenberg, lecturing in the spirit of the Renaissance. In spite of their differences, he became Luther's trusted friend; he was influential in shaping Luther's thought in a more rational and systematic form.

In the *Oxford Dictionary of the Christian Church*, F. L. Cross writes about Melanchthon's role in the German Reformation. "The leading figure at the Diet of Augsburg (1530), he was mainly responsible for the Augsburg Confession, and great hopes were placed on his conciliatory spirit as basis of restoring peace and unity." He would also have a role when the Reformation would expand to include Calvin, Ulrich Zwingli, and others. Melanchthon's irenic nature made him a natural candidate to patch up differences with not only other Reformational leaders, but with Roman Catholics as well.

We will meet Melanchthon again, along with a number of other Reformation and Roman Catholic scholars and leaders who would meet to address the developing rift between the two groups. The meeting to be examined is the Conference of Regensburg, which convened shortly before the Council of Trent.

Another scholar, David C. Steinmetz, would comment in *Reformers in the Wings* on Melanchthon's further activity in the development with the expanding Protestant Movement. "[If] ... it is possible to believe that the Reformation took a plurality of legitimate forms, then it must be noted that Melanchthon performed a variety of important services for the Lutheran camp ... Furthermore, he listened to the teaching of the Fathers and tried to incorporate their insights into the teaching of the Lutheran church." His philosophical skills, which Luther lacked, would serve the Movement well.

JOHN CALVIN

We now turn to the second development of the Reformation, the Reformed/Calvinistic wing. In 1509, John Calvin was born at Noyon in Picardy, France. His father was well off, and because he wanted his son to become a lawyer, he paid for his education in Paris.

Calvin became acquainted with humanism and also was aware of the doctrines of Wycliffe, Hus, and Luther. He studied theology, but having doubts concerning a priestly vocation, switched to law. He studied at Orleans and later at Bourges, where he joined a group of Protestants.

While not as irenic as Melanchthon, Calvin's skills were in systematic theology. In *Church History in Plain Language*, Bruce L. Shelley makes the following comments on Calvin's break with Rome: "[h]is studies brought Calvin into touch with reforming ideas circulating in Paris, and shortly thereafter one of those 'events' in Calvin's life turned him in a new direction. He called it an 'unexpected conversion.'"

In 1534, Francis I, King of France, who until then had shown relative tolerance toward Protestants, changed his policy and the next year Calvin went into exile in Basel, Switzerland. He wished to study Scripture and write about his faith. To this end, he began a literary project, *The Institutes of the Christian Religion,* which would become the major textbook of Reformed Theology. The original effort was six chapters and would ultimately end up 80 chapters published in Latin and French.

Calvin arrived at Geneva in 1536, intending to stay briefly and then move on to Strasbourg, but his supporters convinced him to stay. The citizens of the city had notoriously lax morals and Calvin wanted Geneva to be like the Kingdom of God on earth. This system is known as a "theocracy"—or a government by God—and became instituted as the governing body at Geneva. In the history of the Church, we find this system used by medieval popes, in Oliver Cromwell's England, and in Scottish Presbyterianism. It hasn't had a long shelf life.

In 1553, Calvin had his infamous dispute with Michael Servetus. The problem arose with Servetus's view that rejected the doctrine of the Trinity, a position now known as Unitarianism. Servetus was tried and arrested for heresy by the Catholic Church in France, but escaped to Geneva, where he was arrested and found guilty of heresy. Servetus was ultimately burned at the stake, which was at this time the penalty for this offense. Some held this event against Calvin; however, other historians questioned Calvin's culpability in the incident. Even though Christians should oppose false doctrines, these extreme measures used in early church history are inappropriate.

Calvin's activity in the Protestant Reformation was more logical and theological than Luther's, but was not as well received as the German reformer. He maintained a simple lifestyle, but riled even some of his supporters with his condescending demeanor.

During his time in Geneva, Calvin's disposition improved, and his ability as an ecclesiastical statesman and an educator, along with his theological insight, made him well known throughout Europe. His lectures brought students from near and far. His Bible commentaries are still considered classical. Calvin's *Institutes* are considered the highest authority in the non-Lutheran Protestant Churches.

ULRICH ZWINGLI

Ulrich Zwingli was born in 1484 in the small Swiss village of Wildhaus, Switzerland. His father was a farmer and chief magistrate. Zwingli's family was well off and he received a good education in the classics at the University of Vienna and later at Basel.

Zwingli was ordained priest and was pastor at Glarus from 1506–1516. He immersed himself in the writings of Desiderius Erasmus, taught himself Greek and some Hebrew, and read the Church Fathers. Using Erasmus' newly available translation, Zwingli increased his knowledge of the Greek New Testament and improved his skills as a preacher.

In 1518, Zwingli was elected People's Preacher at the Old Minster in Zürich, where he remained for the rest of his life. It can be said that the Reformation in Switzerland owes its beginning to his lectures on the New Testament, which differed from Lutheran and Calvinistic theologians.

Zwingli and Luther agreed on many issues such as justification by faith, indulgences, and the primacy of Scripture. The problem between them arose over the understanding of the communion sacrament. Roman Catholics believe in "transubstantiation," the view that during communion when the priest consecrates the elements, the bread and wine become the Body and Blood of Jesus Christ.

In contrast, the Lutheran view is "consubstantiation," which holds that Jesus Christ comes "alongside" of the elements. Zwingli believed that the Eucharist was merely a memorial meal. They disagreed so strongly that Luther told Zwingli, "You have a different spirit than I." The Roman Catholic and the Lutheran positions on the Eucharist were similar, but not completely identical. This theological difference on this issue was never resolved during the Reformation period.

Finally, although Zwingli served as military chaplain to Swiss mercenaries in the Papal service and was present at the Battle of Marignano, he later turned against service by Christians in armed conflict. However, the same Reformer who had worked to eliminate the mercenary service now again took up arms, convinced it was necessary in the service of God and the Gospel. He was killed in 1531 at the battle in Kappel, Switzerland; his body was hacked to pieces and disgraced by the enemy.

HEINRICH JOHANN BULLINGER

Not much is written about Heinrich Bullinger's place of birth and early life. What is known is that he was Zwingli's disciple and successor within the Swiss Reformation. Bullinger received his spiritual formation by reading the Bible and the Fathers and by studying the writings of Luther and Melanchthon. In 1529, Bullinger became pastor of Bremgarten, and following Zwingli's death, he was appointed to succeed him as chief pastor of Zürich.

In 1549, he partnered with John Calvin in the production of a treatise on the Lord's Supper. The understanding of that work caused great consternation among the Reformers, especially the Lutherans. Bullinger also produced the Second Helvetic Confession, which became a standard text for the Swiss Reformation.

Bullinger joined Calvin, Luther, and Zwingli as leaders in the Protestant Movement. Bruce Gordon agrees and in his book, *The Swiss Reformation*, offers these words. "It is generally accepted that the Second Helvetic Confession is a mature expression of the theology of Heinrich Bullinger, leader of the church in Zurich and the dominant churchman of the Swiss Reformation from 1532 until his death in 1575." He saw in the Reformation the thinking of the apostolic church and the theological formulations of the early Councils and Creeds.

As to the value of Bullinger's writings, Franklin H. Little, in the *Origins of Sectarian Protestantism*, observes: "The writings of Bullinger may be taken as authoritative for Reform churches. Again and again he returns to attack those who spread dissention and factionalism in the church." Little makes the point that Bullinger also cautioned against criticism being employed when dealing with another group in the Movement.

It seems that Bullinger performed in the same moderate spirit as his Reformed colleagues in Switzerland that Melanchthon did in Germany with his fellow Lutherans.

ANABAPTISTS

The next branch of the Reformation had a number of titles: Anabaptists—"re-baptizers"—and Reformation radicals, to name two. In the sixteenth century, these groups did not permit their children to be baptized. Instead, the groups reinstituted believer's baptism, which they believed was the authentic mode described in the New Testament.

They also repudiated the name "Anabaptists," insisting that infant baptism did not constitute "true" baptism—hence they were not in reality "re-baptizers." These believers came from the major Protestant groups, but believed that Luther, Calvin, and Zwingli didn't distance themselves enough from Catholicism.

Zwingli at first sympathized with the movement, but later denounced it, declaring that Anabaptists were "Pelagians," who laid too much stress on Jesus as "example" and paid too little attention to His resurrection. He ridiculed them as "Killjoys," anti-intellectuals whose distain for dully constituted government was dangerous.

F. L. Cross comments on the way that mainstream Protestants treated Anabaptists in *The Oxford Dictionary of the Christian Church*. "The Anabaptists were vigorously denounced by M. Luther, H. Zwingli and J. Calvin and severely persecuted by both Roman Catholics and Protestants. Those put to death probably ran into tens of thousands."

Some of the Anabaptist leaders included Thomas Monzer, Balthasar Hubmaier, and Menno Simons. Anabaptist descendants today can be found in the Mennonites, Amish, Hutterites, Brethren in Christ, and other groups.

JOHN KNOX

We will conclude the Reformation period by moving from Europe to the British Isles. John Knox was born in 1513 and was reared in Haddington, 17 miles from Edinburgh, Scotland. Not much is known of his early life; he was educated at Glasgow and perhaps at St. Andrews.

Knox was possibly ordained as a priest and in 1544, he became a tutor. He shortly became attached to an early reformer in Scotland, George Wishart, and subsequently embraced the principles of the Reformation. R. Tudor Jones speaks of the danger that the early Reformers faced in their activities. Jones notes in his volume, *The Great Reformation*, "Wishart had no more fervent admirer than John Knox, who had followed the reformer as a self-appointed bodyguard, armed with a two-handed sword."

After Wishart was burned at the stake at St. Andrews, Scotland was looking for a new leader. The path to leadership would be a painful one for Knox. After the French captured St. Andrews, he served as a slave for 19 months and became a chaplain upon his release. Mary, queen of Scots, became queen of England, she was heard to say, "I fear the prayers of John Knox more than all the assembled armies of Europe." Knox fled and took refuge in Geneva. There he became a follower of John Calvin, both of his form of theology and church government.

Knox returned to Scotland in 1555, was condemned for heresy in Scotland the next year, and departed to Geneva. He became pastor of the English-speaking church in Geneva and only returned to Scotland five years later. Finally, the Scottish church that he envisioned came to pass. Knox is reported to have said, "Give me Scotland, or I die."

Back in Scotland, John Knox seized the opportunity to begin the Reformation in his country. His administrative skills, personality, and writings, including the *Scottish Confessions* and the *Treatise on Predestination,* led to the forming of the Church of Scotland. Knox soon was installed as minister at the High Kirk of Edinburgh St. Giles, where he often preached to huge crowds.

LADY JANE GREY

On October 12th, 1537, news in London announced that Jane Seymour had given Henry VIII his long-hoped-for heir who would be named Edward. On the same day another birth occurred at Bradgate Manor in Leicestershire: a daughter of Frances and Henry Grey, whom they named Jane.

Lady Jane Grey had Tudor blood in her veins—the great niece of that most infamous of English Kings, Henry VIII. The Tudors were the royal house that ruled England from 1486–1603. Jane lived in a time of great change in which the Reformation, which had its birth in Europe, had developed a foot hold on England.

Scholars who would have important roles in the development of the Reformation would be on the scene, including Desiderius Erasmus and Heinrich Bullinger. Civil unrest and violence were always a threat between Roman Catholicism and the newly emerging Protestant movement.

Edward VI, upon the death of his father, Henry VIII, would succeed the throne in 1547. This period was critical for the Church of England. During Edward's reign, the state took a Calvinist direction. Here the story is confused by the divorces and remarriages surrounding Henry VIII.

According to Henry's will, his daughter Mary was the rightful heir to the throne. However, Jane's ambitious parents and John Dudley, father of Jane's husband, along with other supporters, had other plans. So, four days after Edward's death, Jane Grey was proclaimed Queen of England. Meanwhile, Mary was gathering support in Suffolk. She and her followers rode into London nine days later and imprisoned Jane and her supporters. Jane and her husband were held in the Tower of London and were executed after a second ill-fated uprising in their name.

A modern film portrayal distorts Jane's last words. Nothing is said about her spiritual commitment. Before her execution, she said loudly and with great dignity, "Lord, into thy hands I command my spirit." The film has not done justice to the deep and personal faith of Lady Jane Grey and her husband. This young girl possessed a deep theological truth and faith in Christ. I would encourage you to obtain Faith Cook's book, *Lady Jane Grey: Nine Day Queen of England* and read the debate between Fr. John Feckenham, Queen Mary's personal chaplain, and Jane. He attempted unsuccessfully to cause Jane to renounce her evangelical faith and return to Catholicism.

Queen Mary soon earned the title, "Bloody Mary." She had hundreds of Protestants martyred between 1553–1558.

ENGLISH REFORMATION

Events which began in the fifteenth century prepared England for the Reformation. As in the rest of Western Europe at this time,

England was beset with corruption. Many of the monks were idle and ignorant, while large numbers of priests had concubines.

The writings of Luther were available to people who had grown weary of the religious conditions that existed in Europe. William Tyndale had studied under Luther and completed his translation of the New Testament in 1526. Copies were smuggled into England and William's life was in danger. John Wycliffe wrote tracts and preached sermons throughout the country and earned the title of the "morning star of the English Reformation."

To understand the impact of the Reformation in England, one must deal with Henry VIII. Prior to his infamous marital difficulties, the Lollards had been spreading the teachings of John Wycliffe. Henry VIII was a handsome, cultured prince who spoke a number of languages and was a learned lay theologian. His wife Catherine could not produce a male heir for the throne, and having fallen in love with Anne Boleyn, Henry wanted to divorce his wife and marry Anne.

In 1522, the Church of England was established. Thomas Cranmer became Arch-Bishop of Canterbury and aided the King in divorcing three of his wives. Cranmer could be called one of the chief architects of Anglicanism. He embraced justification by faith and became more and more Protestant. He was central in the composition of the Book of Common Prayer and the Thirty-Nine Articles, which are the core beliefs of the Church of England.

It has often been said that the Reformation in England was essentially an act of state. When Queen Elizabeth died in 1603, she declared her successor to be James, who was already King of Scotland. Elizabeth had tried to follow a course between conservatives in the Church of England and Calvinist Protestants who wanted to structure the church closer to biblical norms.

These Protestants were called "Puritans," those who wanted to purify the Church. These people opposed such things as the use of the cross and priestly garments, and they stressed the need for a sober life. Many insisted on the need to keep the Lord's Day and were also critical of attending the theater.

One group affirmed that each congregation should be separate from all others and were called "Independents." They believed that baptism ought to be restricted to believing adults. These people came to be called "Baptists" and drew their inspiration from Calvin, Zwingli, and some from the Anabaptist tradition.

After inheriting Elizabeth's crown, James called a conference where an attempt was made to reconcile the different church groups but was unsuccessful. Instead, James' lasting contribution to Christian thought was the commission to translate the Bible into English, namely the King James Version. This translation remains popular to this day.

When the Protestant Queen Elizabeth I died in 1603, she was buried in Westminster Abbey in the same tomb as her Catholic sister Mary. Although united in death, during their lifetimes, they resided on opposite sides concerning the Reformation.

There is now in Westminster Abbey, a plaque that makes this request of those who visit there: "Near the tomb of Elizabeth and Mary remember before God all those who, divided at the Reformation by different convictions, laid down their lives for Christ and conscience sake."

Counter-Reformation Christianity

The Counter-Reformation is a term usually used to refer to the revival of the Roman Catholic Church in Europe. It extended from the middle of the sixteenth century to the period of the Thirty Years War from 1618–1648.

Prior to the Protestant Reformation, it was understood that the Roman Catholic Church needed to be reformed. Many Catholic scholars acknowledged that the Church was in a state of moral and spiritual disarray.

We will be treating a number of conferences that occurred prior to the Council of Trent. These conferences were held to determine if reunification between Catholics and Protestants were possible. The Council of Trent will be covered as well.

PRE-TRENT CONFERENCES

There were three conferences leading to the Council of Trent. Charles V was the eldest son of Philip of Burgundy, and when elected Emperor in 1519, he was the most powerful man in Europe. The major problem he faced was the rise of Lutheranism. He decided to address the issue of the Reformation and attempted to repair the fissure between Rome and Protestantism.

A number of meetings between Catholics and Protestants occurred prior to the Council of Trent. Paul Johnson, a British Catholic historian, comments on them in *A History of Christianity*. "There were, indeed, a great many reformers who believed a split in the Church was tragic and avoidable, just as there were many Catholics who were deeply disturbed by the Church's merit-theology and it's teaching about the use of the sacraments, and were anxious to embrace the Lutheran correctives." These efforts were not productive. The three Conferences leading up to Trent will now be discussed.

THE CONFERENCE OF HAGENAU

The gathering at Hagenau in 1540 was convened by Emperor Charles V to discuss the dispute between the Catholics and Protestants in Germany. It was unsuccessful because of poor preparation. It was arranged that the participants would meet at Worms.

DISPUTATION OF WORMS

This colloquy was called for the continuation of the matters discussed at Hagenau. It was concluded that there would be eleven representatives from each side. This was decided to be a bit too cumbersome, and it was finally agreed that one theologian should speak for each side; Johann Eck was to represent the Catholics and Philipp Melanchthon would speak for the Protestants. In 1541, an agreement was reached on original sin, but the final resolution would be put off until the forthcoming conference at Ratisbon.

THE CONFERENCE OF RATISBON/REGENSBURG

This was a conference convened by Emperor Charles V. It consisted of three Catholics—Johann Eck, Julius von Pflug, and Johann Gropper, and three Protestants—Philipp Melanchthon, Martin Bucer, and Pistorius. The Ratisbon Conference was chaired by Gasparo Contarini, who was the papal representative.

Contarini was a fascinating person in his own right. As a layman, he was very popular at Rome; he was made a bishop and then became a cardinal appointed by Paul III in 1535. He came full of good will, and like Luther, had come to understand justification though the teachings of Augustine.

The gathering reached significant agreement on most issues, including the doctrine of justification. However the subsequent hostility of Luther, as well as cultural issues, ultimately doomed any chance for reconciliation. When Melanchthon returned to Germany, Luther lamented, "I should have known better than to send a philosopher to debate with Roman Catholics." For his part in the event when Cardinal Contarini returned to Rome, he was censured for having compromised Catholic doctrine. It is ironic that both leaders were criticized for reaching out to the other side at Regensburg.

THE COUNCIL OF TRENT

Pope Paul III convoked the Council of Trent, which officially met in 1545. It was the most important council since the fifth century and reflected the positions of the Counter-Reformation.

The pre-Trentian conferences had not been successful in effecting reconciliation between Catholics and Protestants. This council was convened with the task of addressing the problem of Protestantism. The Reformation had spread its influence throughout Europe and had shown no indication of abating. New groups were forming, and furthermore, the Reformation had revealed ethical issues that clearly needed to be dealt with.

The Council of Trent was held in Northern Italy and the proceedings were as follows: Period I set the basic agenda, Period II dealt with Protestant views of the Eucharist, and Period III saw the influence of the Jesuits increase and any hope of peace between Catholics and Protestants disappeared.

A number of theological schools were represented at Trent: the Thomists, the Augustinians, the Jesuits, and several forms of the *via moderna*—the nominalism of William of Ockham. Also it is interesting to note that there was a group of theologians who have been named "Reform Catholics." Although these men cannot be understood as Protestants, they were interested in the Reformed view of justification. However, they were few in number and too small a group to be effective. Following Trent when their views were made known in Rome, they were held in derision by their critical colleagues.

ISSUES ADDRESSED AT TRENT

Here we can only mention the most important issues addressed at Trent:

- Justification—While Trent condemned Pelagianism and

semi-Pelagianism, it considered justification to be both an event and a process. It occurs "by infusion" with children at baptism.
- Apocrypha—These books (seven whole and parts of existing books) were officially added to the Catholic canon.
- Scripture—The old *Latin Vulgate* was the only version authorized and only the Church could interpret the Scriptures.
- Sacraments—Seven were established: Baptism, the Holy Eucharist, Penance, Matrimony, Extreme Unction, Confirmation, and Holy Orders.
- Purgatory—Exists to cleanse believers who die with venial sins on their souls. The prayers and works of the living faithful can assist those in purgatory.

The final result of Trent was the rejection of the doctrines that had emerged from the Reformation. Protestants, therefore, declared that Catholicism denied the Gospel and was apostate. Both of these positions would make dialogue difficult in the future. Happily, the situation changed somewhat by the last half of the twentieth century. We will address this in Part Five.

RENE DESCARTES

Not much is written about Descartes' early life. He was born in 1596 in Central France. His father and elder brother were officials in provincial parliaments. His mother died soon after his birth, and the boy's own health was unstable.

Young Rene early on displayed a keen mind. He was sent to study at the Jesuit College in La Fleche in Marine from his eighth to his sixteenth year. The school emphasized Roman Catholic doctrine, but also included classic literature and study in mathematics.

The experience of a dream led Descartes to pursue the study of philosophy. He became known as one of France's most famous philosophers. Even though he challenged some of his church's traditional doctrines, he remained a Roman Catholic. The significance of Descartes was his method; the ground of his philosophy was his own self-consciousness—"*Cogito, ergo sum*"—I think, therefore I am.

Descartes attempted to learn truth, not by reliance on authority or the experience of the senses, but by using mathematical data reached by intuition and deduction. The later process was helped by his memory. He experimented himself and was familiar with the intuitions of contemporary scientists. Descartes has been called the father of modern philosophy.

As to his faith, Descartes believed God is the Creator, who is immutable, undeceiving, and knowable. Negatively, his view of rationalism constructed a dualism between mind and matter. However, concerning mathematical logic, analytical geometry, and speculative philosophy, Descartes has stood the test of time.

PETER CLAVER

In 1581, Peter Claver was born the son of a Catalonian farmer in Verdu, a town near Barcelona, Spain. When Claver was twenty, he entered the Jesuit order at Tarragona. Later, he studied philosophy at Majorca, an island off the coast of Spain.

While at the college on Majorca, Claver came under the influence of Alphonsus Rodriguez, a respected professor at the school. Rodriguez recognized in his young associate a number of gifts and a level of spirituality that would serve him well as a missionary.

Rodriguez exhorted his charge to consider becoming a missionary in the Spanish possessions in America. Peter agreed and in 1610, landed at Cartagena, a city in Columbia on the Caribbean. This town had become the main location to facilitate the slave trade in the New World. For the next forty-four years, Peter Claver would be known, as "the apostle for the African slaves."

Slavery had been around for a long time. It is an error to think that it was accepted in the Old Testament; the situation there was "serfdom." Slavery in the sixteenth and seventeenth centuries had been opposed by popes and the Third Lateran Council with little affect. The missionaries could not end slavery, only alleviate it, and no one labored harder in this effort than Peter Claver.

Every month, when the slave ships would land at Cartagena, Claver visited the slaves and distributed food and delicacies. They had been cooped up in the hold of the ship, crazed by suffering and fear. He would visit each one and made them understand that he was their friend and benefactor. Claver tended the sick and preached the Gospel with good effect, and it is reported that he baptized 300,000 slaves.

These efforts caused Claver severe trials, not only from the slave merchants, but from upper class women of Cartagena. They charged him with excessive zeal in giving the Sacraments to creatures that barely possessed a soul. He persevered, however, and lacking the support of men, Peter received the strength of God.

Claver was canonized in 1888 by Leo XIII and in 1889 was proclaimed "the special patron of all the Catholic missions among the Negroes." Given his efforts, Fr. Peter Claver joins Anselm of Canterbury, who in 1102 preached against the slave trade, and William Wilberforce, who was active in the ending of slavery in England.

BROTHER LAWRENCE

Brother Lawrence was born Nicolas Herman in 1605. As a youth, Lawrence became a soldier, was wounded in battle, and became a hermit.

In 1649 at Paris, he entered the Carmelite monastery and became a lay brother. Being crippled from his battle injury, Lawrence was put in charge of the kitchen, a job he disliked. After fifteen years in the kitchen, he became lame from his war injury and was transferred to the cobbler shop, where he could sit down to work.

It is important to note that during the time Lawrence lived, Quietism, an approach which stresses contemplative passivity, was practiced among French Catholics. Quietism is closely associated with Mysticism, the belief that seeks a personal knowledge of God by means of a loving encounter with Him. Both of these beliefs may have been combined to influence Brother Lawrence to lead a life of constant prayer and reflection to gain the presence of God.

Brother Lawrence wrote a few letters and a number of meditations. Abbe Joseph de Beaufort, the superior of the Parisian monastery, gathered these materials that provide the picture of this unforgettable and holy man. Among those writings in the devotional treatise that has become one of the most highly regarded works in Christian literature, *The Practice of the Presence of God*.

This book is popular with Roman Catholics and Protestants as well. One of the most popular parts in the book deals with how Lawrence relied on God's help when faced with a difficult task to perform. Lawrence writes: "My God, I would not be able to do that, if thou didst not help me."

Asked about the method he had used to arrive at God's nearness, Lawrence replied that he had read about different methods, but they did nothing but trouble his soul. He said, "... thoughts count for little, love does everything."

Brother Lawrence's maxims were quoted by Archbishop Francis Fenelon, who shared with Lawrence many views on mediation and the presence of God. In this sophisticated age, perhaps Quietism and Mysticism are not as practiced as they were with Brother Lawrence. We might be missing out on something.

BLAISE PASCAL

Blaise Pascal, born in 1623, was the son of Etienne Pascal, a man of culture involved in the local government. Blaise was born at Clermont-Ferrand, France. His mother died when he was four and within a few years, his father moved the family to Paris. Pascal and his two sisters were educated by his father. He indicated a high level of maturity and while in Rouen, he participated in a number of mathematical experiments, the result of which led to the invention of the barometer.

The family left Rouen and returned to Paris in 1650. Pascal continued his scientific experiments and involved himself in the culture of Paris. As a youth, he had been taught to regard matters of faith as beyond reason. However, coming into contact with Jansenism, a sect within Roman Catholicism, he experienced his "definitive conversion" discovering "the God of Abraham, Isaac and Jacob, not of philosophy and science."

Pascal, in addition to his newfound faith, continued to pursue scientific projects, including experiments with conic sections and the mathematical theory of probability. It is also reported that, when encountering heavy traffic in Paris, he drew on a napkin the traffic pattern which is still used today in Paris.

Pascal was involved in controversy with the Jesuits in his *Provincial Letters,* which takes exception to the order's casuistry and other theological issues. Pascal's *Pensees,* or thoughts, were a collection of notes and aphorisms intended to be used as an *Apology for the Christian Religion.* However, ill health and an untimely death in 1662 prevented Pascal from the realization of this project.

Pascal was emphatically Christocentric in his theological thinking. This was his normal state as he walked the streets of Paris. Frank N. Magill's "Pensees," found in *Master Pieces of Christian Literature,* clarifies Pascal's thinking. "Not only do we know God by

Jesus Christ alone, but we know ourselves only by Jesus Christ. We know life and death only through Jesus Christ. Apart from Jesus Christ we do not know what is our life, nor our death, not God, nor ourselves." Voltaire ridiculed Pascal and was reputed to say: "Pascal is the wisest man France has ever produced and all he wants to do is read his Bible." One wonders if Voltaire now wishes he had read the Bible more closely.

One could learn much from Pascal's understanding of the relationship between faith and reason.

JOHN BUNYAN

John Bunyan was born in 1628 at Elstow in Bedfordshire, England. His family was poor and his father was a tinker, an occupation John himself followed. He developed his proficiency in the English language probably from reading the Bible. He was converted through writings recommended by his godly wife. He joined an independent Baptist Church at Bedford and in 1657 accepted a position as preacher. He became quite successful.

In 1660, when the Church of England returned to Roman Catholicism, Bunyan, an unlicensed preacher, was imprisoned from 1660–1672. It was during this period that he penned his spiritual autobiography, *Grace Abounding in the Chief of Sinners.*

In this book, Bunyan records the struggles he experienced from his childhood through his first time in prison. It was, in many ways, comparable to Augustine of Hippo's autobiography, *The Confessions*, which also details Augustine's spiritual journey from childhood through licentious living to his conversion.

Bunyan wrote about his own fears and how God delivered him from them to help his congregation when he was in prison and not with them. As a child, Bunyan was beset with thinking about his soul's damnation. He writes remembering how God's help in difficult circumstances is support to the Christian in times of temptation.

Upon release from prison, Bunyan was called to be the minister at Bedford Nonconformist Church. These churches rejected episcopal and hierarchical forms of church government.

The second book Bunyan wrote became a Christian classic, *The Pilgrim's Progress,* written during a second confinement in 1676 and published two years later. This work is an allegory. The central person in Bunyan's story is Christian, who is fleeing his family and the "City of Destruction" to the "Celestial City." Along the way, he meets a number of interesting figures who impact, for good or for bad, his Christian spiritual formation.

Bunyan at once realized that he has produced something special. He had written a story that reflected many of the doctrines that came out of the Reformation, including justification by faith and the availability of the Bible to everyone. It shows that without a true dependence on Christ religious symbols are just a nice story.

Like most Puritans, Bunyan understood Christianity through the eyes of Paul. Charles Spurgeon said that Bunyan's blood was "Bibline." Bunyan's writings show that to the person immersed in spiritual warfare, what matters most is the salvation of the soul.

JOHN LOCKE

John Locke was born in 1632 in Summersetshire, England. He was the son of a small country land owner and lawyer. He attended Oxford, studied medicine, and earned a MD degree. He was introduced to the works of Rene Descartes and his emphasis on reason made a positive impression on him.

Locke traveled to France in 1675, returning to England four years later. He then moved to Holland in 1683. While there, he met a number of Arminian theologians and completed his first philosophical treatise, *An Essay Concerning Human Understanding* and his *Letter on Toleration.*

In his treatise, *An Essay Concerning Human Understanding*, John Locke makes the point that knowledge is obtained through human reason—natural revelation. God's existence can be known by reason as well. Rules of conduct also can also be perceived by God's Law.

Locke's Christian orthodoxy is displayed in *The Reasonableness of Christianity as Delivered in the Scriptures,* written in 1695. He writes that the only true test for Christianity is its reasonableness and he believed that the miracles revealed in the Bible were evidence of its divine source. Finally, the heart of the Christian faith is the acceptance of Christ as the Lord, who came into the world as the Messiah and to spread the truth about God and tell us about our duties.

Locke's theological approach was similar to that of Augustine, Anselm, and Aquinas; he defended miracles, Christ's deity and resurrection, and the Bible as the Word of God. Concerning his view of government, Locke believed that because we are made in the image of God, we have certain responsibilities toward each other. Norman Geisler, in *Baker Encyclopedia of Christian Apologetics,* linked Locke's theological approach with our founding forefathers. "This same view was expressed by Thomas Jefferson in the *Declaration of Independence* when he wrote: 'We hold these truths to be self-evident, that all men are created equal, that they are endowed by their Creator with certain unalienable Rights, that among these are Life, Liberty and the pursuit of Happiness.'" Toward the end of his life, John Locke devoted himself to the study of Scripture.

SIR ISAAC NEWTON

Isaac Newton was born in 1642 at Woolsthorpe, near Grantham in Lincolnshire, England. He was elected a Fellow in Trinity College, Cambridge in 1667 and two years later became Lucasian Professor of Mathematics.

Newton represented the university in the House of Commons on two different occasions. He moved to London and was appointed Master of the Mint in 1699. Newton was knighted by Queen Anne in 1705.

Colin Brown discusses Newton's scientific discoveries in *Christianity and Western Thought, Vol 1.* "Newton's scientific achievements included the formulation of the laws of motion and gravitation, the discovery (apparently coincidentally with Leibniz) of differential calculus, and the first correct analysis of white light. Newton's laws of motion helped to establish the mechanical view of the universe which dominated physics down to modern times." Sir Isaac's scientific approach is similar to that of Galileo, Copernicus, and Roger Bacon.

Sir Isaac Newton has been acclaimed as one of the foremost scientific intellects of all times. In addition to his many scientific accomplishments, he was involved in the study of Christian theology, the Scriptures, and Hebrew and Jewish mysticism. However, Newton departed from classical Christian orthodoxy by holding that the message of Christianity went astray in the fourth century with the Council of Nicaea's statements on the nature of Christ and the Trinitarian doctrines. He did, however, possess a deep religious sense, and Newton venerated the Bible and believed the account of creation found in the book of Genesis.

Enlightenment & Skeptics of Christianity

The Enlightenment—some call it the Age of Reason—appeared in eighteenth century Europe. It was indeed the birth of secularism—illustrated by reason being elevated over revelation. We shall examine some of the men and their thinking that was involved in the movement.

THE ENLIGHTENMENT

Although the term "enlightenment" is a translation from the German, it is now used to identify ideas which developed in eighteenth century Europe. It reflected distrust in authority. Those who held to tradition believed that truth could be understood though reason, observation, and experimentation.

The Enlightenment is often confused with the Renaissance—the latter movement was treated earlier. They were quite different. The Renaissance produced "humanism," and the majority of its practitioners were theologically orthodox, using the developing scientific discoveries in a positive way.

The movement under consideration here was different. Rodney Stark, in *For the Glory of God*, trashes the Enlightenment. "Turning to an assessment of the 'Enlightenment,' I show it to have been conceived initially as a propaganda ploy by militant atheists and humanists who attempted to claim credit for the rise of science."

The Enlightenment embraced people with a wide spectrum of views. Some were atheists, most were probably deists. By attempting to accommodate Christian thought to these new ideas, a "theology of reason" developed, discounting a "theology of revelation." The Enlightenment was the source of many unorthodox notions and movements that continue to plague the Church.

VOLTAIRE

Voltaire was born in 1694 in Paris, France, to a well-to-do family. He had a burning desire for social reform; he wrote poems and tracts that were critical of society. At an early age, Voltaire was hailed as the best playwright in France. He was educated by the Jesuits but throughout his life was violently opposed to the Catholic Church, believing their institutions to be filled with deceit, superstition, and fanaticism. Probably the only thing that he and Pascal had in common was a dislike for the Jesuit order.

The eighteenth century has been known as the "age of Voltaire." Not only in France, but in western civilization, his name expresses a direction of thought. This can be demonstrated by a number of dictionaries that define "Voltairism" as signifying infidelity or skepticism when dealing with religion.

Voltaire's thought was not systematic and contributed little to the history of philosophy. He was, however, a genius for presenting ideas to common people. Voltaire railed against superstition, bigotry, and injustice. He was also guilty of unscrupulous tactics and shameless writing.

Voltaire, while opposed to all types of Christianity, threw his support behind the French Protestants because he opposed all religious persecution. He seems to have favored Deism, which is the view that while God is the original creator, He stands outside of his creation. God built the machine, but it now runs its predetermined course, independent of its maker. Also, God is unconcerned with us personally, according to Deism.

DAVID HUME

Born in 1711, Hume was a native of Edinburg, Scotland, where he was schooled. At an early age, he was drawn to study philosophy. While he resided in France, he developed his skeptical ideas. Hume had been raised as a Scottish Presbyterian, but early in his life rejected his faith and ultimately came to argue against religion of any form. He wrote on morals and ethics, and his most well received work were two volumes called *Essays Moral and Political.*

Hume understood reason as coming from experience thus negating its claim to authority. His skepticism is clearly stated in his *Essay on Miracles.* He not only rejected Christianity, but Deism as well. He questioned the Deistic position that monotheism was the original religious view of mankind, and held that polytheism came first.

JEAN-JACQUES ROUSSEAU

Rousseau was born in 1712 in Geneva, the son of a French refugee family. He was brought up a Calvinist, but embraced Catholicism through the persuasion of a woman, herself a convert from Protestantism. She became his mistress. They ultimately both embraced Deism.

Rousseau was self-taught and read extensively the works of Descartes, Leibniz, Locke, and Pascal. The Christian content that was present in his reading, however, hardly changed his thinking. His personal life was a disaster; he sent his five illegitimate children to an orphanage.

As to his spiritual legacy, Rousseau's proponents assert that he proclaimed the fundamentals of Christianity among unbelievers of his time. However, one could argue the opposite. Due to his denigrating original sin and thus the need for grace through faith, he militated against biblical Christianity by promulgating dependence on reason, conscience and free will, paving the way for humanistic liberalism.

IMMANUEL KANT

Born in East Prussia in 1724, Kant was one of the most important philosophers of modern times. During his early life, he was attracted to the study of mathematics and physics and retained interest in the natural sciences throughout his life. For Kant, the traditional Christian view of Revelation—God revealing Himself in history and personal experience through events and His Word—is replaced by reason.

Kant was embedded in the Enlightenment period, when thinkers struggled to free themselves from what they considered to be the bondage of outdated thinking. He claimed to be freed from his "slumbers" by reading debates, which the Scottish skeptic David Hume had with his opponents.

Christian scholars who follow Thomas Aquinas are very critical of Kant. He held that all knowledge came from nature. Kant attacked the basis of traditional metaphysics, including, of course, Christianity, which claims to provide data that nature alone does not.

FRIEDRICH SCHLEIERMACHER

Friedrich Schleiermacher was born in 1768 in Breslau, Silesia. He was the son of a Reformed army chaplain. After his parents' conversion to the Herrnhut Brethren, Friedrich was educated at their college and seminary at Barby.

Friedrich found the teaching at Barby too fundamentalistic for his independent thinking and in 1787, he entered the University of Halle and was exposed to the philosophy of Immanuel Kant and Aristotle. It was this experience that brought him to the belief that religion was based on intuition and feeling and that religious language is only an expression of religious self-consciousness.

Schleiermacher was ordained as a Reformed pastor in 1794 and later held theological positions at Halle and Berlin. In spite of functioning in orthodox religious settings, he is known as the father of modern liberalism. Schleiermacher thought that religion was "the feeling of absolute dependence." There was no need for a number of intellectual propositions and dogmas, which the would-be convert would be asked to accept. Although verbal forms of the faith would develop, he believed they would be secondary; they had changed and would change again.

Early American Christianity

Columbus' discovery of America in 1492 and the beginning of

the Reformation are separated by only twenty-five years. All of the churches to develop from the Reformation, and later the Roman Catholic Church, would be established in America.

In the spring of 1607, the permanent colony of Jamestown, in what would become the state of Virginia, was established. A chaplain was among the settlers, who anticipated that the Church of England would soon follow. Some wanted Puritan principles to rule the new colony, but King James hated the Puritans and would not allow it.

In 1620, 101 settlers boarded the Mayflower and sailed for the new land. They arrived at Plymouth in December and founded a Puritan colony. While they had fled England to escape persecution, they soon expelled those who differed with them on religious matters.

THE GREAT AWAKENING

The "Great Awakening" was a religious movement that occurred in the American colonies from 1725–1760. It addressed rationalism, formalism, and pastoral indifference that had crept into Protestantism, including Reformed churches, Congregationalists and Baptists.

While the Great Awakening caused fractures amongst some denominations, it had the positive result of encouraging outreach to the Indians and the founding of a number of universities including Princeton, Dartmouth, and Brown. The Second Great Awakening began at the end of the eighteenth century. We will cover the efforts of some of the prominent revivalists next.

ISAAC WATTS

Born in 1674, Isaac Watts was born in Southampton, England. He exhibited his aptitude with English verse while still a youth and turned down an opportunity to study at the university. Instead,

Watts chose to attend a dissenting academy at Stoke Newington, under the instruction of Thomas Rowe.

Watts became attached to Rowe's church and began to compose hymns. In 1702, he became pastor of an evangelical chapel, but health problems prevented his ability to discharge his responsibilities. Watts then directed his energies to writing hymns, poetry, and theology.

Watts occupies a very high standing among English hymnwriters. His hymns speak to his deep Christian faith and introduced hymn-singing as a powerful force in the nonconformity churches in England. Of his 600 hymns, many can be found in current hymnals today, including 'Jesus Shall Reign Where'er the Sun,' 'When I Survey the Wondrous Cross,' and 'Our God, Our Help in Ages Past.' Two collections published are *Hymns and Spiritual Songs* and *Psalms of David*.

DAVID BRAINERD

David Brainerd was born in 1718 in Haddam, Connecticut and became an orphan at the age of fourteen. He was converted to Christianity and entered Yale College with the hope of becoming a Congregationalist minister.

Brainerd became a leader at Yale of the Great Awakening; however, he was dismissed from the college over a disagreement with a professor. He continued to study for the ministry and in 1744 was ordained by the Presbytery of New York.

He then began a work which would identify Brainerd's special talent, evangelizing among Indians in New York, Pennsylvania, and New Jersey. Brainerd conduced a revival in Eastern Pennsylvania among the Delaware Indians and by 1746, 130 of them accepted Christ.

During a visit the following year with his mentor Jonathan Edwards, David Brainerd died at the age of twenty-nine of tuberculosis, which had afflicted him for years. When mention is made of evangelistic efforts among American Indians, David Brainerd's name comes to the forefront.

JONATHAN EDWARDS

Born in 1703, Jonathan Edwards was drawn to philosophy from an early age. This interest, prompted by his study of John Locke, appeared in his essay in 1717. After coming to faith in Christ, he was ordained as a Congregationalist minister and became pastor of the church in Northampton, Massachusetts.

His preaching skills soon become apparent, and they stimulated the Great Awakening. Edwards was concerned with the influence that Arminianism was having in his church. His efforts to stem the tide led to a religious revival, which he discussed in his work *Faithful Narrative of the Surprising Works of God*, published in 1737.

From 1751, Edwards ministered in Stockbridge, including an outreach to the Indians. He was a Calvinist, which caused him real difficulty in a theological climate which was exposed to a more "moderate" approach. After much persuasion, he became the president of Princeton Theological Seminary in 1758. Unfortunately, during that same year he died a month after receiving a smallpox vaccination. Jonathan Edwards was considered the foremost theologian and philosopher of American puritanism. He also believed that Christianity, after developing in America, would spread throughout the whole world.

GEORGE WHITEFIELD

George Whitefield was born in 1714 in Gloucester, England. In 1734, he was admitted to Oxford's well-known Pembroke College, where he paid his way by serving meals to wealthier students. While at Oxford, Whitefield would meet the brothers John and Charles Wesley. Their friendship and piety would have a lasting effect on Whitefield's life. While disagreeing with them on predestination and free will, he accepted their teaching on piety and necessity of spiritual regeneration.

The Wesley's influence caused Whitefield to consider the ministry and in 1737, he was ordained a preaching deacon in the Church of England. He preached not only in local congregations but far and wide over the countryside proclaiming the necessity of receiving Christ as Saviour.

Whitefield's theology raised criticism from his fellow Anglicans and in 1739, he took his ministry to America. Here his theatrical style was enthusiastically received. While in Georgia, Whitefield began an orphanage; in Philadelphia, he preached to crowds as large as 20,000. Even Benjamin Franklin was impressed.

It was fortuitous that in God's timing, Whitefield would arrive in America when the Great Awakening was in its peak. He was arguably the greatest English-speaking preacher in the eighteenth century and perhaps never equaled as a revivalist.

SAMUEL DAVIS

Samuel Davis was known as the founder of the Presbyterian Church in the U.S., the Southern Presbyterian Church. Born in 1723 in Delaware, he was ordained as an evangelist in 1747 and was involved in the Great Awakening in Virginia and North Carolina.

Davis raised support for the College of New Jersey that later became Princeton. In Virginia, he faced opposition from Anglican officials, who felt that he came short of their ecclesiastical standards. Solving that difficulty, he was soon holding worship services over a five-county area. Davis visited Britain with Gilbert Tennent, and made a great impression there with his preaching. Davis succeeded Jonathan Edwards as president of Princeton University in 1759.

COUNT VON LUDWIG ZINZENDORF

Count Zinzendorf was born in 1700 in Dresden and raised in pietistic circles. He studied law at Wittenberg and then entered Saxton government service. He provided shelter to a group of Bohemian refugees on his estate and this resulted in the formation of the famous Christian community, Herrnhut.

Count Zinzendorf left the government. He was ordained as a Lutheran pastor in 1734 and became a bishop three years later. From Herrnhut he sent missionaries abroad; John Wesley recounts that when he encountered the Moravians on one of his journeys, he found his heart "strangely warmed." Wesley held that this experience completed his conversion. Against the rejection of Christianity, as well as 'dead' orthodoxy, Zinzendorf traveled worldwide ministering in America and England. One cannot overestimate the contribution that Count Von Ludwig Zinzendorf made to the modern missionary movement.

JOHN WESLEY

John Wesley was born in 1703 in Epworth, Lincolnshire, England. He was the fifteenth child of Anglican rector Samuel Wesley and was educated at Charter House, London, and Christ Church Oxford. Ordained in 1728, he joined his father in Wroote as curate.

After his father's death, Wesley returned to Oxford where he became director of the "Holy Club," which was a group of serious students who were called "Methodists." They performed works of piety and charity and were ridiculed by their more worldly fellow students.

Wesley embarked for America on a missionary endeavor in Georgia, which turned out to be a disaster. Returning to London, he had an experience which he called a final conversion at a meeting on Aldersgate Street. This experience changed his life.

John Wesley is best known as the founder, along with his brother Charles, of the Methodist denomination. What is unknown to many is that he never officially left the Church of England.

Let Daniel G. Reid, in *The Dictionary of Christianity in America,* give us some information about him and his influence. "John Wesley, through men like Francis Asbury, Thomas Coke and others, established a tradition among the Methodists that sought to emphasize justification by faith as the gateway to sanctification or 'scriptural holiness.'" The brothers also came to America and were instrumental in laying the framework in this country for Wesleyanism.

Those whom he assigned to work toward strengthening the Methodist presence in America saw in this country what Wesley had developed in England.

CHARLES WESLEY

Born in 1707, Charles Wesley was the eighteenth child of Samuel and brother of John Wesley. He was educated at Westminster School and Christ Church, Oxford. Along with John, Charles became active with the Oxford Methodists.

After ordination, he joined John and traveled to Georgia in 1735, where he became Secretary to Governor Oglethorpe. Charles and John returned to England the following year. Charles came under the influence of the Moravian Herrnhut gathering, the famous Christian community, and along with John, experienced Christian conversion.

Charles and John became revivalist preachers in Bristol and they took turns preaching at the City Road Chapel in London. Charles Wesley wrote more hymns than anyone England had ever known. Not only is the music recognized in Christian circles, but the biblical content of the words are stellar. I attend a Presbyterian church, and if the hymns that Charles Wesley composed were removed from our hymnal, we would indeed suffer the loss.

ISAAC BACKUS

Isaac Backus was born in 1724 at Norwich, Connecticut, a son of Samuel and Elizabeth Backus, respectable members of the Congregational Church. His father was a descendant of one of the earliest settlers of Norwich and his mother of the Winslow family that came from Plymouth in 1620.

It was in the midst of a revival that George Whitefield was holding that Isaac received his first religious experience. He joined the Congregational Church in his native town, in spite of concerns about their laxity in regard to the admission of members to the congregation.

Backus formed the New Light Church in Titicut, Massachusetts. In 1751, he came to the conviction that adult baptism was more biblical than infant baptism. This position put Backus and his church in conflict with the Congregationalist establishment and therefore, five years later, he became the pastor of the Baptist Church in Middleborough, Massachusetts.

During his life, Baptists were subject to persecution from the civil authorities of Massachusetts. They were taxed to support the state Congregational Churches and when they refused to pay, their houses, land and possessions were confiscated. Some were put in prison for refusing to support the state-sanctioned religion.

While pastoring the church in Middleborough, Backus organized evangelistic tours and petitioned for the cause of religious freedom. His most famous tract, *An Appeal to the Public for Religious Liberty Against the Oppression of the Present Day*, was published in 1773. It was called the best evangelical concept of the separation of church and state produced in the eighteenth century.

Backus spent the next five years writing articles to explain the need for complete religious liberty. Although he saw some relief, the entire fruit of his labor was not appreciated until after his death. Isaac Backus is remembered for his efforts in the cause of religious liberty.

FRANCIS ASBURY

Francis Asbury was born in 1745 near Birmingham, England to Anglican parents who had joined the Methodist society. He did not receive any formal training and became a blacksmith apprentice at age sixteen. Asbury was converted soon after and shortly became a local Methodist preacher in 1767.

Joining his parents, Francis Asbury became associated with the Methodist movement in the Church of England. He became a street preacher at an early age and soon became associated with John Wesley. Five years later, he answered Wesley's appeal for missionaries to go to America.

For forty-five years, Asbury traveled some three hundred thousand miles, preaching sixteen thousand sermons. He had no permanent home, once instructing a correspondent in England to address letters to him simply "in America." Being distressed by the lax attitude of American clergy, he established the Methodist system of "circuit riders." Asbury certainly drew everyone's attention to the Methodist Church's growth in this country.

Responding to Wesley's call for preachers to go to America to further the Methodist cause there, Asbury and another volunteer, Richard Wright, arrived in Philadelphia in late October. They set about moving Methodist preachers out of the cities and into the country side.

ARCHIBALD ALEXANDER

Archibald Alexander was born in 1772 in Rockbridge Country, Virginia and was converted at the age of seventeen. He had little formal schooling and studied theology at what would become Washington and Lee University.

In 1812, Alexander became the first professor at Princeton Theological Seminary in America. Under his leadership, it would develop a standard of excellence that would be continued by such Reformed leaders as Charles and A. A. Hodge and Benjamin B. Warfield. Alexander joined Scottish Common Sense philosophy with Reformed theology; this combination, which begins with the use of external evidences for establishing the credibility of Scripture, would lead to what has been called "Princeton Theology."

Alexander was not opposed to the use of reason in the understanding of biblical truth, but took a skeptical view toward mysticism. While at Princeton, he pastored the Pine Street Presbyterian Church in Philadelphia.

Unfortunately, the nineteenth and twentieth centuries have seen the emergence of hostile attacks on orthodoxy by modern theologians, using methods like deconstructionism to attack the reliability of Scripture. Archibald Alexander's teaching and writings reflected a piety and fervor, which had its roots in his revivalist's preaching.

THE CLAPHAM COMMUNITY

The evangelicals in the Church of England were loyal to their church's Episcopal form of government. However, they worked with nonconformist ministers and churches, because they considered the preaching of the gospel central to the church's mission rather than sacraments and rituals.

The Clapham Community was formed in 1790 and was also known as the Clapham Sect. It was so named because a number of the Anglican evangelicals lived near Clapham, in England, and were attenders at the parish church in town. The members were social conservatives who also held to high moral standards and the belief that Christianity must be demonstrated by the practice of good works. They were especially interested in the abolition of the slave trade.

The Clapham Community had in its group a number of influential people, including Lord Teignmouth, the Governor General of India; Charles Grant, Chairman of the East India Company; and William Wilberforce, who will be discussed shortly. A number of evangelical causes were gathered at Clapham: the Church Missionary Society; the British and Foreign Bible Society; the Society for Bettering the Condition of the Poor; the Society for the Reformation of Prison Discipline; and many more.

One of the most interesting persons to be involved with the Clapham Movement was Hannah More. She had been active in London's social and literary circles, but upon meeting John Newton—the former slave ship captain and author of the famous hymn *Amazing Grace*—and hearing him preach, she joined him at the Clapham meeting.

Hannah's new faith and skills caused her to become a leader in the Community. Secular historians have noted Clapham's ability to cross party lines and champion causes that needed to be addressed. Hannah More has been called "the most influential reformer you've never heard of."

WILLIAM CAREY

William Carey was born in humble beginnings in Northamptonshire, England in 1761. He was baptized an Anglican. After working two years for a shoemaker, he experienced a conversion in 1779, which led him to become a Baptist, and he spent part of his time preaching.

For some time, Carey continued his cobbling at night, while operating a school by day and pastoring a church as well. At the same time, he taught himself a number of languages, which would enable missionaries to spread the good news of the Gospel throughout the world.

Carey set sail for Calcutta, India in 1793. The following year, he was put in charge of an indigo plant in Bengali, translated the New Testament into Bengali, and preached in the villages. For twenty-five years, he worked to eliminate the religious practice of burning widows on their husband's funeral pyre, known as sati, which finally led to the banning of the practice. In 1800, he moved to Serampore and became professor of Bengali, Sanskrit, and Marathi at Fort William College and translated Scripture into thirty-five languages and dialects. His efforts gained him the title of "Father of Bengali prose."

WILLIAM ELLERY CHANNING

William Channing was born in 1780 in Newport, Rhode Island. He graduated from Harvard College in 1798 and was a tutor in Richmond, Virginia.

He became the pastor at Federal Street Congregational Church in Boston in 1803 and held that position until his death. Channing is regarded as the founder of the liberal movement, which developed in New England congregationalism, known as Unitarianism. You may remember that John Calvin had a confrontation with Michael Servetus. This event led to Servetus being declared a heretic and subsequently burnt at the stake. Servetus held the same views concerning the Trinity that would become known as Unitarianism.

In his treatise Unitarian Christianity, Channing developed the doctrinal framework that would lead to a separate religious community. Channing was reported to be an eloquent orator, and he produced a number of literary essays dealing with the finer points of Unitarianism. He also was involved in social justice causes, including an early indictment of slavery. In spite of the aforementioned positive comments, "honorable character does not guarantee good theology." One can also find that Unitarianism has made its way into some mainline denominations currently.

WILLIAM WILBERFORCE

Born in 1759, William Wilberforce was a native of Hull and educated at St. John's College, Cambridge. He was the son of a rich merchant, who died when William was eight years old. He went to live with an uncle and aunt who had been influenced by George Whitefield and the Evangelical Movement. They were also friends of John Newton, a former slave trader and a popular hymn-writer. He is famous for his hymn *Amazing Grace*.

While at Cambridge, Wilberforce was very popular, amusing his fellow students with his wit and charm. He became close friends with William Pitt, the future prime minister of England. This friendship would serve Wilberforce in good stead later, when he considered a political career.

At age twenty-one, he entered the House of Commons. John D. Woodbridge offers the following critique in *Great Leaders of the Christian Church*. "Four years later, with Pitt already prime minister, Wilberforce won the important seat of Yorkshire on Pitt's behalf and became a man of political consequence. He was a good parliamentary speaker with an exceptionally attractive voice, his tones 'so distinct and melodious that the most hostile ear hangs on them delighted.'" It is here that Wilberforce developed his speaking skills that would later service in good stead.

In 1784, Wilberforce embarked on a trip to the American continent accompanied by Isaac Milner, who had been his tutor at Hull Grammar School nearly two decades before. Milner was a huge man physically, and possessing a prodigious intellect, Wilberforce looked forward to an enjoyable trip.

Milner not only knew secular topics, but, while not a practicing

Christian, he was interested in theological issues. Wilberforce had a cursory understanding of Christian salvation; knowing "about" Jesus, but not "knowing" Him. The sessions with his former tutor led him to a full conversion experience.

Wilberforce's role in dismantling the slave trade in England has previously been mentioned. Bruce L. Shelley, in *Church History in Plain Language*, gives us an insight into his political acumen. "In 1789, Wilberforce made his first speech in the House of Commons on the traffic in slaves. He recognized immediately that eloquence alone would never overthrow the commercial interests in the sale of human beings." He would not be dissuaded in his dedication to this noble cause.

But the die was cast; in 1807, support for abolition was passed in the House. The story is told that when Wilberforce was a young boy and told about the conditions that slaves experienced, he wondered why it was allowed. He was in the chamber when slavery was officially denounced. Overcome with emotion, Wilberforce, head in his hands and tears streaming down his face, remembered that little boy's question.

And lastly, in the *Encyclopedia of Evangelicalism*, Randall Balmer includes one of my favorite tributes to William Wilberforce where he writes, "[He] was a man of extraordinary piety, and his political importance was such that Parliament insisted he be buried in Westminster Abbey following his death in 1833." William was a gentle man and a wonderful Christian, and he did much to stop a terrible situation in England.

PART FOUR

Modern to Postmodern

19th Century Modern Christianity

Here in *Part Four* we begin by addressing the Modern Era and continue into the so-called Postmodern Era. Many readers today often find these terms somewhat confusing. Joseph Bottum confirms this in his *First Things* article "Christians and Postmoderns" when he writes, "In some sense, of course, these words premodern, modern and postmodern are too slippery to mean much ... they seem to name the periods before, during, and after the Enlightenment." He continues, "It is premodern to seek beyond rational knowledge for God; it is modern to desire to hold knowledge in the structures of human rationality (with or without God); it is postmodern to see the impossibility of such knowledge."

THE RESTORATION MOVEMENT

The Enlightenment, which began in the eighteenth century in Europe, made its way to America as the new nation was forming from 1750–1800. The Christian movement in America soon realized that the tenets of the Enlightenment were counter to its own beliefs.

These Enlightenment notions and denominational unrest prompted a reaction from Christians in America, resulting in the formation of groups such as the Restoration Movement. Campbell and his son Alexander co-founder the Restoration Movement. Thomas was born in Ireland and raised an Anglican. He graduated from the University of Glasgow. He became a Presbyterian, but he was unsettled with the theological disputes among the Scottish Presbyterians and worked tirelessly for unity.

Alexander Campbell grew up in Ireland and was educated by his father. In addition to his general studies, he examined the works of John Locke. He spent ten months at the University of Glasgow, where he studied the Greek New Testament, literature, logic, French, and experimental philosophy. Little did he realize at the time how much he would see this academic preparation in the work with his father in America.

In 1809, Alexander arrived in Pennsylvania, where he found his father, who had emigrated two years earlier from Ireland. Alexander discovered his father had departed from Presbyterians over the Reformed closed communion practices and other disagreements with Calvinism. The younger Campbell, coming to the same conclusions as his father, started the Brush Run Church in 1811. Thomas was appointed an elder and Alexander was ordained to preach. The Restoration Movement was beginning to take shape.

Barton Warren Stone was an important leader who became involved in the Restoration Movement. He was born near Port Tobacco, Maryland. He was converted to Christianity at age nineteen and became a member of the Orange Presbytery. He preached in a number of Southern states, but he was most successful in Concord and Cane Ridge, Kentucky, the center of the Great Revival.

The Restoration Movement came into existence in America as a reaction to Enlightenment precepts that were beginning to surface. Randall Balmer, in the *Encyclopedia of Evangelicalism*, addresses the Movement as follows: "Stone had long expressed reservations about the Calvinist doctrine of election, which he viewed as a hindrance to revival. In 1803, he and four other revivalists withdrew from the Presbyterian Synod of Kentucky rather than face censure for their views." A number of churches would join the group. Stone became leader of an independent group, and in the 1830s, they joined the Disciples led by Thomas and Alexander Campbell. The group became known as the Christian Church/Disciples of Christ.

In the 1906 federal census of church denominations, a third group of churches made its appearance arising out of the Restoration Movement. Its name was Churches of Christ, Non-Instrumental. These churches were quite legalistic and disagreed on other theological issues coming out of the Restoration Movement. They were not inclined to be open to other Christian groups.

However, the Christian Church/Disciples of Christ has remained orthodox in doctrine and practice. It is also open to evangelicals who worship in other Christian denominations.

ADONIRAM JUDSON

Born in 1788 in Malden, Massachusetts, Adoniram Judson was the son of a Congregational minister and he graduated from Brown University. While attending Andover Seminary as a nominal believer, he experienced conversion and was involved in the formation of the country's first foreign missionary society, the American Board of Commissioners for Foreign Missions.

Judson and his wife Ann sailed for India in 1812, and during the trip, they became convinced that their baptisms as infants were unbiblical; therefore, on their arrival in Calcutta they experienced adult baptisms and were immersed. The Congregationalists back home took exception to this theological change on the part of the Judsons and they were recalled from India.

This led the Judsons to move to Rangoon, Burma, where they gathered a group of converts and started the task of learning the language and translating the Scriptures. War erupted between England and Burma in 1824, and Judson was imprisoned at age thirty-six. His confinement was severe, complicated by the knowledge of his wife's travails over the birth of their child and several diseases. Ann Judson died in 1826, not long after Judson's release.

In 1834, he married the widow of a fellow missionary, but she died in 1845 after working with her husband on the translation of the Bible and literary work that became Judson's legacy. One year later, he again married a young writer, Emily Chubbuck, who survived him by only a few years.

For spending over thirty-three years as a missionary, receiving only one furlough, experiencing seventeen months incarcerated, and losing two wives to untimely deaths, one imagines that Adoniram Judson will be handsomely rewarded at the judgment seat of Christ.

JOHN NELSON DARBY

John Darby was born in 1800 in London, England, of wealthy Irish parents and named in honor of Admiral Lord Nelson. Darby was schooled at Trinity College, Dublin, Ireland.

He practiced law for a time and after a conversion experience, Darby joined the Church of England and became a successful parish priest in County Wicklow, Ireland. However, he found that the state church was immersed in religious formalism which stifled his spiritual life.

Darby began meeting in Dublin, Ireland with people who gathered for worship, Bible teaching, and the breaking of bread that differed from the ecclesiastical form found in the Church of England. He left that church in 1831 and moved with his followers to Plymouth, England founding a movement known as the Plymouth Brethren.

The Plymouth Brethren Movement was so called because its first church was formed in Plymouth, England. It was also known as the "Christian Brethren Church." It became popular among American evangelicals after the Civil War. The movement still has no salaried or ordained clergy, and its meetings are conducted by the laity. Members reject the formalism found in the established churches and attempt to reflect the simplicity of New Testament Christianity.

Darby addressed his distinctive views of Dispensationalism through conferences and Bible study. As the founding leader of the movement, he shaped their theological perspective. After 1837, Darby traveled worldwide spreading his ideas. He made seven trips to Canada and the United States, where he influenced men such as D. L. Moody of Chicago and A. J. Gordon of Boston. In the twentieth century, Dispensationalism made a significant impact on the spread of evangelical Protestantism in America and elsewhere.

THE OXFORD MOVEMENT

The Oxford Movement began within the Church of England, centered at Oxford. Its primary goal was to address the damage that Protestantism and Nationalism had inflicted on the Church of England and to restore the High Church ideas of the seventeenth century. It also opposed Erastianism, which handed ecclesiastical jurisdiction to the state.

The original leaders of the movement were John Keble, Edward Pusey, and John Henry Newman. However, Newman, who had increasingly been attracted to Roman Catholicism, finally made the move. In 1845, he was received in the Catholic Church and was subsequently ordained in Rome.

As to the reasons some were attracted to the Oxford Movement, founded in 1833, Catholic historian Paul Johnson writes in *A History of Christianity*: "The Movement began by assuming that they were safe within the Church of England, at any rate as they conceived it, 'a true branch or portion of the one Holy, Catholic and Apostolic Church of Christ.'" These Anglicans wanted a mechanism to address the theology that had crept into the organization without being forced to leave the Church of England.

A great volume of literature supporting these ideals included *Tracts for the Times,* produced by Newman in 1833. Some changes were made in doctrine, and new vestments and rituals were introduced into the services of the church. In many cases, the "new" was a revival of the patristic or the medieval. The Oxford Movement has become Anglo-Catholicism, and it still is a force in Anglicanism.

ORESTES BROWNSON

Orestes Brownson was born in 1813 in Vermont and, in his early years, he was attracted to Puritanism and later to the revivals in upstate New York. When he decided his spiritual life needed some tightening up, he investigated Presbyterianism. Upon learning about the stern doctrines of Calvinism, he went to the other end of the theological spectrum and embraced Universalism in 1826. He was licensed as a preacher in his new-found religion and edited one of their publications: *The Gospel Advocate.* Then followed a time of radical humanism, and Brownson began to work for social reform.

In the 1830s, he combined his spiritual journey with his quest for social reform. He edited *The Philanthropist*, became a Unitarian preacher, and often wrote in Unitarian publications. He also was attracted to Transcendentalism.

Coming to the conclusion that New England Unitarianism was not meeting his spiritual needs, Brownson started his own "Church of the Future" in Boston. To link up American democracy and religion, he published his Marxist *Essay on the Laboring Classes* and developed P. Leroux's notions on communion of life. You might think that Orestes had just about run out of new and exciting religious options—hold on—the last one is coming.

Finally, after looking at a number of ecclesiastical groups, the Roman Catholic Church caught his eye. He was baptized a Catholic by Bishop Fitzpatrick of Boston in 1844. In *The Dictionary of Christianity in America,* Daniel G. Reid speaks to Brownson's position as a Catholic. "Brownson defended Catholic doctrine against Protestant thinking, such as the Mercersburg theology and even certain Catholic writers such as John Henry Newman (1801-1890) of England, whose views on the development of dogma Brownson found dangerous and unorthodox." He was not content to address the evils of Protestantism, but criticized doctrines that were held by Catholic theologians at the time. Orestes Brownson finally found an ecclesiastical tradition which met his spiritual needs. Brownson spent the remainder of his life arguing for the compatibility between Roman Catholicism and American democracy.

JAMES GIBBONS

James Gibbons was born in 1834 in Baltimore, Maryland, and moved with his family to Ireland at the age of three. He returned to the United States at age nineteen and worked as a grocery clerk in New Orleans.

Gibbons entered St. Mary's Seminary and was ordained in

1861. Thereupon he ministered in pastoral duties in the Catholic archdiocese of Baltimore for four years. He caught the attention of archbishop Martin Spalding and became his secretary. The following year, Gibbons was appointed assistant chancellor and assisted Spalding in preparing for the second plenary council of Baltimore in 1866. Two years later, Gibbons was made a bishop and assigned the task of pastoral care over the newly created vicariate of North Carolina. He was the youngest bishop to attend and participate in the First Vatican Council. Gibbons was rapidly ascending the ecclesiastical ladder.

Gibbons became bishop of Richmond in 1873, and three years hence, produced his best known work, *Faith of Our Fathers*, a presentation of Catholicism based on his decade of pastoral experiences. Bishop Gibbons walked a fine line between remaining a loyal Roman Catholic prelate while attempting to convince his church that some of the restrictions that had been in place for many years had outlived their usefulness. He became the second American cardinal in 1886.

In 1917, President Theodore Roosevelt said that Cardinal James Gibbons was "the most respected and venerated and useful citizen of our country." He is one of the best known Catholic bishops in United States history.

FREE METHODIST CHURCH

The Free Methodist Church was founded by Benjamin Titus Roberts. He was a member of the Methodist Episcopal Church and was expelled for causing controversy in the Genesee Conference in western New York. The expelled group founded the Free Methodist Church, which was considered a sister denomination of the Wesleyans.

The denomination was founded in 1860 because of objections arising over the "new school" movement, which had infiltrated the doctrinal structure of mainline Methodist theology. The Free Methodist leaders held to the need of returning to primitive Wesleyan doctrines, including an emphasis on the deity of Christ, the importance of conversion, and complete sanctification.

Apart from the stress on total holiness—some have called it "sinless perfection"—the Free Methodist Church adheres to classic Christian orthodoxy in its theology. In 1995, the denomination reported 1,068 churches with 74,707 members. Headquarters are located in Indianapolis, Indiana.

FRANCIS THOMPSON

Francis Thompson was born in 1859 at Preston, Lancashire into a middle class family. His father was a provincial doctor, and his mother died in his boyhood. His parents being Catholics, Thompson was educated at Ushaw. He originally intended to become a priest, but later he unsuccessfully studied medicine at Manchester. In 1885, he went to London, living on the streets in destitution. Three years later, his poetic talents were discovered by Wilfred Meynell, editor of Catholic magazine *Merry England*. Meynell would remain Thompson's friend and benefactor for the rest of his life.

Thompson composed a number of poems, most of which reflected the asceticism of mysticism, the liturgy, and a sacramental blending of nature with unity. Thompson's time living on the streets, hungry and sick, led him to turn to drugs, and he became addicted to opium. When his longtime friend, Meynell, undertook the task of helping Thompson, he was successful. During his recovery, Thompson penned his best known poem, *The Hound of Heaven*, which is autobiographical in its description of the pursuit of the soul by God. Because of the support of his friend Meynell and the proceeds of his literary efforts, Francis Thompson was never again without food, clothing, shelter, or firewood.

LORD ACTON

John Emerich Acton was born in Naples, Italy in 1834. His father, Sir Richard Acton, descended from an established English line. His mother, Countess Marie Louise de Dalberg, came from a Rhenish family, which was considered to be second in status only to the imperial family of Germany.

Three years after his father's death in 1837, his mother remarried and moved the family to Britain. With his varied upbringing, Acton was at home in England or on the Continent, and grew up speaking English, German, French, and Italian.

He was prevented from taking classes at Cambridge University, because Catholics were not accepted, so he was sent to Germany and attended the Munich University. He studied under Ignaz von Dollinger, a well-known church historian.

Early in his teaching, Dollinger was an adherent of "ultramontanism"—a movement which held a strong emphasis on the authority and leadership of the pope. He would later become antipapal in both politics and theology. Dollinger would have a strong impact on Acton throughout his life, especially during the 1st Vatican Council.

Interaction with Professor Dollinger would broaden his understanding about the similarities and differences between Catholic and Reformed theology. Through his studies and his experiences, Acton became aware of the danger of any type of religious or political persecution.

In 1859, Acton became editor of the English Journal, *The Rambler*, which was the organ of the "Liberal Catholics." *The Rambler* would facilitate discussion of social, political and theological issues and ideas. At this time, he also entered politics and joined the House of Commons.

The later part of the nineteenth century saw the development of Lord Acton's thought on the relationship between religious virtue and personal freedom. He spoke of his work as a "theodicy"—a defense of God's goodness and care of the world. When he died in 1902, Lord Acton was judged to be one of the most learned people of his age. He is known for his famous observation, "Power tends to corrupt, and absolute power corrupts absolutely." All the preceding events would shape the position and goals of the Acton Institute, which would be formed in Grand Rapids, Michigan in 1990 by a Roman Catholic priest and will be treated later.

GEORGE MATHESON

George Matheson was born in 1842 in Glasgow, Scotland. Sadly, Matheson was almost blind by age twenty. The doctors told him that there was nothing they could do to address the blindness; nevertheless, he embarked on studying for the ministry.

Matheson became a minister and served the parishes of Innellan and St. Bernard's Edinburgh. His success as a pastor was treated by J.O. Douglas, Walter A. Elwell, and Peter Toon in *The Concise Dictionary of the Christian Tradition.* "Great crowds flocked to hear the blind preacher with a rare gift of language. Alexander Whyte hailed Matheson's *Studies of the Portrait of Christ* as a work of genius. His verse is haunting and winsome."

Christians who love hymns may recognize Matheson by the hymn: "O Love That Will Not Let Me Go." Even though he was blind, he felt the Lord's blessing, bringing him to a church where he preached to over 1,500 people each week.

There is a story of how years earlier, he had been engaged until his fiancee learned that he was going blind, and she told him that she could not go through life with a blind man. Heartbroken, he retired to his small apartment and penned the following words:

> *O Love that will not let me go, I rest my weary soul in thee; I give thee back the life I owe,*

That in thine ocean depths its flow, May richer, fuller be.
O light that followest all my way, I yield my flickering torch to thee;
My heart restores its borrowed ray, That in thy sunshine's blaze its day May brighter, fairer be.
O Joy that seekest me through pain, I cannot close my heart to thee;
I trace the rainbow through the rain, And feel the promise is not vain,
That morn shall fearless be.
O Cross that liftest up my head, I dare not ask to fly from thee;
I lay in dust life's glory dead, And from the ground there blossoms red,
Life that shall endless be.

ALEXANDER MACLAREN

Alexander Maclaren trained at Glasgow University and Stepney College. He ministered for twelve years in Southampton and then moved to Manchester, where he preached for forty-five years at Union Chapel. He drew huge crowds who came to hear "the prince of expository preachers." Maclaren came to be known worldwide for his sermons and writings.

When addressing missionary tactics, he often spoke on the presence of "general revelation." This is the term used to state that God can reveal something about the divine nature through the created order. A missionary arrives on the field, expecting to find perhaps an indifferent audience. Instead, he is welcomed, the people exclaiming, "We knew someone would come with the words of God." The Canadian pastor, Don Richardson, has written a book entitled *Eternity in Their Hearts*, which discusses this phenomenon.

In a time when Christians rarely fellowshipped across denominational lines, Maclaren maintained good relations with Roman Catholic and Anglican bishops. Twice President of the Baptist Union in 1875 and 1901, he also directed the first Congress of the Baptist World Alliance four years later.

EDWARD M. BOUNDS

Edward M. Bounds studied law and was apprenticed as an attorney, but rather than undertaking a legal career, entered the ministry in his early twenties. In 1859, he was ordained as pastor of the Monticello Methodist Church in Missouri.

Bounds studied extensively in the Scriptures and was greatly inspired by the writings of John Wesley. During the Civil War, Bounds served as a chaplain in the Confederate States Army. He was captured by Union troops in a scrimmage in Franklin, Tennessee and held with other non-combatants in prison for a year and a half. Released in a prisoner trade, he returned to the chaplaincy with the Confederacy.

After the war, Bounds worked as Associate Editor of *The Christian Advocate*, the official weekly paper for the Methodist Episcopal Church. Bounds also returned to Franklin and started weekly prayer sessions.

During his ministry, he wrote seven books on prayer and its essentials, which include necessity, power, purpose, and reality. It is said that he spent a minimum of three to four hours a day in fervent prayer. While he never attracted attention or gained the reputation one might expect, E. M. Bounds is now considered the most prolific and fervent author on the subject of prayer.

DAVID LIVINGSTONE

David Livingstone was born in 1813 in Blantyre, Scotland, in the midst of the British Industrial Revolution. From the age of ten, he worked a fourteen-hour day. He attended night school and became a voluminous reader. His drive for hard work and quest for knowledge was driven by a deep, personal Christian faith.

Upon reading an appeal for medical missionaries, Livingstone decided to train as a doctor on the mission field. After studies at Glasgow in medicine and theology, he was accepted by the London Missionary Society for further training. Contact with Robert Moffat, the well-known missionary in South Africa and Livingstone's future father-in-law, led him to accept a missional position in South Africa.

Livingstone began his missionary career at Kuruman in 1841. From Kuruman, he soon moved farther into the interior to work with people unreached by missionaries. Next, Livingstone pushed on to the north with the hope of finding a route for trade, which he believed was the only way of driving the slave trade from the area. He followed the course of the Zambezi River to its mouth on the Indian Ocean, arriving in 1856—a journey of almost 2,500 miles.

Upon returning to Britain in that year, he found that he was a national hero. Livingstone's African journeys had been accomplished in the name of a cause dear to the hearts of British evangelicals—the elimination of the slave trade. He returned to Africa two more times, but he encountered difficulties with his companions. The crowning blow was the death of his wife Mary in 1863.

While David Livingstone was an explorer and a missionary, he shared one common goal with another Englishman who lived some years earlier. I speak, of course, about William Wilberforce. The goal they shared was the end of the slave trade. While embarked on the missionary journey and following the discovery of the Victoria Falls, Livingstone made such a commotion over the slave trade that his expedition was cancelled.

For years during Livingstone's travels, his whereabouts were unknown to the world. Expeditions were sent to find him. In

1871, Henry Stanley, foreign correspondent for the New York Herald, found Livingstone, desperately ill. He never fully recovered and died in the village of Ilala, Africa, in 1873. His native assistants carried his body 1,500 miles to the coast, and one of them was in the huge crowd at his funeral in Westminster Abbey.

The story is told that when Livingstone's body arrived in England, it was missing its heart. His native assistants said, "England may have his body, but his heart belongs to Africa."

SEVENTH-DAY ADVENTIST CHURCH

The Seventh-Day Adventist Church began with the movement founded by William Miller. Miller was born in 1782 in Pittsfield, Massachusetts and grew up in Low Hampton, New York. Self-educated, he married in 1803 and moved to Vermont, where he became a sheriff and the justice of the peace.

In 1816, Miller experienced conversion from Deism and undertook a study of the Bible. He was particularly interested in the Old Testament, and he developed an eschatological system that predicted the Second Coming of Christ in 1843.

When that prediction failed, Miller began to receive criticism from established churches. He came up with new dates for the Lord's return. Eventually, continued failure caused the movement to fracture.

The arrival of Ellen Gould White revitalized the movement. She and her husband James together constructed the doctrinal system that would identify Adventism.

The denomination is distinguished by its keeping of Saturday, the Jewish Sabbath, as the day of worship. The church holds other doctrines such as baptism of believers by immersion, the imminence of Christ's return, soul sleep—the idea that between death and resurrection the person is in a state of unconsciousness,—and foot washing, which was practiced in biblical times when a host wanted to honor his guests.

Randall Balmer, in the *Encyclopedia of Evangelicalism,* comments further on the Adventist's list of doctrinal distinctives. "There is a special emphasis on Old Testament law, especially the Ten Commandments. Believing that the bodies of believers are temples of the Holy Spirit, Seventh-day Adventists members abstain from eating foods declared in Scripture to be unclean, and they foreswear the use of alcohol and tobacco." Some believe this group holds to some quirky ideas. However, Seventh-Day Adventists are concerned with maintaining a healthy lifestyle and sponsor many top rated hospitals and medical facilities.

While most Adventist doctrines are orthodox, including the Trinity, creation *ex nihilo,* and salvation through the work of Christ on the cross, many evangelicals have considered them to be a cult.

In the early 1960s, two prominent evangelical scholars, Dr. Donald Grey Barnhouse, publisher of *Eternity Magazine,* and Dr. Walter Martin, founder and director of the Christian Research Institute, undertook a thorough reevaluation of the theological system of the Seventh-Day Adventist Church.

After meeting for several weeks with Adventist leaders, they concluded that whereas the denomination holds doctrines which are in error, they are not heretical. Those interested in more information on the Seventh Day Adventist Church will find Walter Martin's *The Kingdom of the Cults,* Appendix: "The Puzzle of Seventh-Day Adventism" informative.

SOREN KIERKEGAARD

Soren Kierkegaard was born in 1813 into an orthodox Lutheran family in Copenhagen, Denmark and lived his entire life there. He was educated at the University in Copenhagen and at age twenty-five inherited enough money to indulge himself in intellectual issues.

Kierkegaard was sickly as a child, and in spite of academic prowess, he suffered from bouts of anxiety and anguish—hence the description of him as the "melancholy Dane." As he grew to manhood, his relationship with his father fluctuated between affection and resentment.

However, in 1838, a reconciliation occurred between father and son restoring Soren's faith. He made the connection between the healing that occurred between him and his earthly father and that which transpired between him and his heavenly Father.

Kierkegaard produced a large number of essays and books including philosophical and Christian subjects. He felt divinely called to criticize the national church, which he was convinced was more a servant of the state than of Christ.

This Danish thinker is thought by many to be the founder of existentialist philosophy. Existentialism emphasizes "existence" over "essence"—does it exist? rather than, what is it?

Because of his philosophical attachment to existentialism, some evangelical scholars question his commitment to Christian orthodoxy. In spite of Kierkegaard's existentialism, he rejected confidence in human reason and detachment from struggle, which was held in his day. The Gospel was reduced to ideas, and persons were blind to the separation between the Creator and the creature. Kierkegaard held that Christianity demands Christians take action, not play the role of a spectator.

Before God we are sinners, and our best as well as our worst is under God's judgment and needs God's pardon. In spite of the philosophical differences between some evangelicals and Kierkegaard, he held to the doctrines that comprised what has been known as classical Christianity. He has been said by some to be the "greatest Christian thinker of the nineteenth century."

JOHN HENRY NEWMAN

Born in 1801, John Henry Newman was the eldest child of John and Jemima Newman. His father was a banker, and the home was a happy one. At the age of seven, he was enrolled in a boarding school where he did well in his studies.

In 1816, the family experienced a financial setback, and around this time, Newman experienced conversion. The event was not highly emotional, but accompanied by the reading of Christian texts.

He entered Trinity College, was a Fellow of Oriel, and was ordained a deacon in the Anglican Church in 1824. The following year, Newman was appointed vice-principal of Alban Hall and then, in 1828, vicar of St. Mary's, Oxford.

He became a Tractarian, which was the first stage of the Oxford Movement. Newman wrote *Tracts for the Times*, which defended the view that the Church of England occupied a position against modern Romanism on the one hand and liberal Protestantism on the other.

However, Newman began to question the claims of the Anglican Church. In 1841, he abandoned his position in Oxford. He lived in retirement with a few friends and, in 1845, he entered the Roman Catholic Church. Newman then issued his *Essay on the Development of Christian Doctrine*, which was a defense of his change of allegiance.

When he returned to England after being ordained in Rome, Newman's life became entangled in a number of controversial issues, about some of his writings and the rupture of relations between friends. When the First Vatican Council was held, Newman was in Rome as a member of the liberal minority at the Council—joined by J. J. I. von Dollinger from Bavaria and others. In 1879, Leo XIII made John Henry Newman Cardinal-Deacon of St.

George in Velabro.

Newman's approach to basic Christian doctrine is helpful for both Catholics and Protestants. He held, contrary to liberal views, that religious beliefs were real. He also stressed an appeal to historic, objective evidence as necessary to apprehend biblical truth in Christianity.

KARL MARX

Karl Marx was born in 1818 in Trier, Germany, to a Jewish family. Marx's father, a lawyer, later converted to Lutheranism as Jews were not allowed to practice law in Germany at the time. A gifted student, Marx earned a doctorate from the University of Jena.

Karl Marx is best known as the one who provided the philosophical framework which would be used to form the Communist Party. Radoslav A. Tsanoff, in *The Great Philosophers*, speaks to this fact. "Marx combined jurisprudence and history with idealistic philosophy during his university studies. His own materialistic bent was shown when he wrote his doctoral dissertation on Epicurus."

The Communist revolution that assumed control in Russia in 1917 was led by Vladimir Ilyich Lenin. This system of government came to be known as the Marxism-Leninism. Since this volume is about church history, we must examine the effect that Marxism has had on Christianity. Communism has targeted Christianity in every country it has taken over, and we are only now seeing some recovery.

Lenin believed that Communism would most likely occur in the developing world and not in the industrial societies of Western Europe. He also held that Communism could succeed only if the government was controlled by a single Communist Party. Lenin was followed in Russia by Joseph Stalin, whose system was known as Stalinism.

Marxist-Leninist states include the former Communist states of Eastern Europe, such as Poland, Hungary, and Germany. Also, Marxism developed in China, which came to be known as Maoism, after the first Chinese communist leader, Mao Zedong. Communist persecution toward persons of faith will be discussed when we address two Christians who lived in Russia during this era—Fr. Alexander Men and Aleksandr Solzhenitsyn.

FR. ALEXANDER MEN

This presentation not only tells about a brilliant and pious individual, the priest Fr. Alexander Men, but also a side of Russian life—the inter-relationship of the church and state. Alexander was born into the family of a textile engineer. His father was of Jewish extraction. Though he lost his faith when he was young, he did not become a militant atheist.

On the other hand, Alexander's mother Elena was deeply religious. She also was born of Jewish parents. Elena was taught by her mother to love God as Creator of the universe. From a young child, Elena was attracted to Christianity. At age nine, Elena announced that she wanted to be baptized. Sometime later she began to attend a Baptist church.

After the birth of Alexander in 1935, his mother took little Alik to a friend who was a priest, and he baptized the child. This priest, Fr. Seraphim, died in 1942. However, sometime before, feeling that death was near, he insisted on hearing Alik's first confession. About the event Alik said, "With grandfather (his name for the priest), I felt I was in heaven with God."

Later on, Fr. Alexander was to express his gratitude to his mother for having had the faith to expose him to the Gospel in such difficult times. As a teenager, Alexander read books that were difficult for young students, such as Kant, while his friends were learning that Marxist Leninism was the wave of the future.

Alexander had a personal encounter with Christ, and at that time decided he would become a priest. He began to read the works of Vladimir Soloviev, who was said to be the real founder of twentieth century Russian religious thinking. In 1956, the Communist Party held its 20th congress, during which Khrushchev wrote his famous report on Stalin's crimes. Millions of men and women were set free, including the as yet unknown Aleksandr Solzhenitsyn.

Alexander was introduced to a vicar bishop of the Moscow diocese, who recognized his gifts and ordained him a deacon in the Church before he even started seminary. In 1960, he was ordained priest, and his future in the Russian Orthodox Church had begun.

Throughout his ministry he remained loyal to the Russian Orthodox Church, while maintaining openness to interaction with Christians of different denominations, including Catholics, Baptists, and missionaries who served in Russia.

Alexander's fruitful ministry ended in 1990. While on his way to celebrate the liturgy in the country church he had served for the past twenty-five years, he was brutally struck down by a blow to his head. He was dead by the time the medics arrived.

The culprit has never been found. After the passage of time, no answer has been forthcoming.

ALEKSANDR SOLZHENITSYN

Aleksandr Solzhenitsyn was born in 1918 in Kislovodsk, Russia. Prior to Aleksandr's birth, his mother, Taisiya Solzhenitsyna, was Ukrainian. Taisiya had travelled to Moscow, where she met and wed Isaakiy Solzhenitsyn—an officer in the Imperial Russian Army.

Taisiya became pregnant with Aleksandr, and shortly after, Isaakiy was killed in a hunting accident. Aleksandr's educated mother, who remained unmarried, prompted his literary and scientific leanings and raised him in the Russian Orthodox Church. She died in 1944.

Solzhenitsyn attended Rostov State University while simultaneously taking correspondence courses from the Moscow Institute of Philosophy, Literature and History. At this time, the University was heavily Marxist in orientation. Solzhenitsyn later stated that he did not question the superiority of the state's ideology until he spent time in the labor camp known as the gulag.

During World War II, Solzhenitsyn was an officer in the Red Army and saw action at the front. During this period, his doubts about the moral underpinnings of the Soviet regime increased. This time in his life would provide material for the literary output which would be published later in his life. In 1945, while serving in East Prussia, Solzhenitsyn was arrested for writing negative comments on the way Joseph Stalin was conducting the war. He was accused of anti-Soviet propaganda and taken to Lubyanka prison in Moscow. He was questioned, beaten, and sentenced to an eight-year term in the gulag. This would be the beginning of time spent in a number of different work camps and a "special camp" for political prisoners.

After Khrushchev's speech in 1956, Solzhenitsyn was freed and pardoned from exile. He continued to write, which gathered the attention of the KGB. He had some success in publishing his writings overseas, but little in Russia.

While at the University, Solzhenitsyn had married Natalie Alekseyevna Reshetovskaya. They divorced in 1972. The following year, he was married for the second time to Natalia Dmitrievna Svetova, a mathematician. They had three sons: Yermolai, Ignat, and Stepan.

In 1974, Solzhenitsyn was deported to Frankfurt, Germany. Although not fluent in spoken English, he had been reading English language literature since his teens. He spent two decades in the United States, and his warnings about Communism and the weakening nature of the moral fiber of the West were well-received in Western conservative circles.

Despite his critique of the weakness in the West, he always spoke well of the political liberty that he saw in western democratic societies. He implored the West not to lose these values. With his Soviet citizenship restored, Solzhenitsyn returned with his wife to Russia in 1990. All of his sons became United States citizens.

Solzhenitsyn died of heart failure near Moscow in 2008 at the age of 89. Russian and world leaders paid homage following his death. Anyone not aware of the terrible nature of Soviet Marxism and the millions of lives lost in the twentieth century need only familiarize themselves with Solzhenitsyn's literary output.

CHARLES HADDON SPURGEON

Descended from several generations of ministers, Charles Haddon Spurgeon was born in Kelvedon, England in 1834. He joined the Baptist Church in 1850 and preached his first sermon that year. At the age of twenty, he was called to London, drawing such large crowds that the Metropolitan Tabernacle was built for him.

Spurgeon disliked Calvinism as much as Arminianism, but he was drawn to Puritanism. He became known as "the prince of preachers." On the Day of National Humiliation, he addressed an audience of 23,000, which was said to be the largest religious gathering to that time in the history of Europe.

Spurgeon's habit of speaking his mind landed him in many controversies; he was wary of evolution and the rejection of the inerrancy of the Bible; issues that were making their way into the theology of the day. He also took issue with the Evangelical Party of the Church of England for remaining in a church that taught baptismal regeneration. He had been active in the Baptist Union, but he became concerned with the encroachment of liberalism in the group and when the members refused to address the situation, Spurgeon withdrew from the Union in 1887. This dispute became known as the "Downgrade Controversy."

Spurgeon is known as a Calvinist, but he was not opposed to the doctrine of "freedom of the will." He believed that both God's sovereignty and human responsibility work together. As to his pulpit skills, James L. Garlow makes these observations in *How God Saved Civilization*. "Few preachers in all of church history command the respect of this English preacher/orator who weekly filled a 6,000 seat London auditorium known as the Metropolitan Tabernacle. His services were much more than an experience. The sermons had rich content. So significant were his sermons that they are still popular reading today." He also was interested in providing for people's physical and social needs.

Spurgeon was not only a competent preacher and theologian, but he had a good sense of humor. The tale is told of an elderly woman who greeted him after a sermon. She said, "I enjoyed your presentation, however I must take issue with your disgusting habit of smoking cigars." Spurgeon replied, "Well, sister, the Bible tells us to do all things in moderation." She answered, "What would you consider an immoderate use of smoking cigars?" He answered, "Smoking two at a time." A short time later, Spurgeon saw an advertisement for cigars claiming that they were the ones he used. He immediately stopped smoking cigars.

DWIGHT LYMAN MOODY

Dwight Moody was born in 1837 in Northfield, Massachusetts. His family had ties to the Unitarian Church; however, Moody had little schooling or religious training.

At age seventeen, he moved to Boston and worked in his uncle's shoe store. After attending a Congregational Sunday school class, Moody was converted and joined the church. He moved to Chicago in 1856 and became a successful shoe salesman. He joined Plymouth Congregational Church and rented several pews for his friends and business partners. "Crazy Moody," a name he acquired because of his zeal, began a Sunday school in a poor neighborhood and two years later, left his business to devote his passion to building his religious pursuits.

During the Civil War, Moody worked with the United States Christian Commission throughout the South, doing evangelism and relief activities. Returning to Chicago, he formed the Illinois Street Independent Church now Moody Church, and became president of the Chicago YMCA.

The Chicago fire of 1871 destroyed the YMCA facility, Moody's Church and home. This led him to build a new building, the Northside Tabernacle, used to feed and clothe thousands of people left homeless and destitute. Moody launched out as an evangelist, traveling to Britain, where he enjoyed great success. Moody returned to North America and conducted crusades in Brooklyn, Philadelphia, New York City, Boston, and Chicago.

Moody brought a new level of organization to revivalism. He was always modest and conducted himself as the businessman he was. His sermons were straightforward, emphasizing the love of God over God's wrath. Moody's message was clear: ruined by sin, redeemed by Christ, and regenerated by the Holy Spirit.

Moody was one of the first American revivalists to stress premillennialist views in eschatology. He was known to have said, "I look upon this world as a wrecked vessel. God has given me a lifeboat and said to me, 'Moody, save all you can.'" Although never ordained, Moody preached to more people than anyone else in his time. During Moody's career, he traveled a million miles and preached to more than a hundred million people.

Despite having little formal education himself, he was not a theological neophyte. The story is told about a young man who had recently been converted, approaching Moody on the street in Chicago one day and asking, "Sir, have you been saved?" Moody replied, "Son, I have been saved"—Justification; "I am being saved"—Sanctification; and "I will be saved"—Glorification.

CHARLES DARWIN

Charles Darwin was born in 1809 in Shrewsbury, England. His family was wealthy and respected; his mother was the child of the prominent Wedgwood family, and his father was a physician. From an early age, Darwin held a fascination with living creatures, particularly beetles. It was taken for granted that Charles would follow his father and grandfather in medicine. He began medical courses at Edinburgh, but soon dropped the subject. He then moved to Cambridge to pursue a degree in theology, but eventually decided his interests lay in the natural sciences.

As to Darwin's religion, he began as a Christian theist and was baptized in the Anglican Church. In spite of this, he was sent to a school directed by a Unitarian minister. Darwin is recognized as the person who set the stage for the emergence of evolution. In his book, *The Baker Encyclopedia of Apologetics,* Norman Geisler speaks to Darwin's earlier views. "Darwin recognized 'the extreme difficulty or rather impossibility of conceiving this immense and wonderful universe, including man with his capacity of looking far backward and far into futurity, as the result of blind chance or necessity.'" Unfortunately, this view of Darwin would change in due course. He even would reject the notion that he was a theist.

After Darwin decided that his future lay in the natural sciences, an opportunity arose that would seal his career choice; he joined the crew of the Beagle, a vessel that was to embark on a six-year exploratory voyage to South America and the Pacific Islands. As the journey's recorder, he proved to be equal to the task and took copious notes of his observations, which were published in 1839, titled *The Voyage of the Beagle*.

The issue that puzzled Darwin after the Beagle's expedition was how specific living things manage to survive in different environments. A team of modern scholars had a look at Darwin and the issue of natural selection. Steve Wilkens and Allan Padgett, in *Christianity and Western Thought: Faith and Reason in the 19th Century, Vol. 2*, address this concept. "It begins with the observation that small variations occur in the off-spring of the same parents. In domestic husbandry these variations have been exploited for generations in order to increase production and quality." As Christians, we believe that the changes have been put in place by God, who is the Creator.

As for the subject of Darwin's descent from Theism, a number of factors were in play. While denying ever being an atheist, he claimed to be an agnostic by 1879. The impact of destructive higher criticism led him to distrust the worthiness of the Bible. As an agnostic, Darwin considered the belief in hell to be illegitimate. Also, the death of his beloved daughter Anne caused Darwin much anger toward God and grief at the loss of his child. It should be noted that despite his rejection of Christianity, he was buried in Westminster Abbey.

JAMES HUDSON TAYLOR

J. Hudson Taylor was born in 1832 in Yorkshire, England, into a devout Methodist family. At age seventeen, he was converted to Christ and decided that God was calling him to be a missionary to China. He left for China at age twenty-one, sponsored by the Chinese Evangelization Society.

Arriving in Shanghai, Taylor noticed missionaries from the West wore the same clothing they did at home, which clashed with the way the Chinese dressed. Deciding that style of clothing was not a theological matter, and not wanting to be an unnecessary hindrance to his message of the Gospel, Taylor decided to wear Chinese clothes and his hair in a pigtail. Previously, Jesuit missionaries who served in China during the seventeenth century attempted to adapt Catholicism to the existing culture in the same manner Taylor did. They were condemned by popes for their efforts.

Taylor left the Chinese Inland Mission, married, and formed a church with twenty-one members. He established another mission, which eventually became the Overseas Mission Fellowship—now OMF International.

J. Hudson Taylor was convinced that the standard approach to mission involvement must be changed. In *Encyclopedia of Evangelicalism,* Randall Balmer comments: "Taylor insisted that his new organization be open to any worker, no matter how qualified. The mission field was so great, that 'the eye cannot say to hand, I have no need of thee;' nor yet again the head to the feet, 'I have no need of you.' Therefore persons of moderate ability and limited attainments are not precluded from engaging in the work." Modern missionary models seem to agree with J. Hudson Taylor.

THE FIRST VATICAN COUNCIL

The First Vatican Council was the most eventful Council since the Council of Trent. In the nineteenth century, a movement comprised of Catholics developed in England and Germany. They were intellectual liberals, many of whom took their direction from the Enlightenment. They wanted the Catholic faith to be measured in the light of modern philosophy and new approaches to the study of Holy Scripture.

Pope Pius IX saw the danger in this movement, and issued a Syllabus of Errors in 1864, in which he reminded Catholics to seek spiritual direction from the Church and not society. The First

Vatican Council was held in Rome and was designated as the twentieth Ecumenical Council. These are assemblies of bishops and other ecclesiastical representatives of the whole world whose decisions on doctrine, culture, and discipline are considered binding on all Christians.

The Council addressed such issues as faith and dogma, ecclesiastical matters and canon law, religious orders, foreign missions, and church/state relationships. Two parties were present at the council: the majority group, which was in favor of increasing Papal authority, and the liberal minority, which was presented by J. H. Newman in England and J. J. I. von Dollinger in Bavaria.

After Pius IX opened the Council, nearly seven hundred bishops discussed many issues. The two that stood out and were the most contentious were the dogmas that state the Pope holds supremacy over the whole world—universal jurisdiction and papal infallibility—when the pope defines a doctrine dealing with faith and morals and speaks *ex cathedra,* meaning "from the chair."

Both dogmas were accepted by a majority vote, including those in the liberal minority. The day following the acceptance of the two dogmas concerning the Pope, war erupted between France and Prussia. Consequently, the French troops pulled out of Rome and the Italian soldiers arrived in the city. It also brought the end to the Council. While both J. H. Newman of England and von Dollinger of Bavaria were in agreement against the decision, Newman acquiesced and von Dollinger refused to submit to the conciliar decrees and was excommunicated in 1871.

ABRAHAM KUYPER

Born in 1837 and educated at Leyden (Leiden), Netherlands, Kuyper was pastor of the Dutch Reformed Church at Beesd. After some years as pastor, he became politically active and formed the Anti-Revolutionary Party in 1878.

He became a professor at the Calvinistic University, which he established at Amsterdam and in 1886 was installed as the leader of the strictly Calvinistic Reformed Community. Kuyper attracted support by combining religious orthodoxy and social reform. He was very interested in governmental issues. One idea he advanced was "Sphere Sovereignty," a concept similar to the Roman Catholic doctrine of "Subsidiarity." This idea concludes matters should be handled by the smallest, lowest, or least centralized competent authority before moving to higher units, for example, families before local governments and local governments before national governments.

In 1901, Kuyper became prime minister in a coalition government. Even when he was defeated four years later, he remained politically active, seeing many of his reforms accepted. His ideas about the ways that church and state should interact are in play now in modern governance.

JULIUS WELLHAUSEN

Julius Wellhausen was born in 1844 in Hameln, Northern Germany, and studied at Gottingen. He taught there, and also at Greifswald, Halle, Marburg. He consequently returned to Gottingen as a historian, conversant in a number of languages, including Hebrew, Aramaic, Syriac, and Arabic.

Wellhausen is responsible for creating the approach known as historical-criticism, which has been used to attack the authority of Scripture. This led to the development of the documentary hypothesis. Three authors, Stanley J. Grenz, David Guretzki, and Cherith Fee Nordling, in *The Pocket Dictionary of Theological Terms*, discuss this notion. "Also known as the JEDP theory, the documentary hypothesis arose out of the work of nineteenth century OT scholars K. Graf and J. Wellhausen. They suggested that the Pentateuch (the first five books of the O.T.) was actually a compilation of the work of at least four separate sources, designated at the J (Jehovah) source, the E (Elohim) source, the D (Deuteronomist) source and the P (Priestly) source." Its purpose was to establish the development of the Hebrew religion from an early form to that of the Law.

Wellhausen later turned his efforts to a study of the New Testament using the same approach; however, his efforts in the New Testament were disappointing. As Norman Geisler states in his work, *Baker Encyclopedia of Christian Apologetics*: "Virtually the whole corpus of archaeological evidence has tended to prove Wellhausen's evolutionary theory wrong. Most significant is the earliest findings at Ebla, Syria. The Ebla tablets confirm monotheism extremely early as opposed to Wellhausen's supposition that it was a late evolutionary development from earlier polytheism and henotheism." We will be visiting the institution of Marburg again when we cover Rudolf Bultmann and Eta Linnemann.

20th Century Modern Christianity

The movement known as "Modernism" surfaced at this time. It was an attempt to override ancient doctrines and was especially directed at Christian ethics and theology.

This period began with a war that occurred in the early twentieth century in Mexico. Also examined are Christian leaders, preachers, associations, movements, and some martyrs who were involved in this period. Not all were sympathetic to Christian orthodoxy; however, their impact should be noted.

THE CRISTERO WAR

The Cristero War from 1926–1929, also known as La Cristiada, was a popular movement addressing the anti-Catholicism practiced by the ruling Mexican government. The Mexican Constitution of 1917 had been developed by the former president, Plutarco

Elias Calles. Driven by his atheism, Calles began to persecute the Roman Catholic Church.

Calles decided to enforce the anti-clerical statutes of the Constitution, which resulted in a ten year persecution of Catholics, leading to the death of thousands. Resistance at first was peaceful; however, violent rebellion broke out in 1927. The rebels called themselves Cristeros, using the name of Jesus Christ under the title of Cristo Rey or "Christ the King."

An early leader of the resistance was 27-year-old Rene Capistran Garza, leader of the Mexican Association of Catholic Youth. The formal rebellion began when Garza issued a declaration, entitled *A la Nacion*—To the Nation; "the hour of battle has sounded" and "the hour of victory belongs to God."

However, the most successful leader of the rebellion was General Enrique Gorostieta. At first reluctant to join the fray, he finally agreed to organize a motley group of farmers, students, wives, and even some priests to oppose the government forces. Gorostieta was a retired military mastermind and a brilliant tactician.

Unfortunately, in June 1929, Gorostieta was killed in an ambush by a federal patrol. However, the rebels had some 50,000 men under arms at this time, and the momentum was on their side. Gorostieta's children said in an interview that while their father was not the most devout Catholic, he believed ardently in religious freedom.

Perhaps only people familiar with Graham Greene's 1940 novel, *The Power and the Glory*, will recognize the story line thus far. Graham Greene's novel is about a "whiskey" priest, often tempted to drink the communion wine rather than reserve it for the Eucharistic celebration. He threw his lot in with the rebels during the rebellion. The movie, *For Greater Glory*, reached theaters in 2012. While it leaves out some details of a very complex historical event, it is a good film in what it covers. Cuban-born actor Andy Garcia has the roll of General Gorostieta and does a commendable job. Also, in the film is the Irish actor Peter O'Toole, who plays a Catholic priest who is put to death for his involvement with the rebels. The director-producer Dean Wright and Garcia both feel that the Cristero War episode, which transpired some 84 years ago in Mexico, can give us insight into separation of church and state issues facing us today.

Concerning the aftermath of the event in Mexico today, the constitution prohibits outdoor worship, which is only permitted in exceptional circumstances; religious organizations are not permitted to own print or electronic media outlets, and ministers are prohibited from being political candidates. Despite remnants of anti-clerical statutes, there is no real enforcement of them, and the Catholic Church enjoys overwhelming liberties from the government, as well as devotion from the people.

WILLIAM (BILLY) SUNDAY

Billy Sunday was born in 1862 on a farm near Ames, Iowa and received little formal school training. He began a major league baseball career and was with the Chicago White Stockings from 1883-1891.

While in Chicago, Sunday experienced conversion and joined the Jefferson Park Presbyterian Church, where he met and married Helen Thompson. She had an important part to play in his future preaching events. She raised four children and was involved in scheduling and the pre-campaign events.

In 1896, Sunday was invited to preach in Garner, Iowa, which proved to be the start of his evangelistic career. Until Billy Graham, no American evangelist reached as many people as did Billy Sunday. He used flamboyant gestures and theatrical antics to attract attention and make him a household name.

Billy preached against alcohol, gambling, and loose living. His delivery from the pulpit was designed to get the message over to the common folks. He often said, "I put the cookies and jam on the lower shelf."

Concerning his view of theology, Billy would say: "I don't know any more about theology than a jack rabbit knows about ping-pong, but I'm on my way to glory."

YOUNG MEN'S CHRISTIAN ASSOCIATION (YMCA)

In London in 1844, George Williams founded the YMCA. This organization emerged from his prayer and Bible study meetings. It has always been a lay and interdenominational movement designed to bring young men and boys to Christ.

This is done by providing activities that develop their physical, mental, and spiritual skills in order to serve God and reach others for Him. Full members are committed to reflect Christ and live for Him. Associates are not held to the same requirements but share the facilities and do not determine policy.

The YMCA soon spread to other countries and located its headquarters in Geneva by 1878. Its services were further extended to serve the needs of the Armed Forces in World War I, and of those young people who work or study while away from home.

While clearly Christian in its message and goal, it has become a service organization that is not limited to any religious boundaries. However, the YMCA holds to an emphasis on mind, body, and spirit (John 17:21) and remains the largest service organization of its kind in the United States.

THE SALVATION ARMY

In 1829, William Booth was born in Nottingham, England. He became a pawnbroker's apprentice in Nottingham and later went to London. Booth came to faith in Christ at age fifteen and became a Methodist minister in 1852. Three years later, he married Catherine Mumford who would partner with him in evangelistic and social programs.

Booth formed the Salvation Army in 1878 and structured the organization along military trappings with "General" Booth in command. William and Catherine raised eight children, all of whom eventually rose to high positions in the organization.

From the beginning, William Booth worked on two fronts—the need to address poverty and the effects of sin. The Salvation Army is active in some seventy countries. It provides shelter for the homeless, food for the hungry, support for unwed mothers, and general help for the needy, all free of charge. The Salvation Army's theological structure is Arminian evangelical Methodist. It is classically orthodox, with the exception of the fact that it has no sacramental system, a distinction which it shares with some Quakers, also known as the Society of Friends.

Still, the Salvation Army has always been an evangelical group. Its social activities have been so successful that many do not realize that it is a holiness church that has as its mission "to preach the Gospel and address human needs without discrimination." It holds all of the doctrines that classical orthodox Christianity believes, derived from the Scriptures and the early councils and creeds.

The Salvation Army has not changed its biblical tenets. In 2014, it claims a global membership of 1.5 million, 450,000 of which are in the United States.

SIGMUND FREUD

Sigmund Freud was born in 1856 in the small town of Freiberg, Moravia, 150 miles from the border of present-day Poland. During Freud's early years, Moravia was an especially devout Catholic area—a fact that would impact his future development. While both of his parents had Jewish backgrounds, his mother Amalia was indifferent to Judaism, and his father Jakob would tell his son biblical stories.

While in Freiberg, the Freud family lived in one room, on the second floor of a two-story house. The meager living space indicates that the family was far from well off. However, the Freuds had a nanny, Resi Wittek, who was a devout Roman Catholic. Her influence would have a significant impact on the remainder of Sigmund's life. She not only took Sigmund to church with her several times a week, but she may have had him baptized as well. For a pious Catholic woman, the death of an unbaptized child who was close to her would be a tragedy.

Sigmund's nanny Resi was dismissed in 1860 for reasons that are not clear. He was devastated by her loss, and the family then moved to Vienna. Scholars have located almost 500 different biblical references in Freud's writings and letters. Perhaps the impact that his nanny had on him, and the readings from the Bible with his father, had a larger effect on him than scholars have realized.

In 1874, Freud began his studies at the University of Vienna. It was there that he met Franz Brentano, a popular teacher, who influenced Freud and a large number of gifted students. At this time, Freud was as atheist, but believed that religion contained some positive features. In spite of these benefits, Freud rejected religion because he believed it was driven by wish fulfillment—"I hope there is a God."

In 1886, Freud married Martha Bernays. Martha was an attractive Jewish girl who fit into Freud's family well. Sigmund settled into his career as a practicing physician, specializing in the psychopathology. He was beginning to suspect that his talents and interest lay more in psychology, not in physiology and anatomy.

During this period, he familiarized himself with the technique of hypnosis and began to appreciate the place of sex in the etiology of neurotic problems. He also became interested in fantasies, dreams, and certain neurotic conditions, such as hysteria.

Freud began using cocaine at age 28, when the drug was almost unknown in scientific circles. He indulged frequently, sometimes in heavy doses. One wonders how such a brilliant person in so many areas could involve himself in such bizarre and destructive behavior.

Finally, we turn to the subject of Freud's atheism and its impact on Christianity. An important issue, Freud's treatment of the *Oedipus Complex,* is discussed by Paul C. Vitz in his book.

PAUL C. VITZ

Paul Vitz was born in 1935 in Toledo, Ohio. He resides in Greenwich Village in Manhattan, with his wife Evelyn Timmie Vitz, who is a French professor at New York University, and their six children. He holds a BA in Psychology from the University of Michigan and a PhD in motivational experimental psychology from Stanford University. Vitz is adjunct professor at the John Paul II Institute for Marriage and Family in Washington, DC. He is a member of the Fellowship of Catholic Scholars and is in active contact with evangelical Protestants, InterVarsity, and several seriously committed Jews.

Paul Vitz has published over one hundred articles, essays, and books. His work focuses on the relationship between psychology and Christianity. Vitz is presently working on the following topics: the Christian theory of personality and the psychology of hatred and forgiveness. We normally treat individuals as they appear in history, but as Paul Vitz is still alive and he is so knowledgeable about Freud's thinking that he fits in well here.

We want to address some of Freud's more controversial notions. First is his use of the *Oedipus Complex.* He used the phrase *Oedipus Complex* after the Greek hero who, through a chain of events, unknowingly had sexual contact with his mother. This phenomenon has become a major theme in psychoanalytic theory.

Freud then uses the *Oedipus Complex* to address the development of the world's religions. Few of his followers supported his view of the relationship of the *Oedipus Complex* theory. His thesis that totemism constituted the earliest form of religion is also disputed by most scholars of the history of religion. Thus his critique of religion suffers from an outdated view of religious origins. He is also subject to the criticism that he misunderstood the nature of religion by lumping all into an attempt to gain power over the universe and its force.

Further, Freud advances the notion that humans do not possess rationality. Concerning psychoanalysis, most of Freud's followers admit the difficulty of claiming impartiality for the psychoanalytic method which Freud acknowledged straight away. Not one of his published cases involved a patient who was a believing Christian or Jew.

Dr. Paul Vitz is well qualified to deal with Sigmund Freud. He is a Roman Catholic scholar who is well versed in theology along with his credentials in psychology. He discusses Freud in his book, *Sigmund Freud: Christian Unconscious*. "The reader may not agree with me that the weight of the psychological evidence makes atheism a more probable symptom of neurosis than theism. However, at the very least, it should be clear the atheism certainly may often be an expression of a psychological pathology ... In the future, as psychology moves (as I believe it will) toward a more honest approach to the question of the existence of God, I propose that at least two important spirits of Freud would wish such a new venture well: the spirit of his intellectual courage, and the spirit of a three-year-old boy with his nanny." This is a superb book, as are the ones mentioned earlier.

ALBERT SCHWEITZER

Albert Schweitzer was born in 1875 in Kaysersberg, Alsace, France. His family was well-known, as his father and maternal grandfather were ministers and played the organ. When Albert was six months old, his family moved to the village of Gunsbach in the Munster Valley.

Albert's father, Louis, was offered the pastor's position at the church in the village. In 1884, Albert began to play the organ in the church and developed his skill in music.

The Schweitzers, seeing Albert's potential, wanted to have him attend a better school than the one locally. This move would be expensive, but great-uncle Louis came to the rescue. He and his wife Sophie ran an elementary school in Mulhausen; Albert would attend and they would look after Albert for nothing.

Albert questioned the Bible from childhood; the miracles in the Old and New Testaments were difficult for him to understand. He then entered the University of Strasbourg, planning to study for two degrees, philosophy and theology. He also studied organ under the famous teacher Charles-Marie Widor in Paris. While in Strasbourg, the following are just a few of his many accomplishments:

- Earned a Doctorate of Philosophy
- Appointed pastor, St. Nicholas Church, in 1899
- Received degree in theology
- Began lecturing at Strasbourg University in 1902
- Became principal of a theological college
- Earned medical degree in 1912
- Pursued a new career as a medical missionary to Africa

While in seminary, he was exposed to the teachings of liberal scholars such as Julius Wellhausen and Rudolf Bultmann, which negatively influenced his later writings. In 1912, Schweitzer married Helene Bresslau, a nurse. Due to his many accomplishments, Albert abandoned the opportunity for a life of plenty and set sail for Africa the following year and opened his jungle hospital at Lambarene.

Because the Schweitzers were German subjects, when World War I began, they were deported to France as prisoners of war. When they returned to Lambarene, they found it in ruins. The Schweitzers returned to Europe from 1927–1939 to raise money for the hospital. Two years later, Helene joined him in Africa.

Schweitzer won the Nobel Peace Prize in 1952, and he was awarded Britain's Order of Merit four years later, only the second non-British person to win the award. Helene died in Switzerland in 1957 and was buried at Lambarene. Schweitzer himself died in 1965 at Lambarene and was buried in a simple wooden coffin next to his wife.

The possessor of three doctoral degrees, Albert Schweitzer accomplished many noble endeavors at his hospital in Africa, giving up a successful academic career in Europe to serve the poor. His legacy has become the model for many missionary outreaches to third-world countries.

THE FUNDAMENTALS

The Fundamentals were a series of booklets published in the United States from 1910–1915. The theological framework in the main-line Protestant churches had become, for the most part, liberal, and *The Fundamentals* were produced to address this situation.

Doctrines defended included the deity of Christ, his Virgin Birth, the substitutionary atonement, the bodily resurrection of Christ, and his literal second coming. Although many of the writers were premillennial dispensationalists, that doctrine was not stressed in this publication. Among the authors were some widely respected conservative Protestant scholars, including Benjamin B.

Warfield from Princeton and James Orr from Scotland.

The idea for the project came from two brothers from California, Lyman and Milton Steward. They financed their publication and created a fund to distribute it to Protestant workers worldwide. The Fundamentals mirror the theological formulations to emerge from the first five centuries of Christianity, including the councils, creeds, and the early church Fathers. Also, the basic content of The Fundamentals can be found in the official teachings of the Roman Catholic Church.

KARL BARTH

Karl Barth was born in 1886 in Berne, Switzerland, the son of Fritz Barth. His father was professor of New Testament Theology at Berne. After studying at Berne, Berlin, Tübingen, and Marburg, Barth became a minister at Geneva, and then was pastor at Safenwil, Switzerland for ten years. In 1921, Barth became professor at Gottingen and later taught at Munster and Bonn.

Upon Hitler's rise to power and the "church's struggle," Barth joined the Confessing Church. This was a group of German Evangelicals who opposed the Nazis-sponsored German Christian Church Movement between 1933–1945. The Confessing Church Movement led to issuing the Barmen Declaration in 1934. This statement laid the foundation for resistance to all attempts to make Evangelical churches an instrument of Nazi policy. By the middle of World War II, Barth was well aware of the dangerous situation in the country.

Karl Barth came on the scene when destructive higher-criticism was at its apex in the theological world. Barth's primary object was to lead theology away from what he believed to be the fundamentally false outlook of modern religious philosophy, and to bring it back to the principles of the Reformation. It was to be a return to the teaching of the Bible, which he believed was the goal of the Reformers.

Karl Barth is receiving a new look currently, especially in neo-evangelical circles. While orthodox evangelicals are pleased that he was on the scene to address the earlier theological situations, they are not happy with his replacement model, namely Neo-orthodoxy.

While Neo-orthodoxy can hold to some orthodox doctrines such as the Trinity, the Virgin birth, and bodily resurrection of Christ, these are accompanied by others that are problematic. One would be that Neo-orthodoxy holds to fideism, which says that theological truth must be accepted by faith rather than reason. While not descending to the level of heresy, it was not held by authorities like Augustine, Anselm, or Thomas Aquinas.

More troubling is the denial of inerrancy, which leads to the notion that the Bible is not free from all error. Inerrancy teaches that the Scriptures as originally recorded are completely free from all error. Some believe that inerrancy extends only to Scriptures that deal with salvific references, but not to matters of history and science. This position is called "limited" inerrancy. This view is defective in that it was not held by the church Fathers, the Reformers, or in the official theological documents of the Orthodox and Roman Catholic churches. The denial of inerrancy is at the root of most of the departures from classic Christianity.

CHARLES HODGE

Charles Hodge was born in 1797 in Philadelphia, Pennsylvania. Both his father and brother were physicians, and Hodge attended medical lectures early in his life. He graduated from the College of New Jersey, now Princeton, in 1815. Here Charles was converted to Reformed Christianity and later attended Princeton Theological Seminary, where he became an instructor.

Hodge was committed to defending Reformed orthodoxy, including Calvinistic theology, evangelical piety, and Scottish Common Sense Philosophy. His studies convinced him that he needed to familiarize himself with an understanding of contemporary theological scholarship; hence, he went on to attend French and German institutions.

When Hodge returned to the United States, he was transferred by Princeton to the chair of exegetical and didactic theology, an office he held until his death. This is the study of the prose portions of the Bible as contrasted with the narrative portions.

Charles Hodge was a Reformed theologian of the "old school" when liberalism had infiltrated the world-wide churches. His three-volume *Systematic Theology* established Hodge as America's leading theologian.

Concerning evolution and Darwinism, Hodge was suspicious of the way some scholars were holding that the Bible should "give way" to whatever the newest scientific notion that was in vogue. In spite of his concern over this issue, he clearly thought that science and theology should interact. B.B. Warfield, who revered his predecessor Hodge, held a more accommodating attitude toward evolution and will be discussed next.

Hodge addressed a number of issues. He commented on theological discussions, both European and domestic. He was a Reformed voice at a time when theological and cultural currents were leaning toward Arminian, revivalist, and Unitarian views. Hodge stated, with pride, that "a new idea never originated in this Seminary."

BENJAMIN BRECKINRIDGE WARFIELD

Born in 1851 to a wealthy Virginia family, B. B. Warfield resided near Lexington, Kentucky. Warfield's father came from good Puritan stock, and his mother was the daughter of Dr. Robert Breckinridge, who taught theology at Danbury Theological Seminary, Kentucky. Warfield graduated from the College of New Jersey and from Princeton Theological Seminary, where he studied under Charles Hodge in 1876. He then traveled to Europe to study for a year. Upon returning to the United States, he accepted the pastorate at Baltimore's First Presbyterian Church.

Warfield began his academic career teaching the New Testament at Western Seminary in Allegheny, Pennsylvania in 1878. When A.A. Hodge died in 1887, B.B. succeeded him as professor of didactic and polemic theology at Princeton. Following Charles and A.A. Hodge at Princeton Seminary, Warfield took up the task of defending Calvinistic theology as demonstrated in *The Westminster Confession of Faith*, which is understood to be the very essence of Reformed Christianity.

Mention should also be made of Warfield's marriage. Shortly before the journey to Europe for study, he married Annie Pearce Kinkead, who was also from a storied family. Miss Kinkead was a descendant of George Rodgers Clark, the famous general of the Revolutionary War. After traveling to Leipzig, tragedy struck. While walking together in the Harz Mountains, the Warfields encountered a violent storm. Annie Warfield was stricken with trauma to her nervous system so severe that she never totally recovered. Her husband spent the rest of their lives together giving her his care and attention until her death in 1915.

B. B. Warfield perhaps was best known for his defense of the doctrine of the inerrancy of the Bible in the original autographs. However, he did encounter criticism from Christians who were disappointed with him for attempting to reconcile Darwinism with Christianity and insisting on Postmillennialism rather than Premillennialism when dealing with eschatology.

THERESE OF LISIEUX

Born in 1876, Therese was born to watchmaker Louis Martin and

Zelie Guerin, in Alencon, Normandy, France, the youngest of nine children. At five, her mother died and the family moved to Lisieux, where she was raised by her older sisters and an aunt.

She received a call to become a Carmelite nun and entered the convent in Lisieux at age fifteen. Donald G. Bloesch, in his book *Therese of Lisieux: An Evangelical Saint?* makes an observation on her time in the convent. "Therese's life was ordinary, but her doctrine appears to be extraordinary, since she contended that sanctity lies not in great experiences but in the little tasks of everyday, which remain hidden from most observers. Therese upheld the 'little way,' daily surrender to God, as opposed to the 'great way,' justification by works." This quote shows that Therese was not the average young woman in the convent who was preparing to become a nun in the Roman Catholic Church.

Because of the spirituality in the above quote, Therese posed a threat to the legalism that was in place at the convent and practiced by the nuns who counted works and acts of virtue as pleasing to God and the way to gain salvation.

These comments are not unique to Therese of Lisieux. In the *Catechism of the Catholic Church*, para. 2011 states: "The charity of Christ is the source in us of all our merits before God. Grace, by uniting us to Christ in active love, ensures the supernatural quality of our acts and consequently their merit before God and before men."

Therese died at twenty-four of tuberculosis in 1897. She was canonized in 1923 and in 1997 was declared a "Doctor of the Church" by Pope John Paul II, becoming the 33rd doctor and third female to receive the title. Doctrinal requirements include: outstanding holiness and sanctity; eminent learning and writings; proclamation by the pope; and a canonized saint.

Her comments about salvation remind us of the Gospel hymn, "Nothing in my hands I bring, only to your cross I cling." In statements from this Roman Catholic Doctor of the Church and in the Protestant evangelical Gospel hymn, Jesus takes center stage.

GILBERT KEITH CHESTERTON

G. K. Chesterton was born in 1874 in London, England into a middle-class family. He attended University College and the Slade School of Art. In regards to his Christian faith, Chesterton experienced a period of skepticism and disillusionment beginning in 1893. As a result, during this time he dabbled in spiritualistic and telepathic approaches, including using the Ouija board and investigating diabolism the worship of, or dealings with, the devil or demons. This period in his life even led him to contemplate suicide.

Chesterton left University College and went to work for the London publisher Redway. Chesterton later regained his Christian faith through the support of his future wife, Frances Blogg, whom he married in 1901. She was instrumental in aiding G. K. in extricating himself from his spiritual dilemma. Chesterton moved with Frances to Beaconsfield, a village just west of London. He continued to write, lecture and travel frequently. Speaking of Chesterton's travels, he was notoriously absent-minded, and frequently was forced to telegraph his wife and ask her where his destination on that day was to be.

In 1922, Chesterton joined the Roman Catholic Church from Anglicanism. He also received honorary degrees from Edinburgh, Dublin, and Notre Dame Universities. While not precisely defined a systematic theologian, G. K. had common sense and spoke to the common man.

Chesterton defended Roman Catholicism, while not being triumphalistic toward Christians from other persuasions. He held to all of the doctrines declared orthodox at the early councils and creeds, including the acceptance of the miracles mentioned in

Scripture, the belief of God as the Creator, the fall of Adam, and salvation provided by Christ on the cross.

G. K. Chesterton was a voluminous writer, producing verse, essays, novels, and short stories. Early in the twentieth century, he published some one hundred books. He is best known for his series about the priest-detective Father Brown, who appeared in fifty stories. He also wrote biographies of St. Francis and St. Thomas Aquinas. Chesterton has been called a Catholic version of C. S. Lewis. Indeed, Chesterton was a man with a multiplicity of talent.

WALTER ARTHUR MAIER

Born in 1893, Walter Arthur Maier lived in Boston and became one of the most influential radio preachers of the twentieth century. While executive secretary of the Walther League, a youth group associated with the Lutheran Church-Missouri Synod, Walter spoke at the leagues convention, which was carried on the radio.

Understanding the potential of this new medium, he began a radio station, KFOU, at Concordia Seminary in St. Louis, Missouri in 1924. At the time, Maier had been professor of Old Testament studies at the Seminary for eight years.

Maier took a leave of absence to become the full-time speaker of The Lutheran Hour, broadcast on CBS for the next twenty years. Maier reached a large audience with his biblically sound sermons and by addressing issues that were current at the time. His aim was to preach the great truths of the Scriptures: Law and Gospel, sin and grace, Christ and His redemption. It was said by the end of the 1940s, Maier was speaking to an estimated twenty million people.

When Walter Maier passed away suddenly in 1950, tributes came from around the world. Billy Graham sent a telegram: "We join with friends who mourn the passing of Dr. Walter Maier, whose Lutheran Hour was a constant benediction and source of strength."

It should be noted that Walter Maier's son, Dr. Paul L. Maier, is a distinguished scholar as was his father. He is Professor of Ancient History at Western Michigan University. Paul Maier is a much-published author of both scholarly and popular works. Included in his academic works are *Josephus: The Essential Works* and *Eusebius: The Church History*. The son has followed in his father's footsteps.

PAUL SCHNEIDER

Paul Schneider was born in 1897 in a little town of Pferdsfeld, in northern Bavaria, Germany. He was the second of three sons born to Gustav-Adolf Schneider and Elisabeth Schnorr. Paul had a strong affection for his mother and respect for his father. Gustav was a pastor and a committed patriot.

Schneider fought in the German Army during World War I and, as a result of the severe battle wounds he received, was awarded the famous Iron Cross. Early on, Schneider indicated his desire to become a pastor, following his father's calling. Schneider began his studies at the University of Giessen. At this time, radical theological liberalism had impacted the church in Germany and, at first, he embraced it. However, God had not given up on Paul; the Holy Spirit brought him into contact with genuine believers and ultimately he came to faith in Christ. He finished his training and was ordained in Hochelheim in 1925. The following year, he married Margarete Dieterich, the daughter of a pastor. Two years later, the Schneiders had their first son, followed by a daughter and four more sons.

When Adolf Hitler became chancellor in 1933, Schneider was the pastor of the Hochelheim church, having succeeded his father after his death. At first, Pastor Schneider had hoped that the new Chancellor, with divine guidance, would bring Germany into a bright future. It was not to be. Schneider soon saw the true character of Adolf Hitler and the Nazi regime. Hitler saw the German Church as a useful tool in spreading his "Nazi gospel." Consequently, Schneider and his family moved to Dickenschied, where he became pastor to the Dickenschied and Womrath congregations.

Pastor Schneider never missed an opportunity to address the evil that Nazism was bringing to the country. In spite of pressure to stay quiet and not stand up for the Gospel, he became the lone advocate for the Truth. He allowed only true Christians to partake of the Eucharist and refused to allow support for the Nazi agenda in his church. Finally, Schneider was arrested and sent to the Nazi concentration camp in Buchenwald, Germany. Despite torture, humiliation, hunger, and terrible suffering, his message did not change. He preached the Gospel from his cell, warning the guards and officers of God's impending judgment.

Finally, Schneider met his martyrdom by lethal injection in 1939. His faithful wife Margarete brought his body back home for burial. In the presence of Nazi guards, the audience heard the following prayer over Pastor Paul Schneider's grave: "May God grant that the witness of your Shepherd our brother remain with you and continue to impact on future generations and that it remain vital and bear fruit in the entire Christian Church." Paul Schneider was the first Protestant pastor murdered by the Nazis.

FR. MAXIMILIAN KOLBE

Raymond Kolbe was born in 1894 in Zdunska Wola, Russian occupied Poland, into a Catholic family. He was the second of five sons whose parents worked as weavers, a trade that provided a meager income.

Kolbe entered an order of Friars in Austrian-occupied Poland in 1907, and received the name Maximilian. He was a brilliant student and earned a PhD in philosophy at the Pontifical Gregorian University in Rome. He would later receive another doctorate, the ThD, in theology. As impressive as Kolbe's academic accomplishments were, it was his piety that caught the notice of his contemporaries. In his early twenties, he wrote his mother: "Pray that I will love without limits." One day in the future, he would have an opportunity to show such love.

Kolbe became director of Poland's largest publishing house, which produced a monthly magazine with a circulation of about one million and a daily paper that reached 125,000 subscribers. After leaving Rome, Kolbe taught in Krakow, Poland and established a mission in Nagasaki, Japan. In 1939, Germany invaded Poland, and Fr. Maximilian was arrested and imprisoned. Upon being released, he returned to the Niepokalanow friary he had founded in 1936, reorganized it, turned the friary into a hospice for displaced Polish Jews, Gentiles and German invaders as well; open to all, the word "enemy" was not in his vocabulary.

Five years later, Kolbe was again arrested and imprisoned in Warsaw. In May, he was transferred to Auschwitz as prisoner No. 16,670. In August, as punishment for the escape of one prisoner, the S.S. chose ten prisoners to be sent to a special bunker and starved to death.

One of the chosen, overcome with the realization of his fate, broke down. "My wife and my children," he sobbed. Then a prisoner several rows back broke out and pushed his way to the front. That man was Maximilian Kolbe. He positioned himself before the officer in charge. "Herr Kommandant, I wish to make a request, please," he said politely in flawless German. Kolbe continued, "I want to die in place of this prisoner." The officer wanted to know why. "I have no wife or children. Besides I'm old and not good for anything. He's in better condition," he added, adroitly playing on the Nazi line that only the fit should live. The request was granted. Fr. Maximilian was stripped naked and put in the starvation bunker.

Fr. Kolbe pastored in the bunker, praying, hearing confessions, and singing hymns. Two weeks passed; one by one the prisoners died, leaving only four, including Fr. Kolbe. The S.S. decided the process was taking too long. A prisoner was sent to the bunker, where upon he gave the four prisoners lethal injections of carbolic acid. In 1941, Fr. Maximilian Kolbe, "the man for others," gave his life for another. His body was cremated the next day.

Thirty years later, the Beatification was begun by Pope Paul VI and in 1982, he was canonized a saint by Pope John Paul II. In following his Savior's example, Fr. Maximilian's sacrifice is an example for all believing Christians. He was indeed "the man for others."

DONALD GREY BARNHOUSE

Donald Grey Barnhouse was born in 1895 into a Methodist household in Watsonville, California. He studied at the Bible Institute of Los Angeles (BIOLA), where he was introduced to dispensationalism. He was enrolled at the University of Chicago, for a short time, and then he left to attend Princeton Theological Seminary.

Leaving the seminary in 1917, Barnhouse joined the Army. After the war was over, he remained in Europe and served as a missionary in Belgium and France. Returning to the United States, Barnhouse settled in Pennsylvania.

He did graduate work at the University of Pennsylvania, and then studied at the Eastern Baptist Theological Seminary, receiving a Master's in Theology degree. Growing up in a Methodist home, being exposed to dispensationalism, experiencing secularism at the University of Chicago, and learning about Reformed and Baptistic theology prepared him well for the ministry that the Lord had waiting for this gifted man.

In 1927, Barnhouse was called to serve at the historic Tenth Presbyterian Church in Philadelphia, where he served for thirty-three years—the rest of his life. His skill as a speaker and writer caused Barnhouse to become one of the leading voices in the Presbyterian Church. In 1949, he began a radio Bible study, starting with the book of Romans, and continued for nearly twelve years until his death.

Dr. Barnhouse's ministry was a varied one. He authored a number of articles and books. He also was founder and editor of *Eternity Magazine*, which was the most informative publication of the time dealing with the cultural and theological issues of the day.

At first, in his ministry, Barnhouse was critical of both liberal Protestantism and Roman Catholicism. However, as part of the neo-evangelical movement of the 1950's, he became more irenic and stated that he was willing to work and fellowship with other Christians. He did lose some ground with many fundamentalists when he supported the publication of the Revised Standard Version of the Bible.

DIETRICH BONHOEFFER

Dietrich Bonhoeffer was born in 1906 in Breslau, Poland, to Karl and Paula Bonhoeffer. They had eight children within ten years, Dietrich being their fourth and youngest son. His father Karl held the chair in psychiatry and neurology at the University and was the director of the hospital for nervous diseases.

Dietrich's mother was a teacher, and both her and her husband's family backgrounds were impressive. Paula's grandfather, Karl von Hase, had been a famous theologian in Jena. Karl Bonhoeffer's lineage was also impressive, including doctors, pastors, judges, professors, and lawyers; perhaps Dietrich might be forgiven for thinking that, to some extent, genes were important.

At age fourteen, Dietrich decided that he would become a theologian. In 1921, he attended his first evangelistic meeting directed by General Bramwell Booth of the Salvation Army. General Booth had held services in Germany before the war, and he returned two years later and ministered to thousands, including many soldiers. Dietrich was very impressed by the response.

Two years later, the Bonhoeffers would move to Tubingen, where Karl would be granted a prestigious research position at the Karl Wilhelm Institute. Dietrich would study at the University of Tubingen before embarking on a trip that would mold his theology for the rest of his life.

In 1924, Dietrich embarked on a trip to Italy, ending in a visit to Rome. He kept a journal of his impressions of what he experienced, including at the Vatican with the Sistine Chapel and Mass at St. Peter's. For Dietrich to understand the church as something permanent would change everything and would set in motion the entire course of Bonhoeffer's remaining life. This "further thinking" would be enhanced later on by experiences in Barcelona as a student pastor and in studies in the United States.

Upon returning from Rome, Bonhoeffer enrolled at Berlin University, where he would study for seven semesters, earning his doctorate at age twenty-one. Bonhoeffer, intent on experiencing how the church functioned throughout the world, accepted a call to be a student pastorate in Barcelona, Spain. In 1929, Dietrich returned to Berlin and found that conditions and attitudes in Germany had changed since he left. The most serious was the anti-Semitism that was rampant in the culture. It was not helpful that Martin Luther adopted this view at the end of his life. Bonhoeffer spoke forcefully on this issue.

Next Bonhoeffer visited America. In New York, he went to

Union Theological Seminary and was not impressed; the most liberal preacher in America, Henry Emerson Fosdick, occupied the pulpit of Riverside Church—a stone's throw from Union. He was, however, pleasantly surprised when he attended the hundred-year-old Abyssinian Baptist Church in New York City, which was a welcome change from Union Seminary and Riverside Church.

Bonhoeffer had criticized the abuses of the Hitler regime since 1933. He finally abandoned his Christian pacifism and decided the answer was to eliminate Hitler. While Bonhoeffer was not directly involved in the plot to kill Hitler, the Nazis discovered his connection with the conspirators. Hitler ordered his execution, which took place at Flossenburg Concentration Camp in 1945.

Postmodern Christianity

Negative influences that appeared earlier in church history affected orthodox Christianity in this time frame. Heresies had arisen and were addressed by the church fathers during the first five centuries.

These heresies resurfaced in the Enlightenment and need to be dealt with when we examine ecumenism. Also, secular humanism is presently a danger to Christian orthodoxy and must be considered as well. Secularism is difficult to nail down and some authorities consider the movement to be an extension of modernism.

DEAD SEA SCROLLS

Discovered in 1947, the Dead Sea Scrolls were composed roughly between 250 BC and AD 70 at Qumran, which was a place at the northwest end of the Dead Sea. A Jewish community near Qumran was most likely populated by Essenes, who produced the scrolls.

Though they were not spoken of in the Bible, the Essenes were a group of Jews who practiced an ascetic lifestyle. We learn of them from Josephus, Philo, and early church fathers such as Pliny the elder. Concerning the value of the Dead Sea Scrolls for authenticating the Old Testament texts, eminent American biblical archaeologist William Foxwell Albright said the scrolls were "the greatest manuscript discovery of modern times." Other scholars, including R. Laird Harris and Gleason Archer, have commented on the value that the scrolls bring to the biblical scholarship.

Little is known for certain regarding the date and composition of the Dead Sea Scrolls. What we know for sure is that they were found in a cave at Qumran. Most importantly, they help corroborate and testify to the authenticity of the Old Testament Scriptures we have today.

Dr. Norman Geisler addresses this important topic *in Baker Encyclopedia of Christian Apologetics.* "The Dead Sea Scrolls provide an important apologetic contribution toward establishing the general reliability of the Old Testament Hebrew text, as well as the earliest copies of part of Old Testament books and even whole books." Discoveries like the Dead Seas Scrolls enhance the truth of Christianity. We are thankful for the facts that they reveal.

ECUMENISM

We will now examine ecumenism and its various meanings. The word itself comes from the Greek and roughly translated means, "the entire inhabited earth." Given the modern concern for unity in Christendom, ecumenism has the understanding of working for unity and reunification.

The term had its origin in 1910 at the Edinburgh Missionary Conference. This was an interdenominational group that gathered to discuss the missionary task of the church. However, the word has developed at least three distinct meanings. The first has been called "ancient" ecumenism. This is the earliest formulation that was developed by the first leaders and theologians of the church to establish the doctrines that would determine the content of Christianity.

The second model is called "old" ecumenism. This should not be confused with ancient ecumenism. In spite of the word "old," it developed much later, with the World Council of Churches and the National Council of Churches. This is the ecumenical model that everyone involved in church life has known for fifty years. Since the majority of evangelical Christianity remains outside the movement, it is not truly ecumenical.

This type of ecumenism often focuses on political ideology; hence, evangelicals have been reluctant to join. A respected theologian and historian, Thomas C. Oden, has examined this issue. What Oden calls "old" ecumenism started with the philosophes of Marx, Freud, Nietzsche, and Bultmann. These "isms" took over when modern ideology replaced classical Christian theology and secular philosophy overtook traditional morals and ethics. This happened when liberalism challenged established denominations to unseat doctrines that were in place during the first five centuries.

The third model is called the "new" ecumenism. It seeks to reestablish ties to classic Christian formulations in spite of old ruptures in Christendom. This working of the Holy Spirit is happening worldwide in local churches, para-church groups, and grassroots minis mission activities. Who would have supposed that Anglican bishops from Africa would travel to America to establish orthodox Anglican missions for Episcopalians who are tired of not hearing the Gospel from their pulpits, but rather comments on current social issues?

SECULAR VS. SECULARISM

A problem exists when these two terms are confused. The former, "secular," refers to action by the state when appropriate; the latter, "secularism," is when the state takes action which infringes on the legal rights of the church. One is reminded of Christ's rebuke to the Pharisees, "Give to Caesar what is Caesar's and to God what is God's." (Matthew 22:21) As St. Thomas Aquinas writes in *Commentary on the Sentences of Peter Lombard*, it is better to obey the secular authorities in cases that do not involve religious issues.

There are secularists in America today who prefer to be called "agnostics," because no one can prove one way or the other the existence of God. However, action implies choice; either one acts as if God exists, or one acts as if he does not.

Closely related to the subject of secular and secularism is humanism. It is of two varieties—secular humanism and Christian humanism. Christian Humanists were believers who used their God given talents to enhance, not detract from, the Gospel. While not comfortable with the Enlightenment, it felt at home in the Renaissance Movement. Secular humanism, however, is a way of life and thought that is pursued without reference to God or religion. This form of humanistic secularism denies classical Christian truth.

Historically, "secularism" meant the transfer of authority and property from the church to the state. In this sense, it is a neutral concept. However, secularism and secular humanism normally is used to mean a shift away from God and toward the world. Enlightenment rationalism, the rise of modern science—currently termed scientism, and the breakdown of the family and the church are indicators of this trend. Nationalism, evolution, and Marxism offer competition as well.

Theologians have attempted to address the modern landscape in different ways. Paul Van Buren's *The Secular Meaning of the Gospel* and Harvey Cox's *The Secular City* are examples from the "God-is-dead" school. Christian scholars have weighed in as well with Jacques Ellul's *The New Demons* and Francis Schaeffer's *How Should*

We then Live?

These evangelical thinkers and others interacted with secularism and secular humanism. From the perspective of the Bible, these movements have "exchanged the truth of God for a lie, and worshipped and served the creature rather than the Creator" (Romans 1:25).

The following words were written by one who claims to be an atheist, but respects the contribution of Judaism and Christianity. John D. Steinrocken wrote "Secularism's Ongoing Debt to Christianity" in *American Thinker*, March 2010. "There can be no such morality without religion. Has there ever been a more perfect and concise moral code than the one Moses brought down from the mountain?" This is an interesting observation from one who claims to be an atheist.

PART FIVE

The Church in Transition

Catholic Christianity

Modern Roman Catholicism began with the pronouncements that emerged from the Second Vatican Council. Positions held in this period by Catholics ranged from the contemporary on the left to the ultra-orthodox on the right. Evaluations of the worth of these new positions depend on one's own personal perspective.

VATICAN II

The idea to hold this Council came from Pope John XXIII, who claimed to have a message from the Holy Spirit. This would be the 21st Ecumenical Council of the Roman Catholic Church. Its purpose was to revive the church without the jettisoning of dogmas developed from the first century, as the ultimate goal of the Council was the unity of all Christian communities.

Pope John was perhaps the most beloved pope in history. In *Roman Catholics and Evangelicals*, Geisler and MacKenzie comment on the Council as follows. "The pope defined the task of the council to be the renewing of the religious life of the church and asked Catholics to pray for the council: 'Renew in our day O Lord, your wonders, as in a new Pentecost.' The portrayal of Jesus as the 'Good Shepherd' deeply impressed him, indeed, 'every description of John XXIII calls attention to this single ambition; he wanted first of all and genuinely to be a pastor.' Pope John's vision extended beyond his own communion to the Christian Church worldwide." Pope John realized that the Roman Catholic Church needed to update its approach, without changing essential doctrines, to meet the current cultural climate.

Vatican II developed as follows:

SESSION 1: October – December 1962

Participants decided their own commission, freeing themselves from the Roman curia. Paul VI replaced John XXIII upon his death.

SESSION II: September – December 1963

Collegiality of the bishops was declared; outreach to non-Christian religions was supported.

SESSION III: September – November 1964

Decrees on Ecumenism and the Eastern Catholic churches were formed. The Blessed Virgin Mary was declared to be the "Mother of the Church."

SESSION IV: September – December 1965

A number of documents were addressed including discipline, religious renewal, and Christian education. On December 4th, a statement on the "Promotion of Christian Unity" was presented; observers and guests as well as delegates participated. The Council concluded on December 8, 1965. In total, Vatican II produced sixteen documents.

THEOLOGICAL POSITIONS AT VATICAN II

It is not surprising to learn that church councils have had participants who represented different theological points of view; Vatican II was no exception. Present at the Council, were delegates who held views that spanned the theological spectrum, from far left to the ultra-traditional right.

A balanced orthodox Catholic, James Hitchcock in *Catholicism and Modernity: Confrontation or Capitulation?* offers an assessment on "New" Catholicism. "One of the great human mysteries of modern times is the amazingly swift process by which the Roman Catholic Church, apparently one of the most solid, self-confident, and enduring institutions in the history of the world, was plunged into an identity crisis of cosmic proportions. The crisis still goes on, with no satisfactory outcome in sight." It seems that Hitchcock believes that his church needs to realize that it has allowed factors to develop that damage its credibility.

Some of the more positive statements made by the council were offered by J. D. Douglas, Walter A. Elwell, and Peter Toon, who were evangelical Protestant historians, in *The Concise of Dictionary of the Christian Tradition*. "Vatican II opened the way for greater participation by the laity in the life of the church and urged them to seek holiness as the people of God. Members of the Protestant Churches were no longer called 'heretics' but 'separated brethren.' The council absolved the Jews from Christ's death, stressed the importance of Scripture and its study, reformed the Roman liturgy, and lessened the tension between Rome and other churches." Of course, these changes were not well-received by Catholics of a more orthodox persuasion. They felt that the Council had been hijacked by progressive members.

CATHOLICS AND EVANGELICALS

Since the Reformation split the Western Church in the sixteenth century, both Roman Catholics and evangelical Protestants have considered each other suspect. Following the schism between the Catholics and Protestants, and before the Council of Trent, there were a number of efforts made to address differences and effect reconciliation between unofficial representatives of the two groups.

One of the most significant was the Conference of Regensburg, convened by Emperor Charles V. The gathering included important theologians from both sides and, although some agreement was reached, the hostility that had developed between the Protestant movement and Rome cancelled out the efforts of Regensburg.

This hostility began to change with the advent of the Vatican II Council. Positions emerging from the Council include that Protestants were no longer called heretics, but "separated brethren." People could be members of the Church in a certain sense without being members of the institution. Catholics and evangelical Protestants often found themselves on the same side concerning such issues as abortion, euthanasia, homosexuality, and secularism in cultural issues.

Protestants reexamined their attitudes toward Catholics as well. When they took a closer look at the topics that caused the Reformation, they realized that the issues were not as easily resolved. The purpose of this treatment is to investigate areas where Roman Catholics and evangelicals have cooperated in the past, and to consider the development of guidelines and principles for future projects that both parties have shared interest in. We will address persons, events, statements, and movements which further these goals. Our interest in this should be to proclaim a spiritual unity, not organizational or ecumenical, that can confess "one Lord, one faith, one baptism; one God and Father of all, who is over all and through all and in all."

LEON JOSEPH CARDINAL SUENENS

Leon Joseph Suenens was born in 1904 to Jean-Baptiste and Jeanne (nee Jannsens) Suenens in Ixelles, a city near Brussels, Belgium. He was baptized by his uncle, who was a priest. His father died when Leon was four years old and he lived with his mother and priest-uncle.

Leon began his studies at St. Mary's Institute in Schaerbeek, near home. Next, he enrolled in the Pontifical Gregorian University in Rome. Through his studies at this university, he earned a doctorate in theology and philosophy and a Master's degree in Canon Law.

Ordained to the priesthood in 1927, Leon served as a professor at St. Mary's Institute and subsequently taught moral philosophy and pedagogy at the Minor Seminary of Mechelen. Leon entered the Belgium Army and served for three months; whereupon, in 1940, he became vice-rector at the Catholic University of Louvain. He was in a group of hostages to be executed, but the Allied Liberation of Belgium transpired before these orders could be carried out.

Fr. Suenens was appointed Auxiliary Bishop of Mechelen and named Archbishop in 1961. Pope John XXIII created him a Cardinal a year later. Cardinal Suenens was included when Pope John called the world's bishops to Rome for the II Vatican Council.

Prior to Vatican II, Cardinal Suenens had been concerned with lack of personal faith that a number of Catholics exhibited. To that end, he quotes a French Bishop in his book, *A New Pentecost?* "We held the Second Vatican Council in the belief it was self-evident that Christians were essentially destined to be missionaries. But that presupposes that they are believers. The delay in the hoped for renewal after Vatican II ... all this can only be explained by the fact that, in our naivete, we believed that the basic Christian message, the Kerygma—'I believe in Jesus Christ, the Son of God, the Saviour'—was accepted and lived by everybody. In fact, this was true only of a few.'" Cardinal Suenens had heard of the Catholic Charismatic Movement and made a speech addressing it at the Council. He felt that the Movement could be a factor in evangelizing members of his church that had not been converted to Jesus Christ.

Perhaps one of the greatest things that has happened in the twentieth century to affect Roman Catholicism is the presence of the Catholic Charismatic Renewal within its midst. Having obtained information about the Charismatic Renewal, Cardinal Suenens determined to see for himself. Stanley M. Burgess and Gary B. McGee in *Dictionary of Pentecostal and Charismatic Movements*, tell us how this happened. "In 1972 and 1973 Suenens first came into contact with the Catholic Charismatic Renewal (CCR) in the United States and visited Notre Dame. He hosted a conference at Malines that attempted to evaluate the CCR and provided Theological and Pastoral Guidelines on the Catholic Renewal (1974). He invited two American CCR leaders, Ralph Martin and Stephen Clark, to develop a CCR International Information Office in Brussels (later moved to Rome)." Cardinal Suenens died from thrombosis in Brussels at age 91 and was buried at St. Rumbold's Cathedral.

MOTHER TERESA

In 1910, Mother Teresa was born Agnes Gonxha Bojaxhiu in Skopje, Macedonia. Her family was of Albanian ethnicity. At a young age, she experienced a call from God, instructing her to become a missionary and spread the love of God. At age eighteen,

Teresa left home and entered the Sisters of Loreto, an Irish community which ministered in India. After training in Dublin for a few months, she was sent to India in 1931, where she took her initial vows as a nun.

For the next seventeen years, Mother Teresa taught at St. Mary's High School in Calcutta. The suffering and poverty she saw surrounding the convent led her to ask her superiors to allow her to leave the school and work with the poor in the slums of Calcutta; they agreed, so she began an open-air school for slum children. Teresa was joined by voluntary workers and financial help was also forthcoming.

In 1950, Mother Teresa received permission to establish her own order, "The Missionaries of Charity," which would love and care for those persons whom no one was interested in. Thirteen years later, Mother Teresa formed the Contemplative Branch of the Sisters and the Active Branch of the Brothers, adding the Priest Branch twenty years after that.

Since then, the Society of Missionaries has spread throughout the world, including the former Soviet Union and Eastern European countries. Service is now provided to help the poor in Asia, Africa, and Latin America. This group offers its help when natural catastrophes, floods, epidemics, and famines occur. Mother Teresa's efforts have been recognized and acclaimed throughout the world. Her many awards and distinctions include the Pope John XXIII Peace Prize in 1971 and the Nobel Peace Prize in 1979.

Mother Teresa was also an outspoken foe of abortion. A renewal group in the Presbyterian Church USA—Presbyterians Pro-Life Movement—brought her to address the General Assembly. Using Scripture throughout her presentation, she spoke movingly about the evil of abortion.

We will close this treatment of Mother Teresa with mention of a situation which occurred during her ministry. In the book *Moth-*

er Teresa: Come Be My Light, letters she had written over several decades spoke of a lack of faith, "a terrible darkness within me," and a sense of being deserted by Jesus. This phenomenon, while not often mentioned in church history, has occurred.

The most notable example that comes to mind is John of the Cross, who used such language as "the dark night of the soul" to describe this disturbing event. Also, Ignatius of Loyola in his manual on prayer, *The Spiritual Exercises*, writes about listlessness and feelings of separation from God. During her final illness, Therese of Lisieux experienced doubts as to what would happen to her after death.

Protestant Christians have also not been immune to this condition. Oswald Chambers, William Cowper, and Martin Luther have reported experiencing these feelings in their lives. The most succinct comment on this phenomenon that occurred to the Christians listed above comes from the preacher of the papal household, Capuchin Father Raniero Cantalamessa, who said that Mother Teresa's inner suffering should not be seen as a denial of God. She knew God was there, but suffered because she could not feel him.

LIGHT AND LIFE MOVEMENT

Franciszek Blachnicki was born in Rybnik, Poland as the seventh child of Jözef and Maria Blachnicki. When the Germans invaded Poland in 1939, Franciszek took part in the September campaign.

After Poland was defeated, he joined the underground resistance movement. He was arrested by the Gestapo and sent to a concentration camp called Auschwitz, where he remained for 14 months. Franciszek was sent to a prison in Katowitz. As a result of his anti-Nazi activities, he was sentenced to death.

Five months later, the sentence was commuted, and Franciszek spent the remainder of the conflict in various prisons and camps.

During his time on death row, he experienced a conversion to Christ, which had a deep and lasting effect on his life. After the war, Fr. Blachnicki entered the Silesia Seminary in Krakow and was ordained to the priesthood in 1950.

Fr. Blachnicki was arrested by the communist government in 1960 and spent four months in prison. The year after his release from prison, Fr. Blachnicki entered the Catholic University in Lubin, Poland. Completing his studies, he remained in Lubin as a researcher in the Institute of Pastoral Theology. Early on, the project that Fr. Blachnicki had envisioned to teach children with the Gospel became known as the Light-Life Movement. The light of God's Word was bringing new life to his people.

In 1977, Bill Bright, the founder of Campus Crusade for Christ, asked Norman Geisler to travel to Poland and teach a Bible survey course to university students in the Movement, which was started by Fr. Blachnicki. Dr. Geisler said yes, and when he returned home he wrote in "Oasis of Living Water," *Christian Herald*. "Thousands of people flock to camps to hear the Gospel ... Churches are full and overflowing morning and evening ... In Poland, long an overwhelmingly Roman Catholic land, but dominated by Marxism for a full generation. I saw them, I ate with them, sang with them, and knelt with them in their churches and chapels. They call themselves Oazi (Oasis). They are an indigenous spiritual renewal group who have retreats, publish (underground) literature and teach people to be born again by personally trusting Christ as Savior."

Dr. Geisler said that his time in Poland was one of the most spiritual events of his career. The students told him that before he arrived, "the Bible was like a room with furniture and no lights. You have turned on the lights for us."

Fr. Blachnicki settled in Germany in a Polish center, Marianum in Carlberg, where he unexpectedly died five years later. In 1994, he received posthumously, the Commander's Cross of the Order of Polonia Restituta; and the following year, he received the Auschwitz Cross medal. The mortal remains of the Servant of God, Fr. Franciszek Blachnicki, were transferred to the Church of Good Shepherd in Kroscienko. He was indeed, a good and faithful shepherd during his time in Poland.

JOHN COURTNEY MURRAY

John Courtney Murray was born in 1904 in New York City and entered the Jesuit order in 1920. He studied at Western College and Boston College. He was ordained a priest in 1933 and four years later became professor of theology at Woodstock College, where he remained until his death.

Murray was an editor of the Jesuit journal *Theological Studies* and, for a brief time, religion editor of *America*. He was visiting professor of medieval philosophy and culture at Yale, and he served as an advisor to John F. Kennedy in his 1960 presidential campaign.

In the Roman Catholic Church, the Jesuit Order was perhaps one of the first to become interested in ecumenism. Since Vatican II, interdenominational activity has become popular church-wide, but it was not so in Fr. Murray's day. He was also concerned with church-state issues and questioned whether his church had a role to play in them.

These views of Murray conflicted with traditional Catholic teachings that were held at the time concerning church-state issues. Since Roman Catholicism was the one true religion, the state should establish it as the state religion. This position has changed within Catholicity, to one which holds that a person should not be coerced by the secular state into embracing a particular faith. The newer view is one which is held by orthodox as well as progressive Catholics.

However, this was not the case with the Catholicism that held sway in Murray's day. Some Roman officials felt that Murray's views minimized the claims of Catholicism and changed a doctrine that had been in place for centuries. In 1954, Murray's controversial views caused his Jesuit superiors in Rome to order him not to address church or state issues.

When Vatican II convened, Murray was still unwelcome among Roman officials, which caused him to miss the opening of the Council. However, help was on the way. Cardinal Spellman was an influential cleric at the time, and he arranged to have Murray become an advisor. Fr. Murray should be remembered as being instrumental in the cause of religious freedom in his Church.

Evangelical Christianity

The term *Evangelical* has references to a Protestant form of Christianity which holds to the full inspiration and authority of the Bible and the presence of a personal conversion to Christ. It also has been applied to non-Protestants, primarily Eastern Orthodox and Roman Catholics, who hold to the aforementioned beliefs.

HENRIETTA MEARS

Henrietta Mears was born in Fargo, North Dakota, in 1890. When her father learned that the baby was a daughter, he exclaimed, "Praise God, it's a girl! I couldn't face rearing another son!" Little did he realize the impact his daughter would have on so many people and on Christianity in general.

Her mother and father were devout Christians, and Henrietta was well liked by her older brothers and sister Margaret. Ethel May Baldwin and David V. Benson, in their book *Henrietta Mears and How She Did It,* state the following. "On Easter Sunday morning, when she was about five years old, Henrietta explained to her mother, as they were getting dressed for church, that she was ready to become a Christian and join their church. Her mother tried to reason with her that everyone would think she was too young to understand what it meant to join church. However, after further conversation indicated that Henrietta knew what she was doing, her mother promised to talk about the matter with their pastor Dr. W. B. Riley of the First Baptist Church of Minneapolis."

She began teaching Sunday School at the age of twelve at her church in Minneapolis, where she saw the class of eighteen-year-old girls grow from five to five hundred. Upon graduating from the University of Minnesota, Mears moved to southern California in 1928, and accepted a position as director of Christian education at Hollywood Presbyterian Church. In less than three years, the church's entire Sunday School expanded from 450 to more than four thousand students.

Mears was to have a special impact on college age young men and was reputed to have encouraged about three hundred men to enter the ministry. Her efforts at Hollywood Presbyterian Church made it one of the better known congregations, not only in California, but nation-wide.

Henrietta counted among her proteges: Bill Bright, who would become the founder of Campus Crusade for Christ; Richard Halverson, chaplain of the U. S. Senate; and Louis H. Evans, Jr., pastor of National Presbyterian Church, Washington, DC. She also influenced a number of Hollywood personalities, including Dale Evans and Roy Rogers.

Henrietta Mears founded *Gospel Light Press* in 1933. It was renamed *Gospel Light Publishers*, to produce her materials, which were well received among evangelical churches. Four years later, she arranged the purchase of Forest Home Camp Grounds, near San Bernardino, California, for use as a retreat center. She never married, choosing rather to devote her entire life to using the many gifts that God had bestowed upon her. Since WWII, many leaders in evangelical America were inspired by her work.

A. W. TOZER

Aiden Wilson Tozer was born in 1897 in the mountainous area of western Pennsylvania. He had an impact on his generation like no other individual. During his lifetime, he was called a twentieth century prophet. Tozer had insight into biblical truth and the condition that prevailed in the state of the evangelical church of his day. He saw the fog that existed in modern Christianity.

Before Tozer was seventeen, he encountered a street preacher on a corner in Akron, Ohio, who said, "If you don't know how to be saved, just call on God saying, Lord, be merciful to me a sinner." Tozer went home and emerged from his house a new creature in Christ.

He was discipled by his future mother-in-law and grew rapidly in the knowledge of God. She counseled him to read good books, study the Bible, and pray. Without a degree, he was called to pastor a small church in Nutter Fort, West Virginia. Tozer and his new bride, Ada Cecelia Pfautz, started a ministry in the Christian and Missionary Alliance that would last for forty-four years.

Tozer received a call from the Southside Alliance Church in Chicago in 1928. He filled that pulpit the next Sunday and, after praying about the opportunity, accepted the call to serve.

From the beginning, his preaching captivated his congregation; it was said that there were only two great churches in Chicago—Moody Memorial Church with Harry Ironside and Southside Alliance Church, where Tozer pastored. The Moody radio station broadcasted a weekly program from Tozer's church study, and his ministry grew. He became the preaching minister of the Avenue Road Alliance Church in Toronto, Canada from 1959 until 1963.

Tozer was involved with denominational issues as well. He urged members of the alliance to move away from the Pentecostal practice of speaking in tongues with his often delivered dictum, "Seek not, forbid not." Self-educated, he read widely, especially in poetry, the Church Fathers, and the mystics of the church.

In a book by Tozer, *The Crucified Life,* the introduction tells the story that Tozer, while browsing in a used bookstore, came upon a book by Archbishop Francois Fenelon, *Spiritual Counsel.* He purchased the book and took it home, and his life was changed forever. Tozer loaned out books occasionally, but this volume never left his study.

Francois Fenelon was greatly attracted to Madame Guyon, who held Quietist views, which is a form of Roman Catholic mysticism in the seventeenth and eighteenth centuries. Both were censured by the church. That an evangelical pastor, before ecumenism rightly understood was fashionable, would find the writing of a Roman Catholic archbishop from the Middle Ages valuable illustrates his desire to learn about other Christians who lived in the past.

C. S. LEWIS

Clive Staples (C.S.) Lewis was born in 1898 in Belfast, Ireland, the second of two sons of Albert James Lewis, a lawyer, and Flora Augusta Hamilton Lewis. His older brother, Warren, said their childhood together "was the greatest happiness of my life."

In 1905, the Lewis family moved to "Little Lea," a large new home. Flora Lewis contracted cancer and died shortly thereafter. It was a difficult time for the family and in the same year, the two boys were sent to school at Wynyard in Watford, Hertfordshire. It was here that Lewis first heard the Gospel, and he began to pray and read the Bible.

Lewis returned to England and Cherbourg House, a preparatory school in Malvern. After obtaining a classical scholarship, C. S. entered Malvern College in 1913. It was here that he developed an interest in Greek mythology, which would lead to his development as one of the most important classical scholars of his era.

The following year, Lewis was tutored by the brilliant atheist W. T. Kirkpatrick, who prepared him for Oxford. During this time, he mastered Greek, Latin, French, German, and Italian. He also read extensively in English and American literature. Lewis developed a liking for great music as well. He was happy with his freedom—as an atheistic pupil of an atheistic tutor—because he had freedom from God.

Lewis began his studies at Oxford in 1917, but when World War I started, he was conscripted into the Army. He was soon commissioned as a Second Lieutenant in the Infantry and shipped to France, arriving on his nineteenth birthday. After his Army service, he returned to University College, Oxford. He was excited to be back in school and began to make many lifelong friends, including Owen Barfield, "Wisest and best of my unofficial teachers." Lewis did well with his studies and in 1925 was awarded a Fellowship in English Language and Literature at Magdalene College, where he remained for the next decade. His friends, including J. R. R. Tolkien, Nevill Coghill, H. V. D. Dyson, and A. C. Harwood, would later become a group of men known as the Inklings, who met to discuss literary issues.

It was about this time that Lewis began to have second thoughts about God. Two of his friends and some of his favorite authors became Christians. By 1931, Lewis was converted to Christ.

After serving at Oxford for many years, Lewis was elected to the Chair of Medieval and Renaissance English at Magdalene College, Cambridge, where he was to spend the rest of his life. In 1956, C. S. Lewis was married to Joy Davidman Gresham. She had been active in the Communist Party in the United States before making a decision for Christ as a result of reading books by Lewis. Joy died in 1960 about two months after the two had returned from a visit to Greece. C. S. Lewis followed Joy three years later, and he is buried in the churchyard of his parish church.

Since his death, Lewis is more popular than ever. And not only was Lewis Christ-centered, he also avoided using the phraseology and jargon of cultural Christians. He knew his audiences, and he pointed them to the theme of themes, Christ.

T. S. ELIOT

T. S. Eliot was born Thomas Stearns Eliot in 1888 in St. Louis, Missouri. He was the son of Henry Ware Eliot and Charlotte Champe Stearns, a former teacher and social worker. He was the youngest of seven children, born when the family was prosperous and secure. Eliot was raised in Unitarianism. His paternal grandfather, William Greenleaf Eliot, graduated from Harvard Divinity School and founded the Unitarian Church in St. Louis.

Eliot was left in the care of his Irish nurse, who occasionally took him with her to Catholic Mass. This mirrors the relationship that Sigmund Freud had with his Czech Catholic nursemaid who took him to church with her. Both men were possibly influenced by these situations later in their lives.

Eliot's parents, guarding their relationship to Boston's Unitarian establishment, took the family back to the North Shore every summer. Eliot began his studies at Harvard in 1906. He attained a BA degree in comparative literature three years later and a MA in English literature the following year. He joined a number of clubs, and his introduction to the works of a number of poets and other literary efforts would result in his poetic vocation being established. He was particularly influenced by Francis Thompson's "Hound of Heaven."

In 1915, while at Oxford, Eliot was introduced to Vivienne Haigh-Wood. At once attracted, he abandoned his normal tentativeness toward women and married Vivienne. She suffered from a variety of physical and mental diseases, and the marriage steadily deteriorated. Vivienne nearly died in 1923 and Eliot, in despair, came close to a nervous breakdown. His wife was committed to the Northumberland House Mental Hospital and remained there until she died in 1947.

Eliot, influenced by reading material written by orthodox Christians, came to find his family's Unitarianism unsatisfying and turned to the Anglican Church. In 1927, he was baptized and joined the Church of England. He stated that he was a "classicist in literature, royalist in politics and Anglo-Catholic in religion." Eliot accepted a Harvard professorship for one year prior to returning to England in 1933.

In 1957, at the age of 68, Eliot married Esme Valerie Fletcher, who was 30. He knew Fletcher well, as she had earlier been his secretary. In contrast to his first marriage, this one was successful, lasting until Eliot's death of emphysema in 1965, after which Valerie dedicated her life to preserving his legacy.

T. S. Eliot produced a number of literary materials, poems, essays, and books, many of which were composed after his conversion, that reflected his new found Christian faith. He also received the Nobel Prize in Literature in Stockholm in 1948.

R. G. LeTOURNEAU

R. G. (Robert Gilmour) LeTourneau was born in 1888 in Richford, Vermont into a Christian family. At the age of fourteen, R. G. left high school; his Christian parents were concerned, but gave him their blessings. He then moved to Duluth, Minnesota, and sometime later to Portland, Oregon. There he worked as an apprentice ironmonger at the East Portland Iron Works.

LeTourneau learned the foundry and machinist trades and at the same time studied mechanics from an International Correspondence School course; however, he never completed any assignments. Later on, when asked what schools he had attended, he replied, "I'm self-educated." Traditional education was not for him.

LeTourneau later moved to San Francisco and worked for the Yerba Buena Power Plant, where he learned welding and the application of electricity. In 1909, he moved to Stockton, California and worked at a number of jobs, including miner, farm hand, and carpenter's laborer, skills which would prove valuable in later life.

Two years later, LeTourneau went to work at the Superior Garage in Stockton. There, he learned about vehicle mechanics and subsequently became half-owner of the company. In 1917, he married Evelyn Peterson. The couple would have five children. LeTourneau worked as a maintenance assistant during World War I at the Mare Island Naval Shipyard in Vallejo, California, where he improved his welding skills.

His experience in maintenance led LeTourneau to begin a business as a road-grading contractor. Combining this skill with earth-moving equipment and manufacturing, his business grew, and he incorporated in California as R. G. LeTourneau, Inc. He was involved in many earth-moving projects during the following decades. One such project was the Boulder Highway to Hoover Dam in Nevada.

LeTourneau's name was synonymous with earth-moving worldwide. His machinery represented nearly 70 percent of the earth-moving equipment used during World War II, and he was responsible for nearly 300 patents.

What is not so well know was his commitment to Christ. With his wife, he founded LeTourneau University in Longview, Texas, and was a generous philanthropist to Christian projects. It was reported that he gave 90 percent of his income to Christian causes, including a camp and conference grounds that bear his name. R.G. LeTourneau avoided high-living often associated with successful businessmen, rather spending his time at the drawing board with his engineers designing new machinery.

In March 1969, he suffered a stroke from which he never recovered, dying at the age of 80. Every time I am on the highway and see one of R. G. LeTourneau's huge earth-moving machines, I am reminded of him.

RUDOLPH BULTMANN

Rudolph Bultmann was born in 1884 at Wiefelstede, Oldenburg, Germany. He studied at Marburg, Tübingen and Berlin. Bultmann married Helene Feldmann in 1917; the couple had three daughters. He taught first at Marburg and then at Breslau and Giessen. Next, Bultmann returned to Marburg in 1921 and became professor of New Testament studies. He remained there for thirty years.

Bultmann's work and the controversies it has produced has earned him the title "godfather" of the higher-critical movement in biblical studies. Another term used by Bultmann in his approach to Scripture is the "demythologizing" process applied to the New Testament. Millard J. Erickson, in the *Concise Dictionary of Christian Theology*, offers this comment, "The theological method, found especially in the thought of Rudolf Bultmann, of interpreting the supernatural elements ("the myths") of Scripture not in a literal fashion, but in accord with the categories of existentialism." Existentialism is an interesting philosophical movement, but it should be used with care, making certain that it does not undercut the authority of Scripture.

Bultmann's approach has been driven by his sense of the unacceptability of the doctrines of New Testament Christianity to people of the twentieth century. Paul Edwards makes the following comments in *The Encyclopedia of Philosophy*, Volume 1. "Other theologians have offered various arguments to show that Bultmann's position is too extreme. They claim that he has underestimated the importance of objective history, that he has made too many concessions to twentieth century skepticism, that his existentialist concepts cannot express the full meaning, the nuances; the complex mesh of associations of the biblical writings, that the myth must be kept intact." This quote makes the same point regarding existentialism that was found in the previous quote.

Concerning miracles in the Bible, Bultmann used phenomenologist Martin Heidegger's idea of existential analysis to the New Testament. Heidegger is an example of a philosopher who used existentialism to interpret Scripture; in effect, severing the Gospel message from the first century worldview.

Trying to get a handle on Bultmann's theological system is very difficult. He merges a number of philosophical, ethical, and theological ideas from different disciplines. Scholars have trouble coming to a conclusion about what he means.

Many hold that he used his brilliance to dismantle orthodox Christianity as it had developed since the councils and creeds. Fortunately, God had raised up men like Augustine, Anselm, Aquinas and, more recently, the Hodges, Warfield, and others to help us sort out and unscramble his efforts. I leave you to ponder one of Bultmann's comments: "Now that the forces and laws of nature have been discovered, we can no longer believe in spirits, whether good or evil."

ETA LINNEMANN

Eta Linnemann was born in 1926 in Osnabruck, near Munster, in northwest Germany. She speaks about her childhood experiences in church, hearing a sermon only once a month, and receiving some teaching in religion. The way Eta describes the setting, it resembles a sort of "cultural Christianity" one can find in a number of mainline denominations currently. After her confirmation, Eta became interested in theology and attended a retreat at the suggestion of her father. The speaker was a young man who was different than the teachers she had encountered earlier in church; he dared to tell the small group that they were sinners and needed a Savior—Jesus Christ. About six or seven of them, including Eta, agreed with him and accepted Christ.

Eta's life changed, and she began to pray and read her Bible. After about half a year, she applied to study at the University in Marburg. This meant that she placed herself under the direction of Rudolf Bultmann, the famous German critical theologian. The most well-known names in higher criticism became her teachers.

She was a bright student and soon decided to attend lectures by Bultmann on 1 Corinthians. When he came to 15:1-5, Bultmann stated that Paul was wrong to speak of the resurrection of Christ as a historical fact. Eta learned quickly and soon began teaching on her own; Bultmann had made a disciple. She discarded her initial experience with the young pastor after her confirmation.

Then, Eta fell into depression due to her reliance on the Bultmannian approach to Christianity replacing her earlier trust in Christ. She fell into destructive addictions, including the abuse of alcohol. But the Holy Spirit had not given up on Eta. She began teaching a class on the miracles that are reported in the Bible. In the providence of God, there were quite a few genuine believers among the students. They were upset with her teaching and started to pray for her. Later, they told her that they thought, "Maybe even a professor is able to repent."

Eta was invited to attend prayer meetings, but she declined. However, she finally went and decided they were sound in their treatment of justification by faith. When the altar call was given, Eta said she knew it was for her. Indeed, even a professor is able to repent. Professor Eta Linnemann eventually went to Batu, Indonesia, as a missionary and taught in a Bible Institute there. She put her academic skills to good use in learning the language and translating Scripture, hymns, texts, and theology into Indonesian.

Now for a word from Eta found in her book, *Historical Criticism of the Bible: Methodology or Ideology?* "'For he spoke; and it came to be; he commanded, and it stood firm.' (Psalm 33:9) But the effectiveness manifests itself only where the Word as it stands is simply accepted in faith. That is why so many miracles happen in places where the age-old cynical 'Did God really say?' (Genesis 3:1), generated today by theological, psychological, sociological, and historical-critical skepticism has not yet penetrated. That is why persons who simply place faith in God's Word experience miracles even here in the West." Christians are enriched when theology that they are taught is drawn directly from the Word of God.

Ecumenical Christianity

The following individuals and organizations tend to promote Christian unity, though some do not. The way *Ecumenical* is used in this section refers to Christians who seek unity and understanding toward and among other faith groups.

J. EDWIN ORR

James Edwin Orr was born in 1912 in Belfast, Ireland, to William Steward and Rose Wright Orr. William was a jeweler and had United States and British citizenship, so his children did as well.

J. Edwin Orr was converted to Christianity at the age of nine, through his mother's guidance. In 1922, his father and infant sister died, and the family experienced financial difficulties. He began his education at the College of Technology, Belfast, and eventually entered and earned a degree from the University of London.

Orr's faith manifested and, in 1930, he and a friend began to hold open air evangelistic meetings in Belfast. In 1932, he was involved in a city-wide evangelistic effort, which increased his desire to lead people to Christ. Orr moved to London and began to meet with Christian leaders as he ministered in various churches. Within three years, he was involved in a number of countries, including Norway, Sweden, the Soviet Union, and Germany.

Orr sailed for Canada in 1935 and preached in Newfoundland, Ontario, at the Peoples Church in Toronto and then in Winnipeg. After that, he began an evangelistic tour of the United States, and he visited all forty-eight states in the next three months, including an appearance at Moody Church at the invitation of H. A. Ironside. The following year he held meetings at Wheaton College in Illinois.

Managing financially to get some time for himself, Orr decided to address some personal issues and asked Ivy Muriel Carol Carlson to marry him. After a brief courtship, she said yes, and they were married in 1937. At his wedding reception, Orr, not one to let a marital event cancel an opportunity to preach the Gospel, gave an evangelistic invitation, and counseled inquirers.

The couple returned to London, where Orr spoke at meetings commemorating the centennial of D. L. Moody's meetings in that city. In his spare time, Orr wrote a number of volumes describing his experiences during his travels and addressing issues relating to the Christian life. A couple years later, the Orrs traveled to Canada, where he served a time as associate pastor at the Peoples Church. He decided to further his education and began studying at Northwestern University in Chicago, where he received his MA.

When World War II began, Orr enlisted and attended chaplain's school at Harvard University. The following year, he received his Th.D. from Northern University and began an extensive tour of duty with the Air Force as a chaplain. When discharged in 1946, he picked up his education again and attended Oxford, receiving his doctorate two years later. He became a professor at Fuller Seminary's School of World Missions—a position he held until 1981.

Dr. Orr suffered from heart disease in his later years, and died the morning after presenting a lecture at a conference in 1987. Billy Graham's introduction in Orr's book *Full Surrender* states: "Dr. J. Edwin Orr, in my opinion, is one of the greatest authorities on the history of religious revivals in the Protestant world. I think God has given him one of the greatest and most unique ministries anywhere in the nation ... I know of no man who has a greater passion for worldwide revival or a greater love for the souls of men."

THE ACTON INSTITUTE

The Acton Institute for the study of Religion and Liberty is named after the great English historian Lord John Acton, who died in 1902. He is best known for his famous remark: "Power tends to corrupt, and absolute power corrupts absolutely." The Institute has been directed by his study on the relationship between liberty and morality.

It was co-founded by Fr. Robert A. Sirico, and he is currently the president. He received his Master of Divinity degree from the Catholic University of America following undergraduate study at the University of Southern California and the University of London. Fr. Sirico was also pastor of St. Mary's Catholic Church in Kalamazoo, Michigan from 2005–2012. The Acton Institute's board of advisors includes: Rabbi Daniel Lapin, author of *Toward Tradition*; Doug Bandow of Cato Institute; Fr. James Sadowsky, SJ, of Fordham University; and Fr. James Schall, SJ, of Georgetown University. Both priests are Jesuits belonging to the order known as the Society of Jesus. Marvin Olasky, editor of *World Magazine*, is a Senior Fellow. Also, John Armstrong joined the Institute as a senior adviser in 2011.

The Institute is ecumenical in the best sense of the term, and promotes a free society characterized by individual liberty and directed by religious principles. Acton is active in America and abroad, working to bring these principles to business leaders and economic knowledge to the community of faith, promoting greater understanding and economic freedom.

MORTIMER ADLER

Mortimer Jerome Adler was born in 1902 in New York City to immigrants who were non-observant Jews. Adler's father was born in Bavaria and raised in an orthodox Jewish family. When he was a child, he accompanied his mother and maternal grandmother to religious services at a Reformed Synagogue on Saturday mornings.

When he came to America, the religious patterns from his childhood persisted. In spite of Adler's father's orthodoxy, the family celebrated Christmas as well as Hanukkah, and Easter as well as Passover. Mortimer enjoyed the four holidays as it meant that he did not have to attend school. When Adler was twelve years old, the time came for him to go through the Jewish rite of passage known as bar mitzvah. He said that he did not remember the rabbis ever asking him if he believed in God.

It was through philosophy that Adler became interested in God—as an object of thought, not as an object of love and devotion. When he graduated from college at age 20, he unknowingly began his journey toward Christianity; he discovered the *Treatise on the One God* in the *Summa Theologica* by Thomas Aquinas. Adler found the intellectual brilliance and precision of that book far superior to all of the philosophical books that he had read up to that time. During the next thirty years, in addition to the *Summa*, Adler studied St. Augustine's *Confessions*, his *City of God* and his essay on Christian Doctrine, as well as St. Anselm's *Cur Deus Homo*.

Mortimer's study of Thomas Aquinas introduced him to Aristotle. While the medieval Jewish and Christian disciples of Aristotle used him as a resource, he was considered a pagan philosopher. However, this did not prevent them from using Aristotle's arguments when they attempted to prove the existence of God.

Adler had become a Thomist without becoming a Roman Catholic, but he became friendly with a number of Catholic scholars and spoke at Catholic institutions as well as secular ones. Many of his Catholic friends wondered why one who declares he is a Thomist did not become a Roman Catholic. His answer was that simply to be able to understand Thomist theology was what Aquinas called "dead faith;" others have stated this situation as knowing "about" Jesus, rather than "knowing" Jesus.

In the 1930s, Adler became a professor at the University of Chicago, where he advocated the adoption of the Classics; however, the faculty refused his request. In later years, Adler helped to found the Institute for Philosophical Research at the University of Carolina, the Aspen Institute, and the Center for the Study of Great Ideas.

After traveling to Mexico in 1984, he became ill and was in the hospital for five weeks, then at home in bed for several months. Father Robert Howell, rector of St. Chrysostom's Church in Chicago, where the Adler's attended, received a letter from the patient stating that after years of affirming God's existence philosophically, he had found himself believing in God personally and praying to him. Father Howell went to his home and baptized him a Christian on April 21, 1984. A year later, Mortimer Adler took the pulpit at St. Chrysostom's Church to give his testimony about his conversion to the congregation of which he had been a nonbelieving member for many years.

Adler believed that students should be required to take a core of classes dealing with Western philosophy, politics, and religion.

Clearly, his approach would do much to correct the secularist model that exists in too many current institutions.

THE TAIZE COMMUNITY

The Taize Community was founded in 1944 by Frere Roger, who was born in Provence, Switzerland. Also known as Brother Roger, he was baptized Roger Louis Schutz-Marsauche. Roger was born the ninth and youngest child of Karl Ulrich Schutz, a Protestant pastor from Bachs, Zurich Lowlands in Switzerland. His wife, Amelie Henriette Schutz-Marsauche, was a French Protestant from Burgundy.

Roger studied Reformed theology in Strasbourg and Lausanne, where he was involved in the Swiss Student Christian Movement. In 1940, he cycled to Taize, some 240 miles southwest of Paris. At the time the region was in unoccupied France, just beyond the zone held by German forces. For two years, Brother Roger undertook the protection of Jewish refugees before being forced to leave Taize.

Returning to Taize in 1944, he established the Community, a group of men living together in poverty and obedience. Since the late 1950s, a great number of young adults from all over the world have traveled to Taize to participate in weekly meetings of prayer and reflection. Taize brothers traveled and conducted meetings in Africa, North and South America, Asia, and Europe, spreading the message of the Community.

The community leader eschews excessive attention, avoiding the possibility of a "cult" to grow up around him. Brother Roger received the UNESOP Prize for Peace Education in 1988. He wrote many books on prayer and contemplation, asking young people to have confidence in God and be committed to their local church and to humanity. He also cooperated with Mother Teresa, with whom he shared a close friendship, on many projects.

Throughout his life, Brother Roger set for himself the task of reconciling the differing jurisdictions within the Christian Church. At a Taize event in Paris, in 1995, he spoke to more than 100,000 young people. His message addressed the need to search for truth through silence and prayer, and get in touch with the inner life. Christ had said, "Do not worry, give yourself."

Brother Roger participated in the Catholic Mass every morning at Taize and received the sacrament from Popes John Paul II and Benedict XVI, which is usually restricted to those who are in full communion with the Roman Catholic Church. As a Protestant, Brother Roger took a unique step that was unheard of since the Reformation; coming into complete communion with the Catholic Church without a "conversion," which would imply a break with his Reformed origins. It bears mentioning that members of the Taize Community were among the observers at the Vatican II Council.

However, tragedy awaited him. In 2005, at evening prayer service in Taize, a young Romanian woman, Luminita Solcan, stabbed Brother Roger several times. She was later deemed to be mentally deranged. Although he was carried from the church, he died shortly afterward.

His funeral was conducted with Horst Kohler, President of Germany and Nicolas Sarkozy, Minister of the Interior of France in attendance. In an unusual move, the funeral of this Protestant monk was presided over by a Catholic Cardinal, Walter Kasper, the president of the Vatican's Pontifical Council for Promoting Christian Unity. Brother Alois Loser, who was Brother Roger's successor prayed: "With Christ on the cross, we say to you, Father, forgive her, for she does not know what she did." Brother Roger is recognized for reaching out to all those in the Body of Christ.

AVERY CARDINAL DULLES

Avery Robert Dulles was born in 1918 in Auburn, New York to Janet Pomeroy Avery and John Foster Dulles. Avery was christened in the Presbyterian Church as Charles Avery Dulles; however, he was called Avery by his family.

Avery's family had a long and distinguished heritage in American political and religious life. His father practiced law and held a special interest in international affairs, which would lead him to become Secretary of State under President Dwight David Eisenhower. Avery's uncle, Allen Welsh Dulles, became head of the Central Intelligence Agency during the Eisenhower era.

In 1930, Avery was enrolled in the Institut Le Rosey, a prestigious boarding school in Switzerland. Two years later, he returned to the United States and entered the Choate School in Wallingford, Connecticut. After Choate, it was time to choose a college, and Avery enrolled at Harvard in 1937. At Harvard, Avery began to study Greek and scholastic philosophy in earnest. Avery felt liberated from the pragmatism, relativism, and subjectivism of modern philosophy. A year later, he became aware of Orestes A. Brownson's journey through a number of religious experiences and finally "swam the Tiber" and became a Roman Catholic in 1940.

Avery's family was disappointed to learn he had converted to Roman Catholicism. He became active as a Catholic layman in a number of activities in promoting religious and intellectual life among Catholic students in the Boston area.

In 1941, Avery Dulles enlisted in the Naval Reserves and applied for a commission as an Ensign. One year later, he was made active duty, sent to the School of Naval Intelligence, and thereafter assigned to duty in the New York City office of Naval Intelligence.

When his time in the Navy ended, Avery decided to become a

Jesuit priest. After an arduous thirteen-year process, he was ordained in the priesthood in 1956. Following four years of study at the Gregorian University in Rome, Avery received the doctorate in Sacred Theology.

Fr. Dulles served on the faculty of Woodstock College from 1960–1974 and the Catholic University of America from 1974–1988. He was a visiting professor at a large number of institutions, including Princeton Theological Seminary, Lutheran Theological Seminary in Gettysburg, Oxford, Catholic University at Leuven, and Yale University. He was the author of over 700 articles, as well as twenty-two books.

Dulles was created a cardinal in Rome by Pope John Paul II in 2001. He served in the College of Cardinals as a priest theologian for the following seven years. Because he was a cardinal, not a bishop, Dulles became an honorary, non-voting member of the United States Conference of Catholic Bishops.

Cardinal Dulles was very interested in Apologetics, which is the defense of the faith. Concerning ecumenism, Patrick W. Carey writes the following in *Avery Cardinal Dulles*. "Dulles became one of the foremost American Catholic ecumenists in the latter half of the twentieth century. Almost as soon as he returned from Rome in 1960, he became involved in ecumenical activities as a theologian seeking ways to articulate the faith for an age seeking more amicable relations and a fuller understanding of the various Christian traditions." Later in this book, we will meet Cardinal Dulles again when he is active in Evangelical and Roman Catholic projects.

In April of 2008, Pope Benedict XVI gave the ailing Cardinal Dulles a private audience during his apostolic trip to the United States. He had been suffering from the effects of polio from his youth; in addition to the loss of speech, he could not use his arms. Cardinal Avery Dulles died in December 2008 at Fordham University.

RICHARD JOHN NEUHAUS

Richard John Neuhaus was born in 1938 in Pembroke, Ontario, one of eight children of a Lutheran minister. After dropping out of high school to work in a gas station in Texas, Neuhaus graduated from Concordia Seminary in St. Louis, Missouri. He was ordained a Lutheran minister in 1960 and became pastor of St. John the Evangelist Church in Williamsburg, Brooklyn.

St. John's congregation was composed of poor blacks and Hispanics. From the pulpit, Neuhaus addressed civil rights and social concerns as well as speaking against the Vietnam War. In the late 1960s, he gained national attention when, Neuhaus founded "Clergy and Laymen Concerned About Vietnam" with Jesuit priest Daniel Berrigan and Rabbi Abraham Joshua Heschel. At this point in his career, he was a garden variety religious leftist. However, a change was coming.

The change was activated by the Roe vs. Wade decision, which was handed down in 1973. Neuhaus became a member of the growing neoconservative movement. He also advocated faith-based initiatives based on Judeo-Christian values such as abortion and later, same-sex issues. In 1990, he founded the Institute on Religion and Public Life. They published an ecumenical journal, FIRST THINGS, which has for its purpose the advancing of a religiously informed public philosophy for the ordering of society.

In that same year, Richard John Neuhaus became a Roman Catholic. A year later, he was ordained by John Cardinal O'Conner as a priest of the Archdiocese of New York. In later years, Fr. Neuhaus compared the pro-life struggle to the civil rights movement in the 1960s. He also advocated the denial of communion to Catholic politicians who supported abortion. Perhaps one of the most significant projects Fr. Neuhaus undertook was the manifesto, Evangelicals and Catholics Together, which he edited with

Charles Colson.

Perhaps the following words written by Fr. Neuhaus in *Death on a Friday Afternoon* best encompasses his theology. "When I come before the judgment throne, I will plead the promise of God in the shed blood of Jesus Christ. I will not plead any work that I have done, although I will thank God that he has enabled me to do some good ... I will not plead that I had faith for sometimes I was unsure of my faith, and in any event that would be to turn faith into a meritorious work of my own ... Whatever little growth in holiness I have experienced, whatever strength I have received from the company of the saints, whatever understanding I have attained of God and his ways—these and all other gifts received, I will bring gratefully to the throne. But in seeking entry to that heavenly Kingdom, I will ... look to Christ and Christ alone."

Fr. Richard John Neuhaus suffered from cancer for some time. He died from complications of the disease in New York at age 72. A funeral Mass was celebrated for him at the Church of the Immaculate Conception, New York City in 2009.

VERNON C. GROUNDS

Vernon Grounds was born in 1914 into a working class, nominally Lutheran family in Jersey City, New Jersey. Both his maternal and paternal grandparents were born in Germany. His maternal grandfather, Richard Heimburg, had strong beliefs and was also a lay preacher. Vernon's paternal grandmother attended a Pentecostal Church. Upon returning home one Sunday, Vernon was asked what he had learned at church and he replied, "All the people there are crazy."

Vernon had one sister, Mildred, and two brothers, John and Raymond. He was an independent lad who especially enjoyed his forays to the library. This liking apparently stuck with him, as it is reported that Grounds' personal library at Denver Seminary contained more than 19,000 books.

Vernon Grounds received a BA from Rutgers University. His BD was granted by Faith Theological Seminary and his PhD by Drew University. Wheaton College awarded him an honorary DD and Gordon College an LHD for his service as a Christian educator and leader.

For 10 years, he was pastor at the Gospel Tabernacle in Patterson, New Jersey, and he also taught at the American Seminary of the Bible and Kings College. From 1945–1951, he was dean and professor of theology at the Baptist Bible Seminary in Johnson City, New York. He joined the Denver Conservative Baptist Seminary in 1951 as dean, becoming president five years later. Retiring in 1979, he continued to teach in areas of ethics and counseling.

Dr. Grounds traveled often, preaching in hundreds of churches and lecturing in institutions nationally, as well as Europe and Latin America. He wrote five books and hundreds of scholarly articles. He regularly contributed devotional material to *Our Daily Bread* for RBC Ministries, Grand Rapids. Dr. Vernon C. Grounds died in 2010 in a Wichita nursing home at 96 years of age.

This Christian man was blessed by God with a number of different gifts, including great intellect, superb teaching abilities, and kindness and compassion as a friend. The church has indeed been blessed.

CHARLES W. COLSON

Charles Colson was born in Boston, Massachusetts in 1931, the son of Inez Ducrow Colson and Wendell Ball Colson. Colson attended Browne and Nichols School in Cambridge in 1949, and then went to Brown University, where he earned his BA with honors, in 1953. He then received his JD, with honors, from George Washington University Law School, six years later.

Colson joined the United States Marine Corps and served from

1953–1955, attaining the rank of Captain. The following year, he worked as assistant to the Assistant Secretary of the Navy. Colson's first marriage with Nancy Billings in 1953 produced three children, but ended in divorce in 1964. He married Patricia Ann Hughes the same year.

Charles Colson's political career began by serving as counsel to Republican presidential candidate Richard Nixon's Key Issues Committee in 1968. Colson himself wrote that he was "valuable to the President ... because I was willing ... to be ruthless in getting things done."

In 1971, Colson became a member of the Committee to Re-elect the President. Colson and John Ehrlichman assigned E. Howard Hunt to a Special Operation Unit, which had been organized to plug leaks in the Nixon administration. Colson was involved in a number of questionable activities during this time frame. In 1974, charges were brought against Colson for conspiring to cover up the Watergate burglary.

Then came the event that would inaugurate the next and final stage in Colson's life. As he was facing arrest, his close friend, Raytheon Company chairman of the board, Thomas L. Phillips gave Colson a copy of *Mere Christianity* by C. S. Lewis. Upon reading the book, he joined the countless thousands of people who embraced the Gospel after being introduced to Lewis' testimony. He ultimately pled guilty to obstruction of justice. In 1974, Colson received a one-to-three year sentence and fined $5,000.

Colson entered prison and was released early in 1975 because of family problems. During his time incarcerated, Colson became aware of injustices done to prisoners and problems in their rehabilitation. When Colson was released from prison, he founded Prison Fellowship in 1976, which is today the nation's largest outreach to prisoners, ex-prisoners, and their families. Ten years later, Colson was presented with the Templeton Prize for Progress in Religion, the world's largest cash gift of over one million dollars, given to the person who has done the most to advance the cause of religion.

Colson spoke out and wrote on a number of contemporary issues from an evangelical Christian perspective, including same-sex marriages; Darwinism, which he claimed opposed Christianity; and abortion, which he decried as the killing of human life. In 2009, Colson was the driving force behind the Manhattan Declaration, which called evangelical Protestants, Roman Catholics, and Orthodox Christians not to comply with rules that go against their religious consciences.

In March 2012, Colson underwent a surgical procedure to remove a blood clot on his brain after he fell ill at a conference. A month later, Colson died in the hospital from complications resulting from a brain hemorrhage.

THOMAS C. ODEN

Thomas C. Oden was born in 1931 in Altus, Oklahoma. He attended the University of Oklahoma and graduated with a BA in 1953. Three years later, he graduated magna cum laude from Southern Methodist University, Perkins School of Theology, with a BD. Oden received a MA from Yale in 1956, and four years later a PhD from Yale Graduate School under the direction of H. Richard Niebuhr. In addition, he holds a number of honorary degrees.

Oden was married to Edrita Pokorny in 1952, and the union produced three children. Dr. Oden was involved with postdoctoral studies in a number of venues, including Heidelberg University and the Ecumenical Institute in Bossey, Switzerland. Also, he studied in the Gregorian University Rome, Oxford University, Oxford Center for Mission Studies, Wycliffe Hall, back to Rome in 1997 at the Augustinianum Patristic Institute. Oden is also active in the Confessing Movement in America, particularly within the United Methodist Church.

In his book, *The Rebirth of Orthodoxy: Signs of New Life in Christianity*, Thomas Oden details what paleo-orthodoxy changes in the way progressive theologians approach their craft. Also, he gives his own personal testimony on how his life was changed by orthodoxy. "In the early 1970's, I went through what seemed to me a lonely, almost solitary pilgrimage ... which took me from obsessive spiritual faddism to stable classic Christian teaching."

Continuing, we look at what caused this turnaround. "The reversal occurred when Will Herberg, my irascible, endearing Jewish mentor and my elder colleague at Drew, held me accountable to my religious heritage. He told me straight forwardly that I would remain theologically uneducated until I had studied carefully Athanasius, Ambrose, Basil, and Cyril of Alexandria." A liberal Methodist scholar becomes an evangelical, helped by a Jewish colleague!

Among the many books and articles Dr. Oden has produced, we will mention two. He wrote an article in *First Things Journal*, April 2012, "Do Not Rashly Tear Asunder." Thomas C. Oden implores the beleaguered "faithful to stay and reform their churches." This addresses the problem that evangelicals in mainline denominations face with liberals attempting to "water down" doctrinal statements in their churches. He uses John Wesley's argument when those in the Church of England wanted to leave and begin a new denomination—the Methodist Church. It is a complicated issue; there are arguments on both sides. However, Oden presents his position well.

Secondly, among his many books, the multi-volume called, *Ancient Christian Commentary on Scripture,* is excellent; he is the general editor, with associate editor, Christopher Hall. We recognize Dr. Thomas C. Oden for following the advice of his Jewish colleague and all of his subsequent activity to renew appreciation for classic Christian orthodoxy.

EVANGELICALS AND EASTERN ORTHODOXY

A group of evangelicals had been studying Eastern Orthodoxy since 1979, and decided to become Orthodox themselves. In 1987, this entire body of the Evangelical Orthodox Church would be brought into full communion with the Orthodox Church by Metropolitan Philip Saliba, Archbishop of the Antiochian Orthodox Christian Archdiocese of North America. The Metropolitan gave the group a new name, the Antiochian Evangelical Orthodox Mission (AEOM).

In 1990, Eastern Orthodoxy received a convert with name recognition, Frank Schaeffer—who later changed his name to Franky—the son of L'Abri founders Francis and Edith Schaeffer. Before his death in 1984, the elder Schaeffer was a significant intellectual influence on conservative Christians in the United States, and his son was active with his father.

After his father's death, a change came over Franky, and he was involved in a number of scorching critiques of evangelicalism and classical Christian theology. He told an audience, "What matters is not belief... because life is not long enough to know anything." He has also criticized his new ecclesiastical home, Greek Orthodoxy. One never knows what disenchantment can occur in spite of one's resume.

We would think that people who were active participants in groups like Campus Crusade, Youth for Christ, and Young Life ministries—which are noted for their biblically based content—would suffice; however, something was missing for Orthodoxy.

One dissatisfaction that AEOM leaders have stated is that the para-church groups, which they were a part of, are missing in church history. I call your attention to the Brethren of the Common Life in the fourteenth century who promoted a high level of

Christian life and devotion. One might say that the Brethren were an early "para-church."

Although some Orthodox leaders would like to see Orthodox worship and the liturgy be in the language of the people, others want things to stay the same "to maintain ethnic identity." This admonition seems to be at cross purposes with Paul in Galatians: "There is neither Jew nor Greek, slave nor free, male nor female, for you are all one in Christ Jesus."

Because Orthodoxy is the least known of the three jurisdictions in Christendom, some of its doctrines have been misunderstood by other Christians. Roman Catholics and evangelicals share a common Augustinian framework on salvation. The Eastern Church comes to the issue from a different perspective. They approach salvation using the concept of "deification," Greek *Theosis*. The term does not imply that a human can ever have the divine essence, but that it is possible to become God-like. Deification has also been spoken of as "Christification," becoming participants in the divine nature in 2 Peter 1:4.

Indeed, Timothy Ware speaks to this topic in his book, *The Orthodox Church*. "The idea of deification must always be understood in that light of the distinction between God's essence and His energies. Union with God means union with the divine energies, not the divine essence; the Orthodox Church, while speaking of deification and union rejects all forms of pantheism." This quote shows that in spite of different terminology, both the East and the West are on the same theological page. Thus, we have many Orthodox brothers and sisters in Christ. Orthodox are indeed, orthodox on the essentials.

EVANGELICALS AND CATHOLICS TOGETHER

Protestants and Catholics have had meetings for some time. For example, the Lutheran World Federation and the Pontifical

Commission for Promoting Christian Unity have engaged in theological dialogue for a number of years. They were addressing doctrines concerning salvation, which were at issue at the Reformation. In 1999, the parties signed a document: The Joint Declaration of the Doctrine of Justification.

Evangelicals and Catholics Together (ECT) is the most ambitious ecumenical project the two groups have put together. Evangelical Charles Colson, founder of Prison Fellowship Ministries, and Fr. Richard John Neuhaus, editor at the time of FIRST THINGS Journal, were involved in the formation of this new venture. Both men had experienced spiritual change in their lives and were prepared to lead this movement. As God would have it, He took both home to be with Himself in the middle of this project—Fr. Neuhaus in 2009 and Colson in 2012.

After their departure, the project continued with a number of Protestant evangelicals and Roman Catholics joining the group. From 1994 to 2012, eight documents were developed addressing doctrines which were important to both groups. Topics included salvation, the importance of Scripture, the Blessed Virgin Mary, and a number of social and cultural issues. The project is ongoing.

ECT has not been without its critics. Those include Michael Horton, "Christians United for Reformation;" the late James Montgomery Boice; "Alliance of Confessing Evangelicals;" and the critique issuing from *"Tabletalk,"* the monthly journal of Ligonier Ministries, whose founder R. C. Sproul is well received by some Reformed evangelicals. And no surprise, David Hunt, representing the fundamentalistic spectrum, likewise responded.

In commenting on some of the reaction to the ECT project, some evangelicals who were involved stated that ECT certainly did not deal with all of the questions. They could have been avoided this problem by being more direct on some points.

Norman Geisler and Ralph MacKenzie, commenting in *Roman*

Catholics and Evangelicals: Agreements and Differences, were troubled and stated: "A serious problem is the document's equating the term 'Roman Catholics' (without a qualifier, such as 'believing' or 'traditional') and evangelicals. It would be equally inappropriate to link the terms 'Protestants' (in general, which includes non-orthodox members) and 'believing Roman Catholics'."

In addition to the problem addressed in the above quote, there are other issues. They are discussed in the aforementioned book in detail. Contents of the Declaration and its various sections are noted. Reactions from both sides—positive and negative—are mentioned followed by an evaluation. Other topics are discussed that impact relations between Roman Catholics and Protestant evangelicals. We pray that any action between the two groups is led by the Holy Spirit.

Although not a part of the ECT project, the evangelical American Tract Society issued a tract in 2003 entitled, "The Road to Heaven: According to Catholic Sources." This presentation used the New American Bible, a Catholic version, and quotes from the *Catechism of the Catholic Church.* The purpose is not to save Catholics out of their church, but within it. This tract follows the same format as Campus Crusade for Christ's "Four Spiritual Laws." Unfortunately, this new tract, which tells Roman Catholics how to get to heaven, has been discontinued.

PART SIX

The New Millennium

Contemporary Christianity

P art Six represents the last section in this volume. It includes ministries with which I have personally been involved. It also treats movements that have had an adverse impact on orthodox Christianity. Furthermore, it describes my trip to Panama to spend some time with a friend from seminary. Finally, it ends with a priest who has a unique ministry at the Vatican.

WILLIAM C. CREASY

Bill Creasy was born in 1947 in Pittsburg, Pennsylvania. Bill's father was a steelworker, and the family attended the Brighton Road Presbyterian Church in Pittsburgh. Bill had a normal childhood. He played sports, joined the Boy Scouts, and worked as a soda-jerk in the neighborhood drug store.

When the war in Vietnam began, Bill joined the United States Marine Corps, serving six years, and then began his academic career. He received his BA Degree *Summa com laude* from Arizona State University in 1974, his MA Degree from Arizona State University two years later, and his PhD in English Literature from the University of California, Los Angeles in 1982.

Dr. Creasy taught at UCLA for twenty years. His class on the

English Bible was always full. When he retired, he began teaching classes on the Bible—Genesis through Revelation, which would become the LOGOS Bible Study Ministry. The classes are held weekly in a number of churches, Roman Catholic as well as Protestant, reaching six thousand people per week. Bill's role model is the well-known evangelical Bible teacher, J. Vernon McGee, who pastored a church in Los Angeles 50 years ago. I have sat under many Bible teachers over the last sixty years and Creasy is the finest verse-by-verse expositor I have ever heard.

Norman Geisler and I were first exposed to Bill in a Los Angeles church. In our book, *Roman Catholics and Evangelicals: Agreements and Differences*, we state: "The two authors were present at St. Paul the Apostle Church for a Monday evening Bible study. We sat fascinated as Creasy taught from the Gospel of John for nearly two hours non-stop. Close to two hundred people (the majority Roman Catholics) followed along attentively, taking copious notes. Chuck Swindoll and John MacArthur would have been impressed." Bill Creasy is also an author of substance. He has produced a beautiful new translation from Latin of *The Imitation of Christ* by Thomas a Kempis. Bill Creasy is clearly a very multitalented Christian.

JOHN H. ARMSTRONG

John Armstrong was born in 1949 in Lebanon, Tennessee, the youngest of two sons of Dr. Thomas H. and Marie F. Armstrong. John's father was a dentist and editor for the Tennessee State Dental Journal. Thomas Armstrong was on the faculty of the University of Tennessee Dental School in Memphis for nearly fifteen years.

He attended Castle Heights Military Academy, where he was an R.O.T.C. cadet officer, and graduated in 1967. John studied journalism and history at the University of Alabama for two years.

John transferred to Wheaton College, where he earned the BA in history in 1971 and the MA in theology and missions two years later. John then studied at Trinity Evangelical Divinity School, Deerfield, Illinois, and Northern Baptist Seminary, Lombard, Illinois. He also earned a DMin degree at Luther Rice Seminary. John is an ordained Minister of Word and Sacrament in the Reformed Church in America. John's mother, deceased in 2008, was the primary influence in hearing God's call in his life and learning to teach the Scriptures.

John is the author of a number of books, including *The Unity Factor: One Lord, One Church, One Mission*; *Your Church is Too Small: Why Unity in Christ's Mission Is Vital to the Future of the Church*; and *Roman Catholicism: Evangelical Protestants Analyze What Unites and Divides Us*. He has also contributed material to more than two dozen volumes and has been published in a number of Christian periodicals.

John is founder and president of ACT 3, a ministry equipping leaders for unity in presenting the Gospel. He is an adjunct professor of evangelism at Wheaton College Graduate School. He joined The Acton Institute for the Study of Religion and Liberty as a senior advisor in 2011.

He and his delightful wife of over forty years, Anita, have two adult married children. Their grandchildren Gracie and Abbie and their miniature dachshund, Nero, all bring special joy to their busy lives. John is also an avid sports fan, especially of the local Chicago White Sox—his only failing.

John and I are close personal friends, being involved in ecumenism—correctly defined. This involves both of us reaching out to those believers, including Roman Catholics and Eastern Orthodox, who have unfortunately been shunned by evangelicals in the past.

John's heart is to bring Christians together as he makes known in *Your Church is too Small: While Unity in Christ's Mission is Vital to the Future of the Church.* "I am convinced that some Christians, and growing number of congregations, are experiencing something previously unknown in American church history: Catholics and Protestants are learning to interact with one another in gracious ways. They are forming friendships not possible before even within the Eastern Orthodox Church, a church very few Americans understand, similar relationships are forming, though on a vastly small scale. Thus, there are people in all three of the great Christian traditions who are actually learning how to love one another. They are finding out that what unites them is much greater than what divides them. I believe this has to be the work of God's Spirit."

DAVID E. BJORK

David E. Bjork was born in Minnesota in 1953. David and his wife Diane met when they attended the Missionary Church in Southern California during their early teens. Their parents were committed Christians, and David and Diane received Christ as their Lord and Savior. Eight months after they married, the couple moved to France, which is considered to be one of the hardest countries in the world to evangelize, to learn the language, and study the culture.

In 1979, they relocated to Normandy, in northwestern France, with their four-year-old daughter and two-year-old son, supported by the Missionary Church. Here their adventure truly begins. After obtaining an apartment, David began a Bible study with some students at a local university. When the class had studied the Gospel for several months, two of the students approached David and asked him to accompany them to their church the following Sunday. With mixed emotions, he entered the Catholic Church; he had visited cathedrals in France, but never attended Mass.

When they left the service, David told his wife, "I am never going to Mass again! I didn't feel comfortable there."

David decided to meet with the parish priest, Father Norbert, and sort out some of the things he was feeling. The priest listened graciously and then shared his testimony, and after that they spent some time in prayer. David writes that it took three and a half years for God to overcome his religious prejudices. David witnessed the vitality of Father Norbert's faith and his submission to the Spirit and the Scriptures.

In *Unfamiliar Paths: The Challenge of Recognizing the Work of Christ in Strange Clothing*, David Bjork further explains the reason he has taken his position on working with Christians from a different jurisdiction. "As I got to know Father Norbert, I began to realize that God's family extends beyond the limits of my own church denomination and reaches even into unexpected places. Perhaps Jesus was alluding to this reality when he said: 'I have other sheep that are not of this sheep pen. I must bring them also.' If we were to come together, it would have to be an agreement over evangelical truths, which are basic to salvation and on our common life in Christ."

Dr. David E. Bjork has been involved in mission activities in France for over three decades since 1979. He has been led to work in Catholic churches that are ministered by pastors like Father Norbert. This approach is not common among many missionary organizations. It seems to be fruitful in France. David and Diane have recently accepted a call to work in French-speaking Africa in Cameroon. Definitely, David is a gifted man who has broken new ground in modern missiology.

THE ALPHA COURSE

Charles Marnham was bent on devising a means for presenting the basic doctrines of Christianity to new believers. As a result, he became a pastor at Holy Trinity, a vibrant Anglican church in Brampton, London. Holy Trinity is a well-attended Anglican Church in the heart of the city.

Marnham devised the Alpha Course in 1977, which asks questions like "Who is Jesus?" and "Why do I pray?" When Charles moved on, new leaders stepped in and made their own changes.

In 1990, Nicky Gumbel took over Alpha, which had become a central part of the church's life. Gumbel had practiced law for six years before being ordained in the Church of England. In 1996, the Bishop of London appointed him as an "Alpha Chaplain." With time, Nicky came to realize that this program could be used to evangelize non-believers, as well as instruct believers. Hence, he worked to make the presentations as friendly and informal as possible, while avoiding the "dumbing-down" of the essentials of the Christian faith.

The Alpha Course is a fifteen session practical introduction to the Christian faith. The courses address topics that answer questions such as: Who is Jesus?; Why did He die?; Why should I read the Bible?; How can I resist evil?; and What are other essentials of Christianity? One problematic point is the issue which comes up when Holy Spirit and His role is covered. Believers who are neither Pentecostal nor Charismatic can be uncomfortable with leaders who often pray for people to receive the gift of tongues. These people who may be uncomfortable are told that they can skip the weekend session where this occurs, if they choose.

Thousands of people around the world have taken part in the Alpha Courses. It is truly inter-denominational. There is even an Alpha for Catholics, which has been accepted by the Catholic Church. The program has been praised by a large number of Christian leaders, including Dr. George Carey, Former Archbishop of Canterbury; J. I. Packer, Professor of Theology, Regent College; Os Guinness, Trinity Forum; Bill Hybels, Willow Creek

Community Church; Bill Bright, Campus Crusade for Christ; and Rick Warren, Saddleback Church, to name a few.

THE ALLIES FOR FAITH AND RENEWAL

The Allies for Faith and Renewal were Christians of different traditions who, facing many of the same challenges in contemporary society, organized to work together. These included evangelicals such as Donald Bloesch, professor of theology at Dubuque Theological Seminary, Iowa; Harold O.J. Brown, professor of Theology at Trinity Evangelical Divinity School in Deerfield, Illinois; and Charles Colson, president of Prison Fellowship International.

Catholic participants involved were William Bentley Ball, an attorney who had been the lead counsel in nineteen cases before the United States Supreme Court, and Stephen B. Clark and Ralph Martin, both involved with the Sword of the Spirit, an international ecumenical community. Also, Michael Scanlan, T.O.R., president of Franciscan University of Steubenville, and Paul Vitz, professor of psychology at New York University, were involved.

Not to be left out were Eastern Orthodox participants such as Fr. Stanley Harakas, professor of ethics at Holy Cross Greek Orthodox School of Theology, and Theodore Stylianopoulos, professor at Holy Cross Greek Orthodox School of Theology.

These Christian leaders from different theological jurisdictions are not attempting to resolve doctrinal differences between confessional traditions. These Catholics, Protestants, and Orthodox stand together against the loss of historic, biblical, Trinitarian teaching throughout the churches and against social pressures that shape Christians' lives according to non-Christian norms.

Allies for Faith and Renewal conferences were held annually by the Center for Pastoral Review, and all orthodox Christians are welcome to attend. Conferences held in the 1980s included "Christianity Confronts Modernity," "Summons to Faith and Renewal,"

"Christianity in Conflict," and "Christian Allies in a Secular Age."

A different group produced *In Search of a National Morality: A Manifesto for Evangelicals and Catholics*, edited by William Bentley Ball, a book that includes some of the same participants who were involved with the Allies for Faith and Renewal conferences.

It contains chapters dealing with topics addressed by Evangelical and Catholic scholars such as secularization, morality, witness-bearing, human life, family, education, higher education, government, and rights. This book is a very comprehensive treatment, showing the areas that Evangelicals and Roman Catholics have interests in common. The volume's importance is highlighted by the fact that Baker and Ignatius decided to publish it simultaneously.

HOMOSEXUALITY AND CHRISTIANITY

Homosexual activity has a long history, to which there has been a number of cultural and moral responses. We will concern ourselves with how this movement impacts the entire Body of Christ today and ways to deal with it. Unfortunately, homosexuality has gathered wide support from heterosexual Americans who agree with its claims on the basis of social justice and tolerance. Evangelicals within Protestant mainline denominations have realized the danger that this movement poses for Christianity.

Homosexual activity is clearly condemned in the Old Testament by violating the integrity of creation (Genesis 2:23-25). In the New Testament, although Jesus never directly addresses homosexuality, He is clear with respect to marriage: heterosexual unions are God's original plan for men and women (Mark 10:1-9). In Romans 1:18-32, Paul places homosexuality in an explicitly theological context. Note that lesbianism is also condemned; both men and women who do these things are indulging in idolatry.

There are two Roman Catholic organizations at cross-purposes in this debate. Of course, the *Catechism of the Catholic Church* (CCC) concludes about this condition: "Basing itself on Sacred Scripture, which presents homosexual acts as acts of grave depravity, tradition has always declared that 'homosexual acts are intrinsically disordered.' They are contrary to natural law."

First, "Dignity USA" began in San Diego in 1969 under the leadership of Fr. Patrick Nidorf. The organization "works for respect and justice for all gay, lesbian, bisexual and transgender (LGBT) persons in the Catholic Church and the world through education, advocacy and support." Further, "As LGBT Catholics, we believe that we can express our sexuality in a loving, life-affirming manner that is in keeping with Christ's teaching." The group advocates a change in the Catholic Church's teaching on homosexuality. However, the *CCC* states, "... they do not proceed from a genuine affective and sexual complementary. Under no circumstances can they be approved."

The Catholic Church's only position in regard to support for individuals experiencing same-sex attraction is "courage to remain chaste." Consequently, "Courage"—the second organization—was founded in 1980 by Terence Cardinal Cooke, Archbishop of New York. The Catholic Church also reached out to family members of homosexuals by counseling them on how they might help in this difficult situation. The CCC makes the distinction between homosexual orientation and homosexual activity; the latter is sinful, the former is not.

EMMAUS MINISTRIES

The ministry Emmaus was founded by John Green, a deacon of the Archdiocese of Chicago. John has been reaching out to men involved in prostitution on the streets of Chicago for over twenty years.

In the foreword of *Street Walking With Jesus*, which details

John's ministry, Francis Cardinal George writes: "I am proud that John Green is a deacon of the Archdiocese of Chicago. I am grateful that he has written this book. I am confident that it will give all who read it and take it to heart new insight and more courage in our common quest to introduce to Christ male prostitutes and all others he died to save."

John Green had worked in New York City, Guatemala City, and Mexico City ministering to adult homeless and runaway youth. John returned to Chicago to complete his BA at Wheaton College in Christian Education. John completed an MA in Educational Ministries from Wheaton Graduate School, and he is a frequent speaker on issues relating to male prostitution and urban ministries. John and his wife Carolyn attend St. Thomas of Canterbury Catholic Church, where he is a Permanent Deacon. I think it is safe to say that John Green is one of the few Permanent Deacons in the Roman Catholic Church with not one, but two degrees from that bastion of evangelical higher education, Wheaton College. John began working with young homeless men, most of who were involved in prostitution. Emmaus Ministries was officially incorporated as a non-profit ministry in 1990. Besides directing efforts to help sexually exploited men to change their lives, Emmaus partners with Wheaton College to provide a semester-long residence program for college students in training for future ministry within this culture.

Emmaus is prayerfully supported by 12 foundations, 30 Protestant and Catholic churches, and 600 individuals. The ministry receives no government funds. One cannot envision a more difficult task than the one God has called on John to perform.

THE SAN DIEGO CHRISTIAN FORUM

In the early twentieth century, there were no conferences in Southern California involving Eastern Orthodox, Roman Catholic, and evangelical scholars. In October 2000, The San Diego Christian Forum was instituted to address cultural and theological issues impacting the community. The Mission Statement was as follows:

"PURPOSE: The San Diego Christian Forum is a ministry, which will address issues impacting the local Body of Christ and the wider community as well. The Forum will build up and under gird individual Christians and congregations, while also presenting the Gospel to the unchurched.

"TACTICS: The Forum will facilitate speakers, conferences and events in which dynamic scholars impact church and society. A speakers' bureau will be provided to the churches. While the form of the message will be irenic and inclusive, the content will be orthodox Christianity—what C.S. Lewis termed *Mere Christianity*.

"GOALS: The Forum will invite the local churches to suggest problems and issues they wish addressed. Our ultimate goal is not to replace existing churches or ministries, but to encourage, enlighten, and strengthen them by presenting the Christian life/worldview to all. Indeed, 'But in your hearts set apart Christ as Lord. Always be prepared to give an answer to everyone who asks you to give the reason for the hope that you have. But do this with gentleness and respect."

The Forum produced a number of seminars addressing the following topics: basic Christian doctrines, social action, Christians working with Jews, and Messianic Judaism. Additional issues were art in the Bible, women in the Church, and the Gospel in the Middle East. The response to the Forum conferences was positive as the attendees appreciated the variety of material presented by the speakers.

CHRIS CASTALDO

The later part of the twentieth century has seen thousands of Catholics converting to Protestant evangelicalism. At least, since Vatican II, there are Roman Catholic leaders, both lay and clergy, who view this departure as an indication of a lack of emphasis on evangelism in Catholic catechesis. One of the reasons for holding Vatican Council II was to inspire Catholics to be evangelists. But this presupposed that they themselves were believers; this was true of only a few. For conversion, a personal encounter must occur.

Chris Castaldo fit this category as do many people in the Protestant mainline churches. He was raised in an Italian Roman Catholic family in St. Joseph's Parish on Long Island, New York; his Catholicism was more cultural than spiritual.

Chris' father became ill, and Chris left his job to manage the family business. A new employee named Jan showed up. He soon learned that she was a born-again Christian. Each day she prepared a Bible verse for Chris. He accepted an invitation to join her at church. After 40 minutes of singing hymns, the senior pastor showed up looking like a combination of Billy Graham and Al Pacino. The text of the sermon was Jesus expounding on John 15:5-6: "I am the vine; you are the branches. If a man remains in me and I in him, he will bear much fruit; apart from me you can do nothing." Because of this message, Chris's spiritual search was over, and his journey had just begun.

Chris Castaldo earned degrees from Moody Bible Institute and Gordon-Conwell Theological Seminary, and he is currently pursuing a PhD at London School of Theology under the direction of Anthony N. S. Lane. Chris lives outside of Chicago with his wife Angela and their four children. He now serves as Director of the Ministry of Gospel Renewal for the Billy Graham Center at

Wheaton College. Chris Castaldo has interviewed hundreds of people, Roman Catholics as well as evangelicals, practicing Catholics as well as former Catholics, to ascertain beliefs and understandings about the other group.

In his book, *Holy Ground*, Chris describes his journey as a practicing Catholic working with bishops and priests before becoming an Evangelical pastor at College Church in Wheaton. The subtitle may cause some confusion: *Walking With Jesus as a Former Catholic*. This might indicate to some readers that Chris is saying that it is not possible to be a Christian if one is a Catholic; this is not what Chris is implying. Throughout the book, he makes clear that he knows many Catholics, including laity, priests, and bishops, who are born again. The book is dedicated to helping Catholic Christians to evangelize cultural Catholics to become genuine believers—saving Catholics in the Church, not telling them to leave. In addition, Chris discusses a number of issues such as identifying different kinds of Catholics: "Traditional" is the Vatican I variety, "Evangelical" is Vatican II, and "Cultural" is the nominal or "cafeteria" Catholic.

Holy Ground is a balanced work including theological positions and church history, which will be of interest to Catholics and Evangelicals. It is highly recommended.

ISLAM IN THE TWENTY-FIRST CENTURY

We addressed Islam when it arose in the sixth century. Currently, however, there are new developments that deserve attention. There are calls from Muslims of the progressive persuasion for a reinterpretation of their religion to bring it into conformity with the present secular culture. However, there is hardly agreement on what this reinterpretation of faith might resemble.

First, we will look at progressive Muslims. In his new book: *Progressive Muslims: On Justice, Gender and Pluralism*, it is the goal of

Omid Safi, that a new generation of Muslims will create a grassroots movement which will not clash with contemporary culture. It goes without saying that the majority of non-Islamists would find this preferable to more 9/11 terrorist attacks on the home front and suicide bombers in the Middle East. We shall see.

Strange as it may seem, given that homosexuality is detested in Islam, there is also a group of Muslims who are gay. It has never been easy being gay in this country, but to step out of the closet and announce one's sexual proclivities causes a double dose of unease. But some gay, lesbian, bisexual, and transgendered Muslims are finding a home in Al-Fatiha, a Washington, DC organization which was founded in 1998. Al-Fatiha provides support for those who want to reconcile their sexual preference with Islam. It is said that there are but three Islamic clergymen worldwide known to be openly gay.

Secondly, we will cover the issue of Muslims who have become Christian. The San Diego Union Tribune had a most interesting story covering this phenomenon. Mosab Hassan Yousef, the eldest son of a prominent Palestinian Islamist who was a Hamas leader on the West Bank, authored a book recounting his conversion to Christianity entitled, *Son of Hamas: A Gripping Account of Terror, Betrayal, Political Intrigue and Unthinkable Choices.*

Yousef became disillusioned with Hamas, in which he had worked with his father, while he was imprisoned in Israel. He had seen how Hamas prisoners treated their fellow Hamas inmates. When released from prison in Israel, Yousef went to work for the Israeli Intelligence Agency, Shin Bet, as a way to curtail violence on both sides. He became a Christian and was secretly baptized in 2005 at the beach near Tel Aviv.

Trying to work both sides became very dangerous for Yousef, and having met Christian missionaries who were visiting Israel, told them of his desire to come to the United States. Yousef ended up in San Diego and contacted Pastor Matt Smith of Barabbas Road Church in La Jolla. They became close friends. He was notified that because of his former ties with Hamas, he had to go to trial and face deportation. Yousef wanted to go public with his story, but he feared retaliation by Islamic terrorists and rejection by his family.

Yousef's story and the possibility of being deported reached Israel and Gonen Ben-Itzhak, a retired Shin Bet agent who had been Yousef's minder when he served in Israel. At his own expense, Itzhak came to San Diego from Israel to act as a sworn witness to validate Yousef's activity as a double agent. Gonen stated, "I came to say that Yousef's actions saved many lives on both sides of the conflict." The deportation trial lasted only fifteen minutes when the government dropped the charges. Yousef said he would continue offering assistance to United States investigators and speak out against terrorism. He also planned to seek U.S. citizenship and apply to Harvard University to pursue a Master's Degree in Middle Eastern studies.

THE AMERICAN ISLAMIC FORUM FOR DEMOCRACY

M. Zuhdi Jasser, M.D. is Founder and President of the American Islamic Forum for Democracy (AIFD). A practicing Muslim, Dr. Jasser founded AIFD after the 9/11 attacks on the United States to provide an American Muslim organization working for the preservation of our Constitution and the separation of mosque and state. He is a first generation American Muslim whose family fled the Baath regime of Syria in the 1960s for freedom in America.

Dr. Jasser earned his medical degree on a U. S. Navy scholarship at the Medical College of Wisconsin in 1992. He spent 11 years as a medical officer in the Navy; his tours of duty included Medical Department Head aboard the USS EL PASO, while deployed to Somalia during Operation Restore Hope; Chief Resident at National Naval Medical Center Bethesda; and staff Internist for the Office of the Attending Physician to the U. S. Congress. Currently in private practice in Phoenix, Arizona, he is specializing in internal medicine and nuclear cardiology.

AIFD's mission originates from a love for America and its founding principles, along with a love of God and his personal faith in Islam. While sharia means God's law for Muslims, the reality is that whenever it is applied by government, it becomes manmade law. The reality is that governmental enforced sharia will always prove to be an undemocratic tool for theocracy or quasi-theocracy. AIFD seeks to counter the ideas of Islamic groups like the Muslim Brotherhood and its network with our own Jeffersonian Muslim ideas of the separation of mosque and state.

Dr. Jasser briefs members of the House and Senate Congressional anti-terror caucuses on the threat of Political Islam. He also treats the extent of radicalization among the American Muslim communities. He has spoken at hundreds of national and international events, including universities and places of worship. Information about AIFD may be accessed at the following website: www.aifdemocracy.org/about/.

CARLI JELENSZKY

I first met Carli Jelenszky while attending Bethel Seminary. The school's student body was made up of almost 50 percent Hispanics, Asians, and others from underdeveloped countries. Their religious backgrounds were Roman Catholicism and Protestantism, with some Buddhism and other religions sprinkled in.

I am a Presbyterian, and because of my understanding of church history am not Catholic-hostile, but Catholic-friendly. This did not set well with my fellow students who were raised Catholic. I attempted to convince them that if they had lived before the Reformation and were Christian, they would have had two choices—live in the East and be Orthodox, or in the West and be Roman Catholic.

At first, I had little success, but finally I convinced some of the former Catholics that the correct approach is to save Catholics within their church, not try and convince them that they must leave Catholicism in order to be truly converted. This would be crucial when Carli graduated and returned to Panama to begin his ministry.

Carli's father, Carlos Jelenszky, a jeweler, had lived in Cuba with his wife and several children. Shortly after Fidel Castro became the new leader in Cuba, they decided to leave the country. They arrived in Panama in 1961 and soon established the nation's most prominent jewelry business. Carli was the oldest son and helped his father run the business.

I contacted the editor at Christianity Today magazine and suggested they do a story on Carli's ministry in Panama, and they agreed. Carli's conversion was described by James A. Beverley in his article, "Gospel Gem" in *Christianity Today* magazine, February 2004. "Jelenszky's journey with Christ began on September 12, 1986, because of misplaced hopes about a drug deal. The previous day he had met Jack Smith at a party. Noting Jelenszky's excessive drinking, Smith asked if he would like to have the same high with no side effects. Jelenszky agreed to meet him the next day in Smith's hotel room. He had no idea the presumed drug dealer was a missionary ... Smith shared the gospel, and after 20 minutes Jelenszky knelt to receive Jesus into his heart. He notes, looking back, that he was ripe for conversion." Things improved for Carli immediately; his marriage became more fulfilling and his relationship with his family members improved. He became more concerned about moral issues in dealing with customers.

As to proclaiming the need for a personal relationship with

Christ for Catholics, Beverley's article continues. "'After my conversion, I was too negative about the Catholic church—probably early on I believed everyone should leave the church,' he says ... Jelenszky began to adopt a more positive approach to Protestant-Catholic relationships while at Bethel West ..." When we both graduated from Bethel West, Carli went east to earn his MDiv and then returned to Panama.

We lost touch with each other; when we finally reconnected, I received bad news. Carli had contracted pancreatic cancer. The disease had metastasized throughout the lymphatic system. I was blessed to spend two weeks in Panama with Carli, where I visited his jewelry business and attended Bible study at his condominium overlooking Panama Bay. I also watched him receive chemotherapy.

I saw first-hand the result of his testimony and the impact on the people that he influenced with his biblical teaching. To see Carli so sick, and yet so cheerful and filled with the love of Jesus was one of the most incredible spiritual experiences of my life. It took me back to our time in seminary when we had so many fruitful discussions. After I returned home, we learned that Carli went home to be with the Lord whom he loved so much on July 2, 2004. He had two funeral services, one at the evangelical church which he had attended and the other at the Roman Catholic cathedral in Panama City. Carli prepared a statement to be read at the services, which testified to his commitment to Christ and was at rest with the eventuality of his death. His final message was a prayer "that each one of his family and friends would have the same personal relationship with God."

When I go to experience "the beatific vision," I will find Carli and tell him how much I valued his friendship.

RANIERO CANTALAMESSA

Raniero Cantalamessa was born in Ascoli Piceno, Italy in 1934. He states that his "journey with the Lord began very early in [his] life." When he was twelve years old, after the war, he was attending a Capuchin College, but had not at that time decided what to do with his life. During a retreat, Raniero heard about the love of God for the first time. At that time, he determined to become a Franciscan priest to serve the Lord full-time. He began his spiritual formation earning a doctorate in divinity and classical literature. Fr. Raniero was ordained a priest in 1958.

He became Professor of History and Ancient Christianity and Director of the Department of Religious Sciences at the Catholic University of Milan. In 1979, he resigned his teaching position, feeling a call to become a full-time preacher of the Gospel. A year later, he was appointed by Pope John Paul II, Preacher to the Papal Household, a position he still holds extended by Pope Benedict XVI. His duties include preaching a weekly sermon in Advent and Lent in the presence of the Pope, the Cardinals, bishops and prelates of the Roman Curia.

What is unique about this academic cleric with advanced degrees in theology, history, and philosophy, is his encounter with the charismatic renewal movement. When he first heard about it, in 1975, Fr. Cantalamessa thought it was a cult. In 1977, he accepted a ticket to attend a large ecumenical charismatic rally in Kansas City. The event was attended by 40,000 people, equally divided between 20,000 Catholics and the rest from other Christian denominations. This huge group sobbed out of repentance over the divisions in the Body of Christ.

Then Fr. Cantalamessa attended a prayer meeting in a house in New Jersey. The theme of the retreat was the Trinity. At this time he had a vision of himself driving a chariot, struggling to get control; Jesus then climbed on-board and asked him, "Do you want to give me the reins of your life?" Fr. Cantalamessa finally said yes and received the baptism of the Holy Spirit.

When he returned to Italy, one person said, "What a miracle! We have sent to America Saul, and they have sent back Paul." Where before he was dedicated to scientific research and quite solemn and reserved, now he always has a smile on his face; it is as he says the Christian life lived in the Spirit. Fr. Raniero has spoken often at Holy Trinity Brampton Church, which is near London.

Finally, in Paul M. Miller's book, *Evangelical Mission in Cooperation with Catholics,* he writes about what Fr. Cantalamessa said at a three-day conference held in the Czech Republic in April 2008. "From the main platform, Fr. Cantalamessa urged the necessity of Catholics to change the way of communicating their faith … Catholics were weak at the point of initial evangelization … 'We tell people all that they most do, but Christian faith does not start by telling people what they must do but rather by telling them what God has done for them.'" From an evangelical prospective, that statement could not be improved upon.

Conclusion

We have taken the reader on a long journey over two thousand years of church history. Beginning with Pentecost in Acts 2:1, then the Early Church, the Middle Ages, the Reformation and Counter-Reformation, the seventeenth through the nineteenth centuries, and finally, the twentieth century to the present.

Persons, events, and movements were addressed which we thought had been under reported on in some history texts. Our volume, while historically accurate, is meant to be of interest to the average Christian lay-person who worships in Orthodox, Roman Catholic, and Protestant congregations.

We have presented much new information while involved in researching the many occurrences and events in church history. I was surprised to learn of the important role that Wesleyan theology had in shaping doctrine and the formation of new denominations in England and later in North America. However, I was pleased to note that when the Restoration Movement began in America in the early 1800s, while Wesleyans were first on the scene, the movement really took shape when the Presbyterians showed up. The church has seen some encouraging changes during the twentieth century and beyond.

THE NEXT CHRISTENDOM

There is no dispute that Christianity is the largest religion on Earth. It is flourishing in Africa, Asia, and Latin America. This is the result of Christian missionary activity worldwide. Philip Jenkins in *The Next Christendom* observes: "If we want to visualize a 'typical' contemporary Christian, we should think of a woman living in a village in Nigeria or in a Brazilian favela. As Kenya scholar John Mbiti has observed, 'The centers of the church's universality [are] no longer in Geneva, Rome, Athens, Paris, London, New York, but Kinshasa, Buenos Aires, Addis Ababa and Manila.'" This comment indicates the spread of the Gospel that did not occur in the West.

One country that clearly reflects this shift is China. Some authorities predict that shortly, one-third of its population could be Christian, making it one of the largest Christian nations in the world. Former Beijing Bureau Chief for *Time Magazine*, David Aikman, has written a volume that addresses this situation.

In *Jesus in Beijing,* Aikman makes the following observation: "In effect, the number of Christian believers in China, both Catholic and Protestant, may be closer to 80 million than the official combined Catholic-Protestant figure of 21 million. But the reality is simply that no one knows for sure." Aikman has commented elsewhere that China may become the largest Christian nation in the world.

Chinese Christians are everywhere—in the government, the armed forces, and as entrepreneurs. One of the richest men in the country is Zhang Jian, age 38, the CEO of Broad Air Conditioners, who has been a Christian for several years. He wants to link up with other Christian businessmen. This book is a "must-read" for those who are looking for information on the topic.

MISSIONARIES TO THE UNITED STATES

Thaddeus Rockwell Barnum was an Episcopal priest for many years. He was involved with a number of fellow clergy who asked for Anglican leaders in Africa and Asia to come to America and address the heresy that has arisen in the Episcopal Church in this country. The call was answered by two clerics from Rwanda,

Bishop John Rucyahana and Archbishop Emmanuel Kolini, who linked the political genocide in their country to the spiritual genocide in America.

In 2000, Bishop Rucyahana, among others, voted to form a movement named the "Anglican Mission in America" (AMIA). Thaddeus Rockwell Barnum, in his book, *Never Silent*, offers the following. "The AMIA soon had several churches across the country in places like North Carolina, Chicago, Denver, Little Rock, and Atlanta. I have several personal friends who were Episcopal priests who have made, or will shortly make, the move to the AMIA."

Many African pastors and leaders coming to speak in churches in the United States thank us for taking the Gospel to their countries many years ago. Some have said that now they are returning the favor.

CATHOLICS AND EVANGELICALS IN DIALOGUE

Are Roman Catholics and evangelicals co-belligerents, competitors, or fratricidal brethren? Since the Reformation split the Western Church in the sixteenth century, both groups have considered each other suspect.

A drastic change occurred at Vatican II. Protestants were now called "separated Brethren;" a person could be a member of the Church in a certain sense without being members of the institution. Catholics and evangelicals share the same views on issues like abortion, euthanasia, homosexuality, marriage, and the impact of secularism in the culture. Catholics were also encouraged to join evangelicals to pray and study the Scriptures. We have covered these issues and noted the activities between the two groups. I now want to provide some personal background material.

A PERSONAL STORY

I was born in Detroit, Michigan in 1932. How did I, a committed evangelical Christian, come to believe Protestants and Catholics should cooperate when possible? My mother was born and raised in a small farming community near Paris, France. As a young woman, she obtained a position as traveling companion for a wealthy American woman. Soon after arriving in the United States, she met my father and subsequently married.

My father was a practicing Freemason, and he was not enthusiastic about his son being brought up in Roman Catholicism, my mother's religious tradition. Therefore, she and I attended an independent Baptist church in our neighborhood. To the best of my recollection, my father never accompanied us, perhaps feeling that his participation at the Masonic Lodge satisfied his religious obligations.

However, when Lent and Advent came around, the spiritual formation that my mother had experienced as a child returned and I would accompany her to the nearest Catholic church. There I was exposed to a liturgical service, which differed greatly from the simple Bible teaching and preaching of the church we regularly attended. Also, the profusion of wood, the vaulted ceilings, the surrounding statuary, the hundreds of flickering candles—not to mention the presence of incense—contrasted with the austere nature of our normal church, and it caught my attention.

At this time, I was not old enough to realize the considerable tension that existed between Catholics and Protestants. Sometime later, I would realize the dynamics at work between the two groups. At this point, I viewed Catholics and Protestants as reflecting different, but not necessarily hostile, perspectives concerning Christianity. These early experiences would be important in the forming of views relating to the possibility of interaction between these two Christian communities.

In January 1953, I met a man my age that would impact my life in a significant way—Donald Moore. Don and I were both married, new parents, and had a number of common interests—not the least of which was sports. My new friend was a committed evangelical Christian who was very "upfront" about his faith. In spite of my church experiences in my youth, I had become quite pagan and took great delight in attempting to de-legitimatize his evangelistic efforts. Don was patient, and when I would raise objections to the Christian faith with which he was unfamiliar, he would research the issue and get back to me. The faith that Don and his wife Sue exhibited had real impact in their daily lives. I finally embraced the Gospel and received Jesus into my life. This volume is dedicated to Don and Sue Moore.

Due to the positive exposure of my youth, I had no latent anti-Catholicism to deal with and therefore read Roman Catholic as well as Protestant sources. I was evangelical in my theology and still am, but I soon realized that—as distasteful the notion is to some evangelicals—prior to the Reformation, if we were Christians, we would have been members of the Catholic Church—unless, of course, we lived in the East and then we would have been Orthodox.

At this time, I met Norman Geisler, who attended the same church as I did. We became friends and shared many of the same views on Catholicism, so we began to meet with Catholics including priests. We discussed—sometimes rather vigorously—the similarities and differences between our two faiths. These meetings were quite rare in those days given the hostility between Catholics and Protestants.

Anti-Catholicism in those days was fueled by two books; the first was *American Freedom and Catholic Power* by Paul Blanshard.

He claimed that the Vatican had sinister designs on our freedoms and religious liberty. He was later recognized as a secular humanist who detested not only Catholicism, but Christianity in general. The second was *Roman Catholicism* by Loraine Boettner. This work was considered the major text on the subject; however, it contains a number of errors—both historical fact and theology—and is a poor source for critiquing Roman Catholicism.

Concerning Eastern Orthodoxy, I taught in the Odessa Theological Seminary, Ukraine in 1997. I attended the Orthodox Cathedral, where the liturgy was the celebration of the circumcision of Jesus. The Metropolitan, known as an Archbishop in the West, arrived with great fanfare and officiated at the service. The sights, the smells, and the a cappella singing were overwhelming. It was an impressing event.

During a break in my teaching in Odessa, I traveled overnight to Kiev with a student as my guide. Founded more than 1,500 years ago, Kiev is one of the oldest and historically richest cities in Eastern Europe. It is considered the birthplace of Slavic civilization. We had a wonderful time visiting the evangelical Christian seminary there as well as a number of Orthodox churches and Cathedrals.

I sense that the Holy Spirit is providing evangelical Protestants, Roman Catholics, and Orthodox Christians with a unique opportunity to evangelize the culture. Concerning this task, evangelical theologian Donald Bloesch offers the following. "We are called to build bridges where they may be built and allow the cleavage to remain where it cannot be overcome." Yes, I am pleased we have come to this juncture in Eastern Orthodox, Roman Catholic, and evangelical Protestant affairs.

Bibliography

Aikman, David. *Jesus in Beijing: How Christianity is Transforming China and Changing the Global Balance of Power.* Washington, DC: Regnery Publishing Inc., 2003.

Ali, Daniel, and Robert Spencer. *Inside Islam: A Guide for Catholics.* West Chester, PA: Ascension Press, 2003.

Armstrong, John. *Your Church is Too Small: Why Unity in Christ's Mission is Vital to the Mission of the Church.* Grand Rapids: Zondervan, 2010.

Baldwin, Ethel May, and David V. Benson. *Henrietta Mears and How She Did It.* Glendale, CA: Regal Books, 1966.

Ball, William Bentley, Ed. *In Search of a National Morality: A Manifesto for Evangelicals and Catholics.* Grand Rapids: Baker Books and San Francisco: Ignatius Press, 1992.

Balmer, Randall. *Encyclopedia of Evangelicalism.* Louisville: Westminster John Knox Press, 2002.

Barker, Kenneth, gen. ed. *The NIV Study Bible.* Grand Rapids: Zondervan, 1985.

Barnum, Thaddeus Rockwell. *Never Silent.* Colorado Springs: Eleison Publishing, 2008.

Beverly, James A. "Gospel Gem." *Christianity Today,* February 2004.

Bjork, David E. *Unfamiliar Paths: The Challenge of Recognizing the Work of Christ in Strange Clothing.* Pasadena, CA: William Carey Library, 1997.

Blanshard, Paul. *American Freedom and Catholic Power.* Boston: Beacon Press, 1958.

Bloesch, Donald G. *Essentials of Evangelical Theology, Vol. 1.* San Francisco: Harper & Row, 1978.

_____. *Spirituality Old and New,* Appendix D, "Therese of Lisieux: An Evangelical Saint?" Downers Grove: IVPress Academic, 2007.

Boettner, Loraine. *Roman Catholicism.* Philadelphia: Presbyterian and Reformed, 1962.

Bray, Gerald. *Creeds, Councils & Christ.* Downers Grove: IVPress, 1984.

Benner, David G, Ed. *Baker Encyclopedia of Psychology.* Grand Rapids: Baker Book House, 1985.

Brightman, F. E. *The Private Devotions of Lancelot Andrewes.* Gloucester, MA: Peter Smith, 1978.

Bromiley, Geoffrey W., Gen. Ed. *The International Standard Bible Encyclopedia.* Grand Rapids: Eerdmans, 1979.

Brown, Colin. *Christianity and Western Thought, Vol. 1.* Downers Grove, IL: IVPress, 1990.

Bruce, F. F. *The New International Commentary on The New Testament: The Book of The Acts.* Grand Rapids: Wm. B. Eerdmans Publishing Co., 1951.

_____. *The Message of the New Testament.* Grand Rapids: Eerdmans, 1972.

_____. *The New Testament Documents: Are They Reliable?* Grand Rapids: Eerdmans, 1988.

Burgess, Stanley M., and Gary B. McGee, Eds. *Dictionary of Pentecostal and Charismatic Movements.* Grand Rapids: Zondervan, 1996.

Cantalamessa, Raniero. *Come Creator Spirit: Meditations on the Veni Creator.* Collegeville, MN: The Liturgical Press, 2003.

Carey, Patrick W. *Avery Cardinal Dulles.* New York: Paulist Press, 2010.

Castaldo, Chris. *Holy Ground.* Grand Rapids: Zondervan, 2009.

Clendenin, Daniel B. *Eastern Orthodox Christianity*. Grand Rapids: Baker, 1994.

Clendenin, Daniel B. *Eastern Orthodox Theology*. Grand Rapids: Baker, 2003.

Cook, Faith. *Lady Jane Grey: Nine Day Queen of England*. Webster, NY: Evangelical Press, 2004.

Cowan, Louise, and Os Guinness. *Invitation to the Classics*. Grand Rapids: Baker Books, 1998.

Creasy, William C. *Translation of Thomas á Kempis' The Imitation of Christ*. Macon, GA: Mercer University Press, 1989.

Cross, F. L., Ed. *The Oxford Dictionary of the Christian Church*. Oxford: Oxford University Press, 1983.

Davis, John D. *The Westminster Dictionary of the Bible*. Philadelphia: The Westminster Press, 1944.

Delaney, John, and James Tobin. *Dictionary of Catholic Biography*. Garden City, NY: Doubleday & Company, 1961.

Douglas, J. D., Walter A. Elwell, and Peter Toon. *The Concise Dictionary of the Christian Tradition*. Grand Rapids: Zondervan, 1989.

Dulles, Avery Cardinal, Ed. by Ralph Martin and Peter Williamson. *Pope John Paul II and the New Evangelization*. San Francisco: Ignatius Press, 1995.

Erickson, Millard J. *Concise Dictionary of Christian Theology*. Grand Rapids: Baker, 1986.

Edwards, Paul, Editor in Chief. *The Encyclopedia of Philosophy, Vol. 1*. New York: Macmillan Publishing Co., Inc., 1967.

Gaebelein, Frank E., gen. ed. *The Expositor's Bible Commentary, Vol. 9, "Acts,"* Richard N. Longenecker. Grand Rapids: Zondervan, 1981.

Garlow, James L. *How God Saved Civilization*. Ventura, CA: Regal Books, 2000.

Geisler, Norman L. *Baker Encyclopedia of Christian Apologetics.* Grand Rapids: Baker, 1999.

_____. "An Oasis of Living Water," *Christian Herald,* 1978.

_____. *Thomas Aquinas: An Evangelical Appraisal.* Grand Rapids: Baker, 1991.

_____. *Chosen But Free: A Balanced View of God's Sovereignty and Free Will.* Minneapolis: Bethany House, 2010.

Geisler, Norman L., and Ralph E. MacKenzie. *Roman Catholics and Evangelicals: Agreements and Differences.* Grand Rapids: Baker, 1995.

Geisler, Norman, and Abdul Saleeb. *Answering Islam.* Grand Rapids: Baker, 1993.

George, Timothy. *Is the Father of Jesus the God of Muhammad?* Grand Rapids: Zondervan, 2002.

_____. *Amazing Grace: God's Initiative—Our Response.* Nashville, TN: LifeWay Press, 2000.

Goerres, Ida Frederike. *The Hidden Face,* trans. by Richard and Clara Wiston. New York: Pantheon, 1959.

Gonzalez, Justo L. *The Story of Christianity: The Early Church to the Dawn of the Reformation, Vol.1.* San Francisco: Harper & Row, 1984.

_____. *The Story of Christianity: The Reformation to the Present Day, Vol. 2.* San Francisco: Harper & Row, 1985.

Gordon, Bruce. *The Swiss Reformation.* Manchester: Manchester Press, 2002.

Green, John. *Streetwalking With Jesus.* Huntington, IN: Our Sunday Visitor, 2011.

Green, Michael. *Evangelism in the Early Church.* Grand Rapids: Eerdmans, 1975.

Grenz, Stanley J., David Guretzki and Cherith Fee Nordling. *Pocket Dictionary of Theological Terms.* Downers Grove: IVPress, 1999.

Hamant, Yves, Translation by Fr. Steven Bigham. *Alexander Men: A Witness for Contemporary Russia.* Torrance, CA: Oakwood Publications, 1995.

Hannam, James. *The Genesis of Science.* Washington, DC: Regnery Publication, Inc., 2011.

Hemmer, Colin J. *The Book of Acts: In the Setting of Hellenistic History.* Winona Lake, Indiana: Eisenbrauns, 1990.

Hitchcock, James. *Catholicism and Modernity: Confrontation or Capitulation?* New York: Seabury Press, 1979.

_____. *History of the Catholic Church: From the Apostolic Age to the Third Millennium.* San Francisco: Ignatius Press, 2012.

Jenkins, Philip. *The Next Christendom: The Coming of Global Christianity.* Oxford: Oxford University Press, 2002.

Johnson, Paul. *A History of the Jews.* New York: Harper & Row, 1987.

_____. *A History of Christianity.* Athenaeum, NY: Macmillan, 1976.

Johnson, Phillip E. "Persian Conversations," *Touchstone Journal.* November 2012.

Jones, R. Tudor. *The Great Reformation.* Downers Grove: IVPress, 1985.

Leithart, Peter J. *Defending Constantine.* Downers Grove: IVPress, 2010.

Lewis, Bernard. *The Crisis of Islam.* New York: The Modern Library, 2003.

Linnemann, Eta, Translated by Robert W. Yarbrough. *Historical Criticism of the Bible: Methodology or Ideology?* Grand Rapids: Baker, 1990.

Little, Franklin H. *The Origins of Sectarian Protestantism.* NY: Macmillan Co., 1968.

Magill, Frank N., ed. *Masterpieces of Christian Literature.* NY: Harper & Row, 1963.

Maier, Paul L. *Josephus: The Essential Writings.* Grand Rapids: Kregal Publications, 1988.

_____. *Eusebius: The Church History.* Grand Rapids: Kregal Publications, 1999.

Marty, Martin. *Martin Luther.* New York: Penguin Group, 2004.

Martin, Walter. *The Kingdom of the Cults, Revised,* Appendix: "The Puzzle of Seventh-Day Adventism." Minneapolis: Bethany House Publishers, 1985.

Massieh, Daniel. *Traitor.* San Diego: Open the Gates Publishing, 2009.

Metaxas, Eric. *Amazing Grace: William Wilberforce and the Heroic Campaign to End Slavery.* New York: Harper One, 2007.

_____. *Bonhoeffer: Pastor, Martyr, Prophet, Spy.* Nashville: Thomas Nelson, 2010.

Miller, Paul M. *Evangelical Mission in Co-operation with Catholics: A Study of Evangelical Missiological Tensions.* Oxford, UK: Regnum Books, 2013.

Morgan, G. Campbell. *Acts of the Apostles.* New York: Fleming H. Revell Co., 1924.

Neuhaus, Richard John. *Death on a Friday Afternoon.* New York: Basic Books, 2000.

Noll, Mark A., and Carolyn Nystrom. *Is the Reformation Over?* Grand Rapids: Baker, 2005.

Novak, Michael. "The Troublesome Term 'Secular'" in *Crisis Magazine,* May 2007.

Oberman, Heiko A. *The Dawn of the Reformation.* Grand Rapids, MI: Eerdmans, 1992.

Oden, Thomas C. *Turning around the Mainline: How Renewal Movements are Changing the Church.* Grand Rapids: Baker, 2006.

_____. *The Rebirth of Orthodoxy: Signs of New Life in Christianity.* San Francisco: Harper Collins, 2003.

_____. Gen. Ed. *Ancient Christian Commentary on Scripture.* Downers Grove: IVPress, 2001.

Reid, Daniel G., Coord. Ed. *Dictionary of Christianity in America.* Downers Grove: IVPress, 1990.

Ruark, James E., editor. *Halley's Bible Handbook.* Grand Rapids: Zondervan Publishing House, 2000.

Safi, Omid. *Progressive Muslims: On Justice, Gender and Pluralism.* London: One World Publications, 2010.

Schreck, Alan. *The Compact History of the Catholic Church.* Cincinnati, OH: Servant Books, 2009.

Shedd, William G.T. *A History of Christian Doctrine.* New York: Charles Scribner, 1864.

Shelley, Bruce L. *History in Plain Language.* Dallas: Word Publishing, 1995.

Shorrosh, Anis A. *Islam Revealed.* Nashville: Thomas Nelson Publishers, 1988.

Sikorska, Grazyna. *Light and Life: Renewal in Poland.* Grand Rapids: Eerdmans Publishing, 1989.

Spitz, Lewis W. *The Renaissance and Reformation Movements: Vol. I—The Renaissance.* Chicago Ill.: Rand McNally, 1972.

_____. *The Renaissance and Reformation Movements: Vol. II—The Reformation.* Revised Edition. St. Louis: Concordia Publishing, 1987.

St. Therese of Lisieux. *Story of a Soul.* Washington, DC: ICS, 1981.

Stark, Rodney. *The Rise of Christianity.* San Francisco: Harper Collins, 1997.

_____. *For the Glory of God.* Princeton: Princeton University Press, 2003.

Steer, Roger. *Guarding the Holy Fire.* Grand Rapids: Baker, 1999.

Steinmetz, David C. *Reformers in the Wings.* Oxford: Oxford University Press, 2001.

Steinrucken, John D. "Secularism's Ongoing Debt to Christianity," *American Thinker*, March 25, 2010.

Suenens, Leon Joseph Cardinal. *A New Pentecost?* New York: The Seabury Press, 1975.

Tsanoff, Radoslav A. *The Great Philosophers*. New York: Harper & Row Publishers, 1953.

Vitz, Paul C. *Censorship: Evidence of Bias in our Children's Textbooks*. Ann Arbor, MI: Servant Books, 1986.

_____. *Psychology as Religion*. Grand Rapids: Eerdmans, 1986.

_____. *Sigmund Freud's Christian Unconscious*. New York: Guilford Press, 1988.

_____. *Faith of the Fatherless: The Psychology of Atheism*. Dallas: Spence Publishing, 1999.

Walker, Williston. *A History of the Christian Church*. New York: Charles Scribner's Sons, 1970.

Ware, Timothy. *The Orthodox Church*. Middlesex, England: Penguin Books, Reprinted 1993.

Warfield, B.B. *Calvin and Augustine*. Philadelphia: Presbyterian and Reformed Publishing, 1974.

Wilkens, Steven, and Allan Padgett. *Christianity and Western Thought: Vol. 2—Faith and Reason in the 19th Century*. Downers Grove: IVPress, 2000.

Woodbridge, John D., Editor. *Great Leaders of the Christian Church*. Chicago: Moody Press, 1988.

Yousef, Mosab Hassan. *Son of Hamas: A Gripping Account of Terror, Betrayal, Political Intrigue and Unthinkable Choices*. Salt River: Tyndale, 2010.

Index of People That Shaped Christianity

Acton, Lord 152
Adler, Mortimer 225
Agrippa, King 28, 29
Alexander, Archibald 137
Andrewes, Lancelot 98
Anselm of Canterbury 71
Anabaptists 108
Aquila 21
Apollos 21
Armstrong, John H. 242
Asbury, Francis 137
Athanasius 47
Augustine of Hippo 55
Backus, Isaac 136
Barnhouse, Donald Grey 193
Barth, Karl 183
Benedict of Nursia 58
Bernard of Clairvaux 74
Bernard of Cluny 75
Bjork, David E. 244
Bonhoeffer, Dietrich 194
Boniface 62
Bounds, Edward M 155
Brainerd, David 131
Brethren, Common Life 85
Brownson, Orestes 148
Bullinger, Heinrich Johann 107
Bultmann, Rudolph 219
Bunyan, John 122

Calvin, John 104
Cantalamessa, Fr. Raniero 259
Carey, William 139
Castaldo, Chris 252
Catherine of Siena 84
Channing, William Ellery 140
Chesterton, Gilbert Keith 188
Claver, Peter 118
Colson, Charles W. 233
Columba 61
Constantine 43
Cornelius 8
Creasy, William C. 241
Cyril 65
Darby, John Nelson 146
Darwin, Charles 168
Davis, Samuel 133
Demon-Possessed Girl 14
Descartes, Rene 117
De Vittoria, Francisco 96
Dominic 79
Dulles, Avery Cardinal 229
Edwards, Jonathan 132
Eliot, T. S. 216
Erasmus, Desiderius 91
Ethiopian Eunuch 6
Felicitas 38
Felix 26
Festus 27, 28

Index of People That Shaped Christianity

Francis of Assisi 77	Locke, John 123
Freud, Sigmund 177	Luke 32
Gamaliel 3	Luther, Martin 101
Gibbons, James 149	Lydia's Conversion 13
Grey, Lady Jane 110	Maclaren, Alexander 154
Gregory the Great 59	Macrina the Younger 52
Gregory the Illuminator 42	Maier, Walter Arthur 189
Grounds, Vernon C. 232	Marx, Karl 161
Hildegard, of Bingen 76	Matheson, George 153
Hodge, Charles 184	Mears, Henrietta 211
Hume, David 127	Melanchthon, Philipp 103
Huss, John 89	Men, Fr. Alexander 162
Ignatius, of Loyola 93	Methodius 65
Jelenszky, Carli 256	Moody, Dwight Lyman 166
Jerome 54	Murray, John Courtney 210
John, The Last Apostle 32	Nero 34
Judson, Adoniram 145	Neuhaus, Richard John 231
Kant, Immanuel 128	Newman, John Henry 160
Kierkegaard, Soren 158	Newton, Sir Isaac 124
Knox, John 109	Nicholas, Bishop of Myra 41
Kolbe, Fr. Maximilian 191	Oden, Thomas C. 235
Kuyper, Abraham 171	Orr, J. Edwin 222
Lawrence, Brother 119	Pascal, Blaise 121
Leo the Great 57	Paul 11, 14, 16, 18, 19, 24, 25, 26, 29
LeTourneau, R. G. 217	Perpetua 38
Lewis, C. S. 214	Peter 8
Linnemann, Eta 220	Philip 6
Livingstone, David 155	Polycarp 37

Index of People That Shaped Christianity

Priscilla 21
Rousseau, Jean-Jacques 128
Saul 7
Savonarola, Girolamo 91
Schleiermacher, Friedrich 129
Schneider, Paul 190
Schweitzer, Albert 181
Seven Sons of Sceva 23
Silas 14, 16
Simeon Stylites the Elder 52
Simon the Sorcerer 5
Solzhenitsyn, Aleksandr 163
Spurgeon, Charles Haddon 165
Stephen 4
Suenens, Leon Joseph Cardinal 205
Sunday, William (Billy) 175
Sylvester II, Pope 66
Taylor, James Hudson 169
Teresa of Avila 97
Teresa, Mother 206
Tertullian 39

Timothy 11
Therese of Lisieux 186
Thomas a Kempis 90
Thomas Aquinas 80
Thompson, Francis 151
Tozer, A. W. 213
Twelve Men w/o the Spirit 22
Tyndale, William 95
Vitz, Paul C. 179
Vladimir of Russia 67
Voltaire 126
Warfield, B. B. 185
Watts, Isaac 130
Wellhausen, Julius 172
Wesley, Charles 135
Wesley, John 134
Whitefield, George 132
Wilberforce, William 141
Wycliffe, John 88
Zinzendorf, Count Von Ludwig 134
Zwingli, Ulrich 106

Index of Events That Shaped Christianity

19th Century Modern Christianity 143	Council of Gentile Believers.................... 11
20th Century Modern Christianity 173	Council of Jerusalem 10
About the Author......................................275	Council of Nicea...................................... 48
Acton Institute 224	Council of Trent..................................... 116
Allies for Faith and Renewal 247	Counter-Reformation Christianity 113
Alpha Course 245	Creedal Christianity................................. 45
American Islamic Forum 255	Cristero War 173
Ante-Nicene Christianity 35	Crusades... 73
Apostles Creed 45	Dead Sea Scrolls 196
Apostolic Christianity 1	Destruction of Rome 35
Apostolic to Post-Nicene............................1	Didache... 36
Ascension of Jesus 2	Disputation of Worms............................ 115
Athanasian Creed 46	Early American Christianity................... 129
Athens...17	Early Church 2
Berea 16	Early Middle Ages Christianity 57
Bibliography 267	Early Modern Christianity........................ 93
Catholics and Evangelicals.....................204	Early Modern to Early America............... 93
Catholics & Evangelicals in Dialogue 263	East/West Schism................................... 70
Catholic Christianity 201	Eastern vs. Western Christianity............. 68
Christianity to the British Isles..................61	Ecumenical Christianity......................... 222
Church in Transition................................201	Ecumenism 197
Clapham Community 138	Emmaus Ministries................................ 249
Conciliar Christianity 48	English Reformation.............................. 111
Conference of Hagenau..........................114	Enlightenment 126
Conference Ratisbon/Regensburg 115	Enlightenment 125
Contemporary Christianity 241	Evangelical Christianity......................... 211
Council of Chalcedon................................51	Evangelicals & Catholics Together 238
Council of Constantinople.........................49	Evangelicals & Eastern Orthodoxy 237
Council of Ephesus...................................50	First Vatican Council............................. 170

Index of Events That Shaped Christianity

Free Methodist Church	150	Pentecost	2
Fundamentals	182	Persecution in the 2nd Century	36
Great Awakening	130	Persecution in the 3rd Century	38
High Middle Ages Christianity	68	Persecution in the 4th Century	41
Homosexuality & Christianity	248	Postmodern Christianity	196
Inquisition	99	Post-Nicene Christianity	51
Islam in the 21st Century	253	Pre-Reformation Period	87
Issues at Trent	116	Pre-Trent Conferences	114
Journey to Rome	30	Reformation Christianity	100
Late Middle Ages Christianity	82	Renaissance	82
Light and Life Movement	208	Restoration Movement	143
Macedonian Call	12	Rise of Islam	63
MacKenzie—Personal Story	264	Salvation Army	176
Middle Ages	57	San Diego Christian Forum	250
Missionaries to the USA	262	Secular vs. Secularism	198
Modern to Postmodern	143	Seventh-Day Adventist Church	157
Next Christendom	261	Taize Community	227
New Millennium	241	Vatican II	201
Nicene Christianity	40	Vatican II—Theological Positions	203
Nicene Creed	46	Vincentian Canon	44
Oxford Movement	147	YMCA	176

About The Author

Ralph E. MacKenzie earned his MA in Theological Studies from Bethel Seminary in San Diego with a concentration in Church History. He then served as visiting professor at Odessa International Theological Seminary in the Ukraine and BIOLA University's School of Apologetics, where he taught Church History and Systematic Theology. He has addressed such topics as current religious trends and the interaction between science and the Christian faith. Finally, he coauthored with Norman L. Geisler, *Roman Catholics and Evangelicals: Agreements and Differences*, published by Baker Books, now in its 11th printing.

www.ingramcontent.com/pod-product-compliance
Lightning Source LLC
LaVergne TN
LVHW051543070426
835507LV00021B/2383

"Ralph MacKenzie has carefully and lovingly exhibited scores of tapestries for the reader's viewing. This book is an esteemed treasure to both personal and institutional libraries. This procession of Christ-followers reveals a pageant of those who lived out their unique callings in real time and place. Thank you Ralph for your labor of love in bringing these personalities and events into better focus."

—*Clifford Anderson*
Dean Emeritus, Bethel Seminary—San Diego

"The 'springtime' of a new ecumenism, an ecumenism that refuses to compromise core convictions while it seeks common cause and collaboration in Christ and his mission, is now impacting Christianity on a global scale. I am profoundly grateful for the scholarship, friendship and support of Ralph MacKenzie, a man who saw the new Catholic-Evangelical moment long before most of my peers. His legacy as a friend of God and all his people is a blessing to so many of us and is, in my estimation, an eternal investment that is bearing great fruit."

—*John Armstrong*
President, ACT3 Network

"Ralph MacKenzie is one of the truly great promoters of Christian unity. He manages to stress unity in Christ without compromising the integrity of other's respective ecclesiastical commitments. In this he serves the Master well and all who desire to follow Him."

—*Mark Brumley*
CEO, Ignatius Press

"I am glad to recommend my personal friend Ralph MacKenzie. He is a reliable scholar, recognized author, and warm-hearted believer. I am happy to offer a good word on his behalf and to commend his writings to publishers and readers alike."

—*Paul Copan*
Past President, Evangelical Philosophical Society

"Ralph is an extraordinarily gifted and enormously learned scholar in his field. His book *Roman Catholics and Evangelicals* with Dr. Geisler is a comprehensive, encyclopedic study of a great divide in the Church, and it forms the basis for bridging the gap. It is a brilliant work, worthy of the praise it receives from both camps. On several occasions, Ralph has served Logos Ministries as a guest speaker on the difficult issues, both theological and historical, that divide the

Church. He is always engaging and respectful of his audience. He has a real gift of explaining very complex issues in lay terms that clarify and illuminate. While never compromising, the truth of the gospel, Ralph seeks to heal the deep wounds in the body of Christ. He is a solid Christian, a fine man, and a gifted scholar. I recommend him enthusiastically."

— *Bill Creasy*
Founder, Logos Ministries

"I have long known and admired Ralph MacKenzie. He is a rarity in the world of Christian work today. A lay theologian deeply committed to the life of the church and a faithful disciple of Jesus Christ. He is also an apologist, strategist, and catalyst—really an evangelist—for Christian unity. I commend his witness and work to God's people everywhere. No one has worked harder than Ralph to build bridges between Catholics and Evangelicals, and his latest book is another important step in that ongoing effort."

— *Timothy George*
Dean, Beeson Divinity School of Samford University

"No one has worked harder than Ralph MacKenzie to build bridges between Catholics and Evangelicals, and his latest book is another important step in that ongoing effort."

— *James Hitchcock*
Professor Emeritus of History, St. Louis University

"I want to let you know that we at BIOLA University have long considered Ralph MacKenzie as our 'go to guy' on a number of important subjects, including church history. For years we have brought him to campus to give special lectures to our graduate students because Ralph is so deeply knowledgeable and clear in his communication. And he is such a wonderful man and elder statesman of the faith, that we love our students to have contact with him. I have heard about his writing project in church history for some time and I can't wait to see the book in print. It will be one we use regularly in our university curriculum. And if Ralph's new book is anything like his previous work *Roman Catholics and Evangelicals: Agreements and Differences*, then it will be something we will use for years to come. The academic community and the community of thoughtful Christian readers are looking forward to reading his latest work."

— *Craig Hazen*
Founder/Director: Christian Apologetics Graduate Program, BIOLA University

"Ralph MacKenzie's efforts for the sake of understanding and greater unity between Christians are commendable. He approaches the issues that divide us with care, humility, and above all with a concern for that Christian unity that expresses the good news of Christ to the world. If our churches were filled with such Christians, we'd be farther down the road to unity."

— James M. Kushiner
Executive Editor, Touchstone: A Journal of Mere Christianity

"At the intersection of genuine conversations among evangelical and Catholic Christians you will find Ralph MacKenzie. He embodies and advocates the kind of ecumenism that celebrates the unity of the Spirit and the bond of peace shared among Christians of every variety. In a time when the world sees only division among the branches of the True Vine of Christ, MacKenzie's voice is well worth hearing. In this new book he capitalizes on the power of story to set hooks in the reader's mind at points in time marked by faithful men and women throughout time. These glimpses into the past give us hope for the future as we seek to live into the calling of Christ in this generation."

— Carmen Fowler LaBerge
President and Executive Editor, Presbyterian Lay Committee

"Your excellent book has spurred the mind of a friend and fellow lover of Christian history and doctrine. This is a great book and has my enthusiastic endorsement. As a pastor, I look forward to its appearing in print so that I may recommend it to my church and to others."

— Barry McCarty
Senior Pastor, Peachtree Christian Church

"Ralph has always been a stimulating conversationalist in things Evangelical and Catholic, for he maintains a vigilant awareness and a solid footing on the true historical traditions. He knows how to listen and when to speak up, and in this book, he does speak up by sharing his historical treasure-trove with the reader. Ralph has been a reliable guide to books and resources, consequently widening my conversation with the global Church. May he faithfully guide you too."

—Paul Miller
Global Businessman, Attorney, YWAM Missionary, and Author

"I first met Ralph MacKenzie as a student in a class I team-taught with J. I. Packer at Regent College on Eastern Orthodoxy and Evangelicalism in Dialogue. From the very start, Ralph distinguished himself as a serious and fair-minded student. His questions were always insightful and consequential to Christian unity-in-truth. I regard Ralph's ecumenical work as a model of cooperation between Orthodox and Evangelical believers."

—Bradley Nassif
Professor of Biblical and Theological Studies, North Park University

"Ralph's previous book, *Roman Catholics and Evangelicals*, was an unusual study for: clarity, insight, fairness, and above all for balance. Those same qualities make him an excellent guide through these important, but neglected, aspects of the church's past. All who read this book will benefit greatly from following such a reliable guide."

— Mark Noll
Francis A. McAnaney Professor of History, Notre Dame University

"Catholics and Evangelicals have in common how we can learn from each other and how imperative it is for us to work together to face the challenge of our times."

— Fr. Anthony Saroki
Pastor, Our Lady of Mt. Carmel

"This is a letter of reference and recommendation endorsing Ralph MacKenzie, whom I have known for over 15 years. I served on Ralph's board for several years for the San Diego Christian Forum and have partnered with him in a number of Christian events in the San Diego area. We have enjoyed many stimulating theological conversations through the years. Ralph has a keen theological mind, a pastor's heart, and an irenic and ecumenical spirit. I can always count on him to encourage positive theological dialogue with others that informs and fosters mutual understanding and spiritual growth. He is an expert in Roman Catholicism who co-authored with Norm Geisler what I would consider to be the best volume available on the agreements and differences between Evangelicals and Roman Catholics. I am pleased to call Ralph my friend and would heartily endorse his work."

— Mark Strauss
Professor of New Testament, Bethel Seminary—San Diego